SEED シード

DESTINY

2

ART BY MASATSUGU IWASE

ORIGINAL STORY BY HAJIME YATATE AND YOSHIYUKI TOMINO

TRANSLATED AND ADAPTED BY
Ikoi Hiroe

LETTERED BY
Ryan & Reilly

BALLANTINE BOOKS • NEW YORK

A Del Rey Books Trade Paperback Original

Gundam Seed Destiny, volume 2 copyright © 2005 by Hajime Yatate, Yoshiyuki Tomino, and Masatsugu Iwase. © Sotsu Agency, Sunrise, MBS.

English translation copyright © 2006 by Hajime Yatate, Yoshiyuki Tomino, and Masatsugu Iwase. © Sotsu Agency, Sunrise, MBS.

Published in the United States by Del Rey Books, an imprint of The Random House Publishing Group, a division of Random House, Inc., New York.

DEL REY is a registered trademark and the Del Rey colophon is a trademark of Random House, Inc.

Publication rights arranged through Kodansha Ltd.

First published in Japan in 2005 by Kodansha Ltd., Tokyo

ISBN 10: 0-345-49275-7
ISBN 13: 978-0-345-49275-3

Printed in the United States of America

www.delreymanga.com

9 8 7 6 5 4 3 2 1

Translator/Adaptor—Ikoi Hiroe
Lettering—Ryan & Reilly

Contents

A Word from the Editor

From volume 2 of Gundam SEED Destiny on, you may notice that a few names are being spelled differently than they were in volume 1 of the series.

Transliteration, or the translation of Japanese characters into the English language's Roman alphabet, is a delicate art, and there is often more than one correct way to spell a name originally written in Japanese characters in our alphabet. We've chosen to change some names in the manga in order to bring our spellings in synch with the "canonical" spellings used in the *Gundam SEED Destiny* anime.

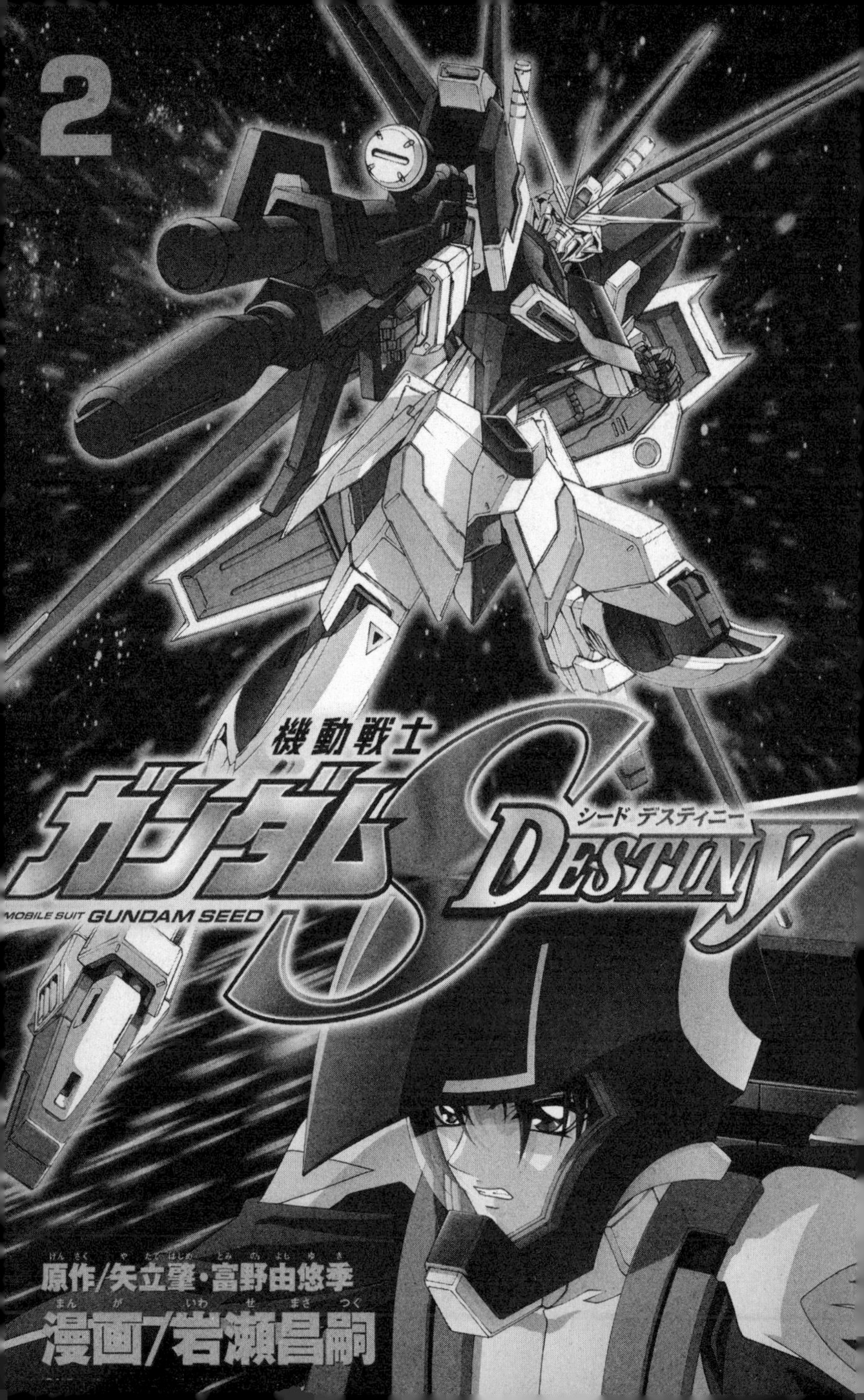
2
機動戦士
ガンダム
MOBILE SUIT GUNDAM SEED
シード デスティニー
SEED DESTINY
原作/矢立肇・富野由悠季
漫画/岩瀬昌嗣

SUMMARY OF VOLUME 1

MARCH, CE 73: THE PLANTs AND THE EARTH ALLIANCE FINALLY AGREE TO A CEASE-FIRE UNDER THE JUNIUS TREATY. ONCE AGAIN, PEACE, SO LONG AWAITED, RETURNS TO THE WORLD. HOWEVER, IN OCTOBER, CE 73, A MYSTERIOUS GROUP CAPTURES A NEW MOBILE SUIT FROM THE ARMORY ONE MILITARY PLANT. LATER, A COORDINATOR TERRORIST GROUP SUCCEEDS IN PULLING JUNIUS SEVEN OUT OF ITS ORBIT AND SENDS IT CRASHING INTO EARTH. THIS INCIDENT WILL BE KNOWN AS "BREAK THE WORLD." ZAFT TROOPS WERE SENT TO DEMOLISH JUNIUS SEVEN BEFORE IT FELL ON EARTH. THE ZAFT FLEET IS ABLE TO MINIMIZE THE DAMAGE FROM THE CATASTROPHE; HOWEVER, JUNIUS SEVEN'S FALL STILL RESULTS IN MAJOR CASUALTIES ON EARTH. THE EARTH ALLIANCE CONSIDERS THE INCIDENT A DIRECT ATTACK AND PROCEEDS TO RETALIATE AGAINST THE PLANTs. WAR RAGES ONCE AGAIN.

ONCE THE WAR HAS BEGUN, ATHRUN ZALA, FORMERLY A BODYGUARD FOR CAGALLI, THE LEADER OF THE ORB, TRAVELS TO SPEAK TO CHAIRMAN DURANDAL OF THE PLANTs. HE THEN REJOINS THE ZAFT AS A FAITH MEMBER, RECEIVES A SAVIOUR GUNDAM, AND IS GIVEN THE RIGHT TO FIGHT FOR HIS BELIEFS WITHOUT HAVING TO ANSWER TO THE MILITARY.

ON THE OTHER HAND, CAGALLI IS NOW UNDER PRESSURE TO MARRY YUNA, THE PRIME MINISTER OF ORB'S SON, AND TO ALLOW HER COUNTRY TO ALIGN WITH THE EARTH ALLIANCE AGAINST THE PLANTs. SHE RELUCTANTLY AGREES IN ORDER TO PROTECT AND STRENGTHEN HER HOMELAND.

THE ZAFT SHIP MINERVA LANDS ON ORB AFTER TRYING TO PREVENT JUNIUS FROM CRASHING INTO THE EARTH'S ATMOSPHERE. HOWEVER, ONCE THE EARTH ALLIANCE RETALIATES AGAINST THE PLANTs, THE MINERVA'S CREW ARE FORCED TO FLEE WHILE BEING ATTACKED BY ALLIANCE FORCES, WHO ARE UNDER YUNA'S COMMAND. WITH SOME HELP FROM SHINN ASUKA, THE MINERVA ESCAPES AND HEADS TO CARPENTARIA.

ON HER WEDDING DAY, CAGALLI CRIES; SHE'S LOOKING TOWARD A FUTURE SHE DOESN'T WANT. HOWEVER, FREEDOM KIDNAPS HER JUST IN TIME, AND ALONG WITH THE INDEPENDENT ARCHANGEL, SHE WILL SEEK PEACE ONCE AGAIN...

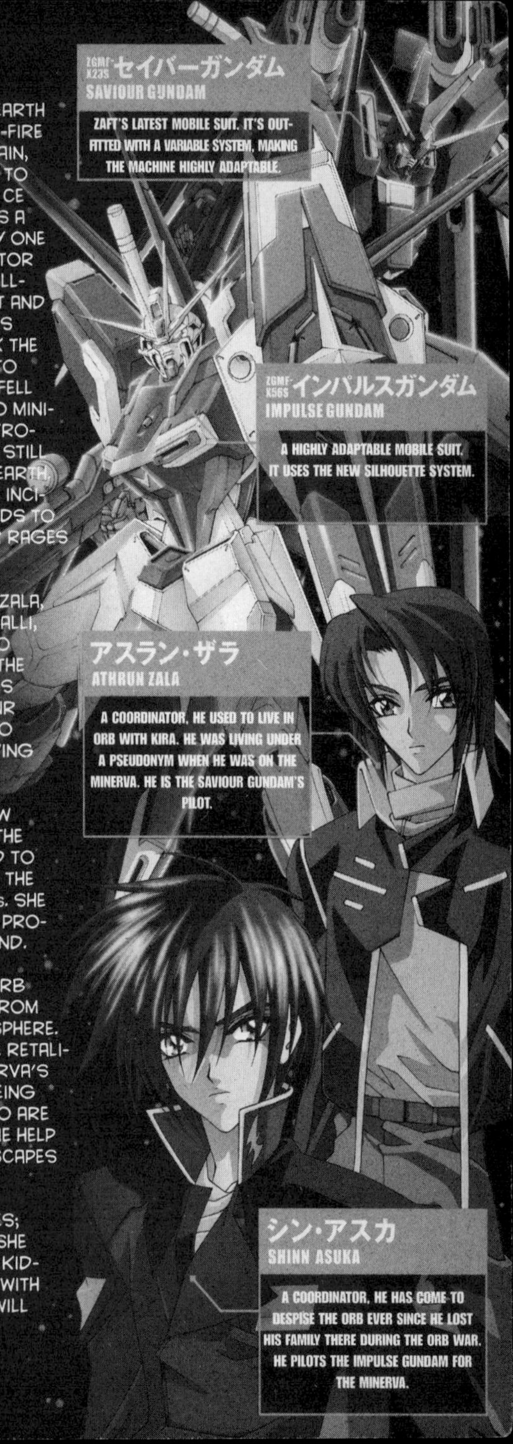
ZGMF-X23S セイバーガンダム
SAVIOUR GUNDAM
ZAFT'S LATEST MOBILE SUIT. IT'S OUTFITTED WITH A VARIABLE SYSTEM, MAKING THE MACHINE HIGHLY ADAPTABLE.
ZGMF-X56S インパルスガンダム
IMPULSE GUNDAM
A HIGHLY ADAPTABLE MOBILE SUIT. IT USES THE NEW SILHOUETTE SYSTEM.
アスラン・ザラ
ATHRUN ZALA
A COORDINATOR, HE USED TO LIVE IN ORB WITH KIRA. HE WAS LIVING UNDER A PSEUDONYM WHEN HE WAS ON THE MINERVA. HE IS THE SAVIOUR GUNDAM'S PILOT.
シン・アスカ
SHINN ASUKA
A COORDINATOR, HE HAS COME TO DESPISE THE ORB EVER SINCE HE LOST HIS FAMILY THERE DURING THE ORB WAR. HE PILOTS THE IMPULSE GUNDAM FOR THE MINERVA.

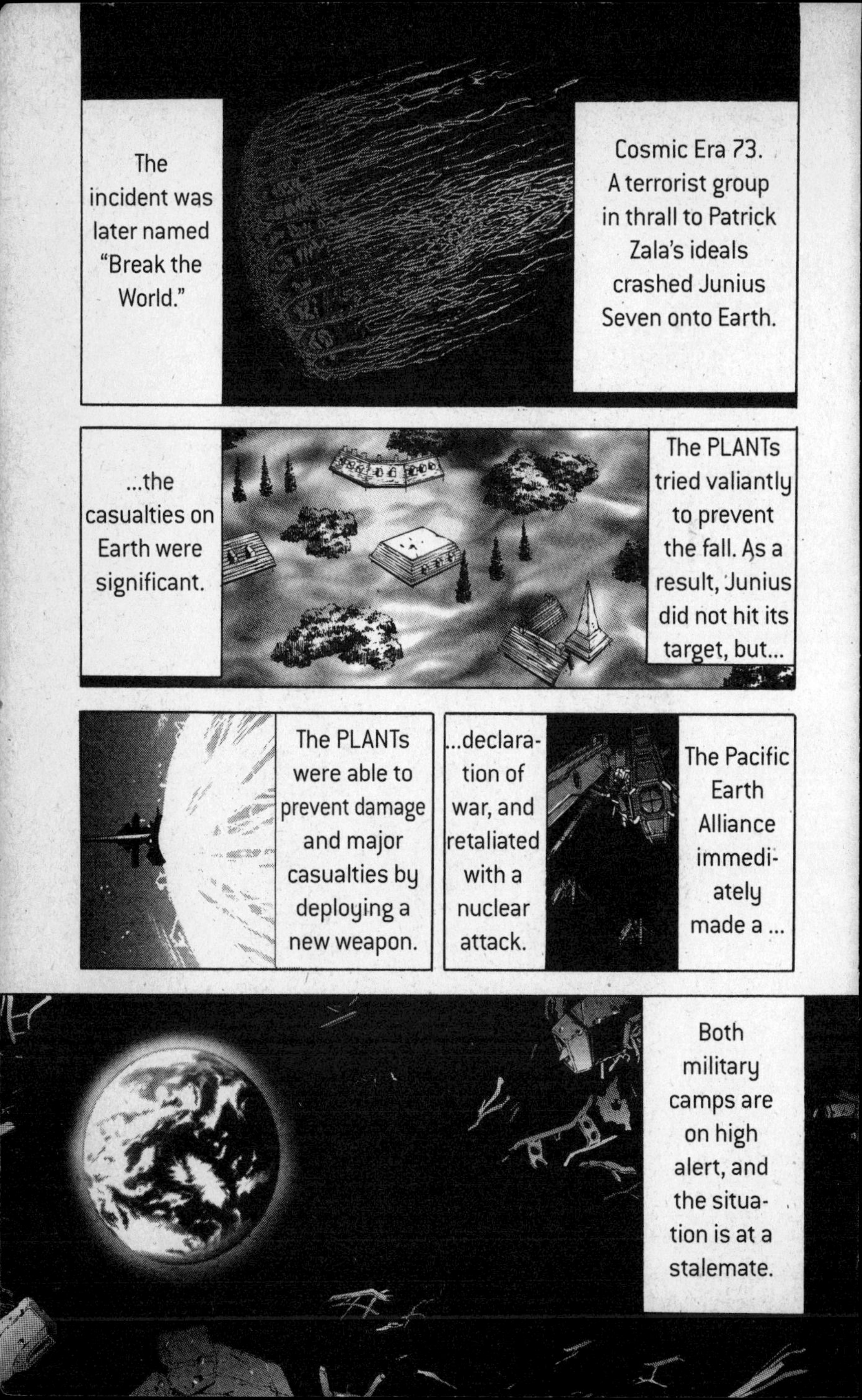
Cosmic Era 73. A terrorist group in thrall to Patrick Zala's ideals crashed Junius Seven onto Earth.
The incident was later named "Break the World."
The PLANTs tried valiantly to prevent the fall. As a result, Junius did not hit its target, but...
...the casualties on Earth were significant.
The Pacific Earth Alliance immedi-ately made a ...
...declara-tion of war, and retaliated with a nuclear attack.
The PLANTs were able to prevent damage and major casualties by deploying a new weapon.
Both military camps are on high alert, and the situa-tion is at a stalemate.

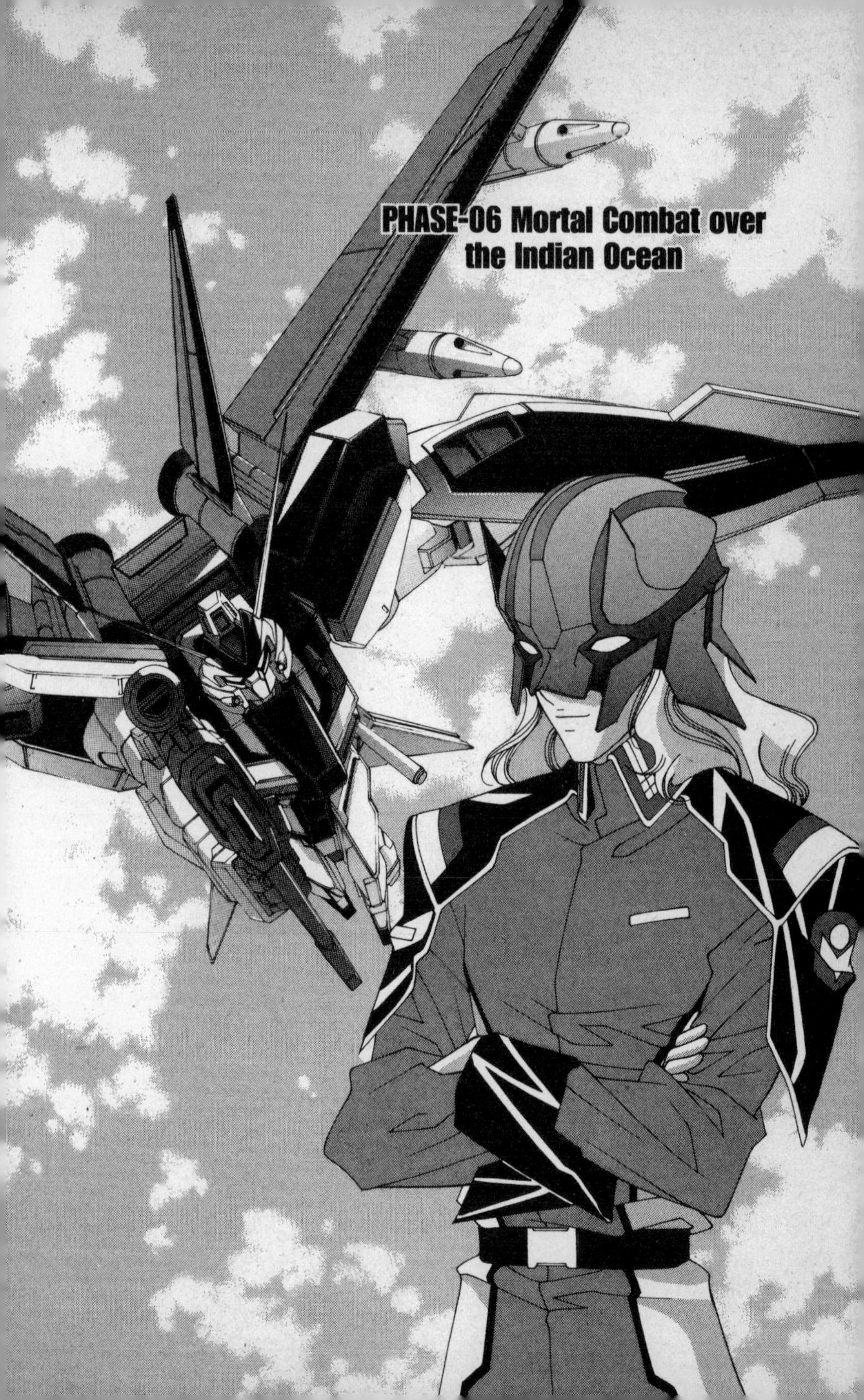
PHASE-06 Mortal Combat over
the Indian Ocean

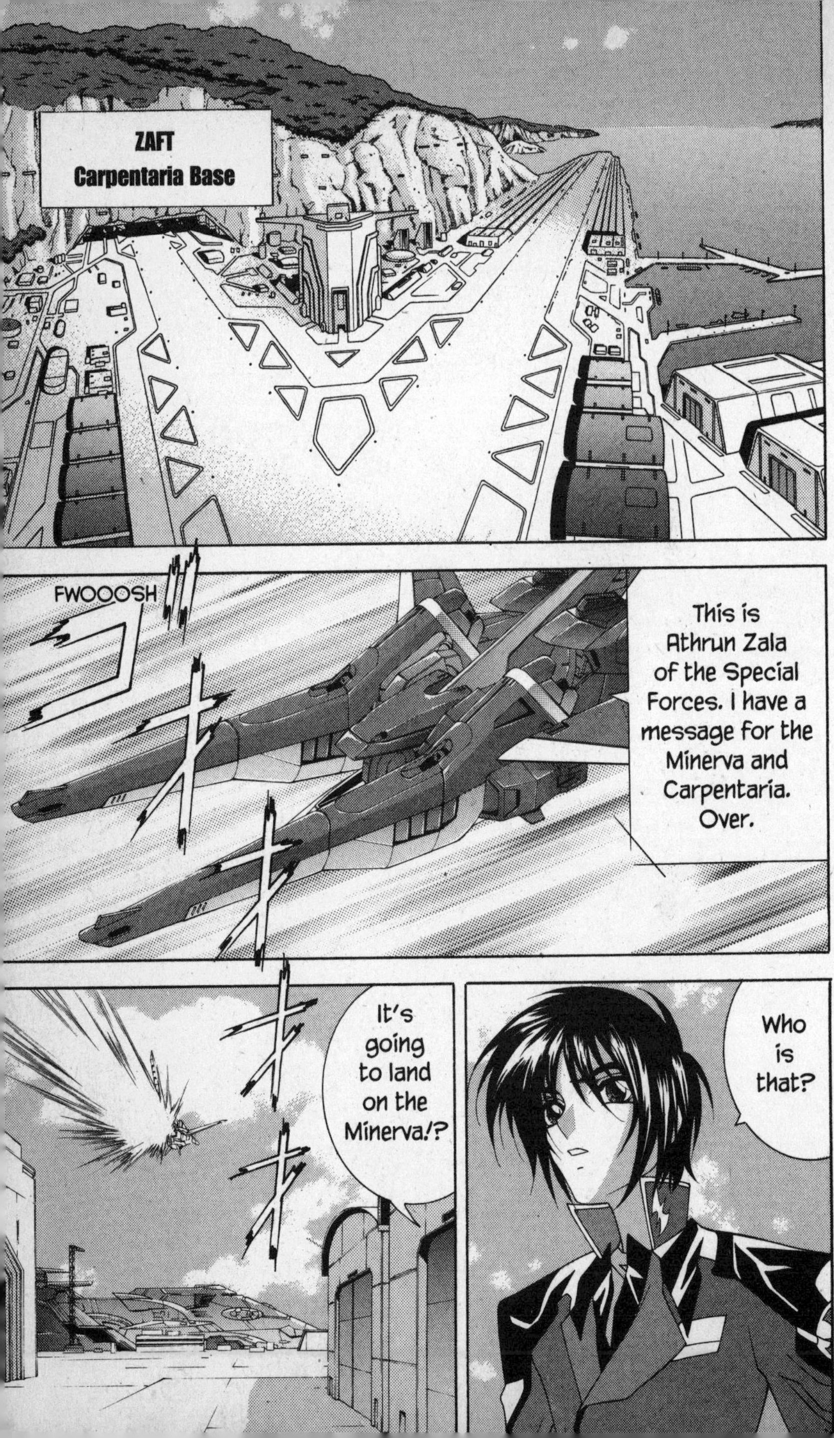
ZAFT
Carpentaria Base
FWOOOSH
This is Athrun Zala of the Special Forces. I have a message for the Minerva and Carpentaria. Over.
Who is that?
It's going to land on the Minerva!?

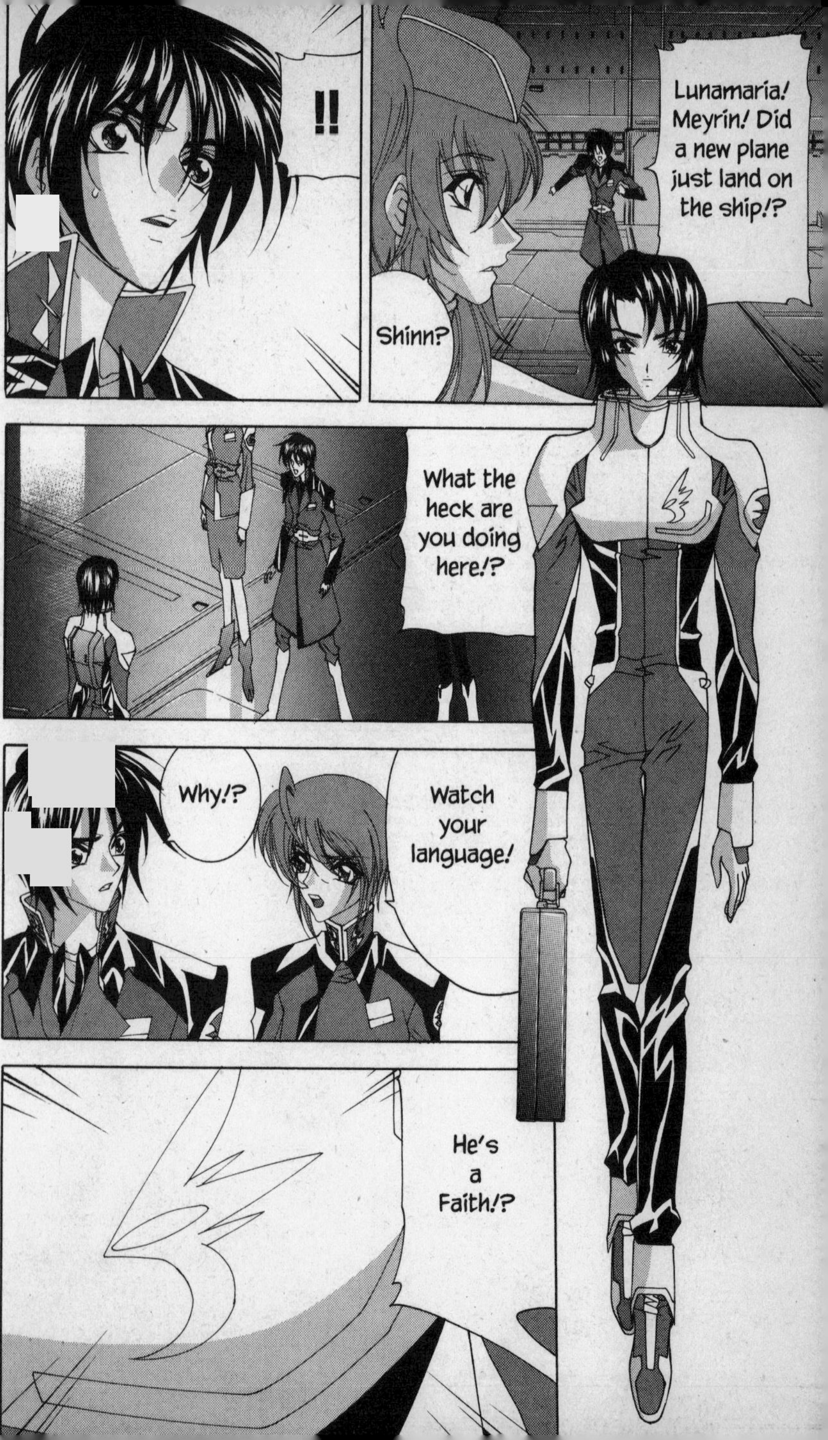
Lunamaria! Meyrin! Did a new plane just land on the ship!?
Shinn?
!!
What the heck are you doing here!?
Watch your language!
Why!?
He's a Faith!?

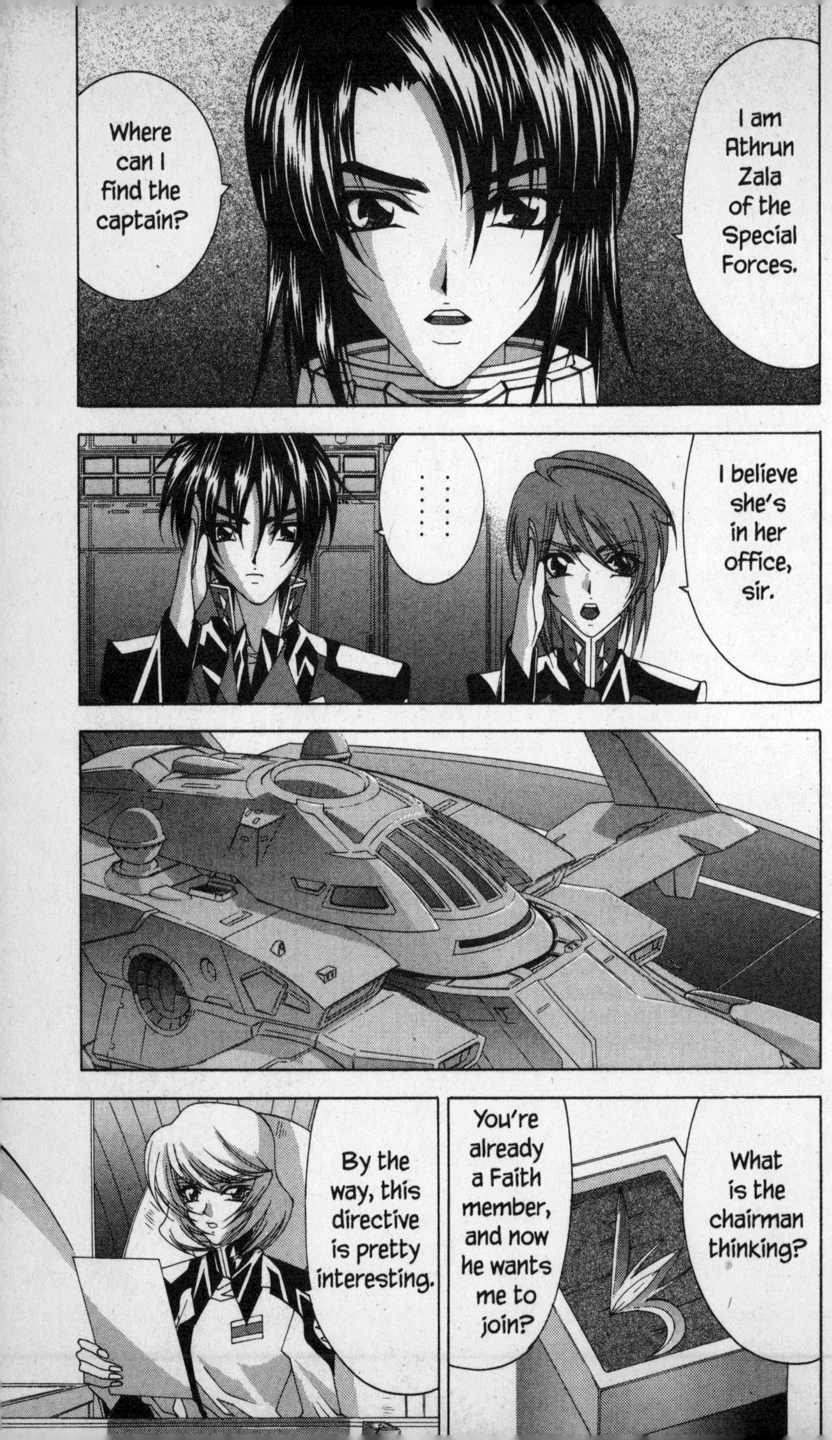
I am Athrun Zala of the Special Forces.
Where can I find the captain?
I believe she's in her office, sir.
......
What is the chairman thinking?
You're already a Faith member, and now he wants me to join?
By the way, this directive is pretty interesting.

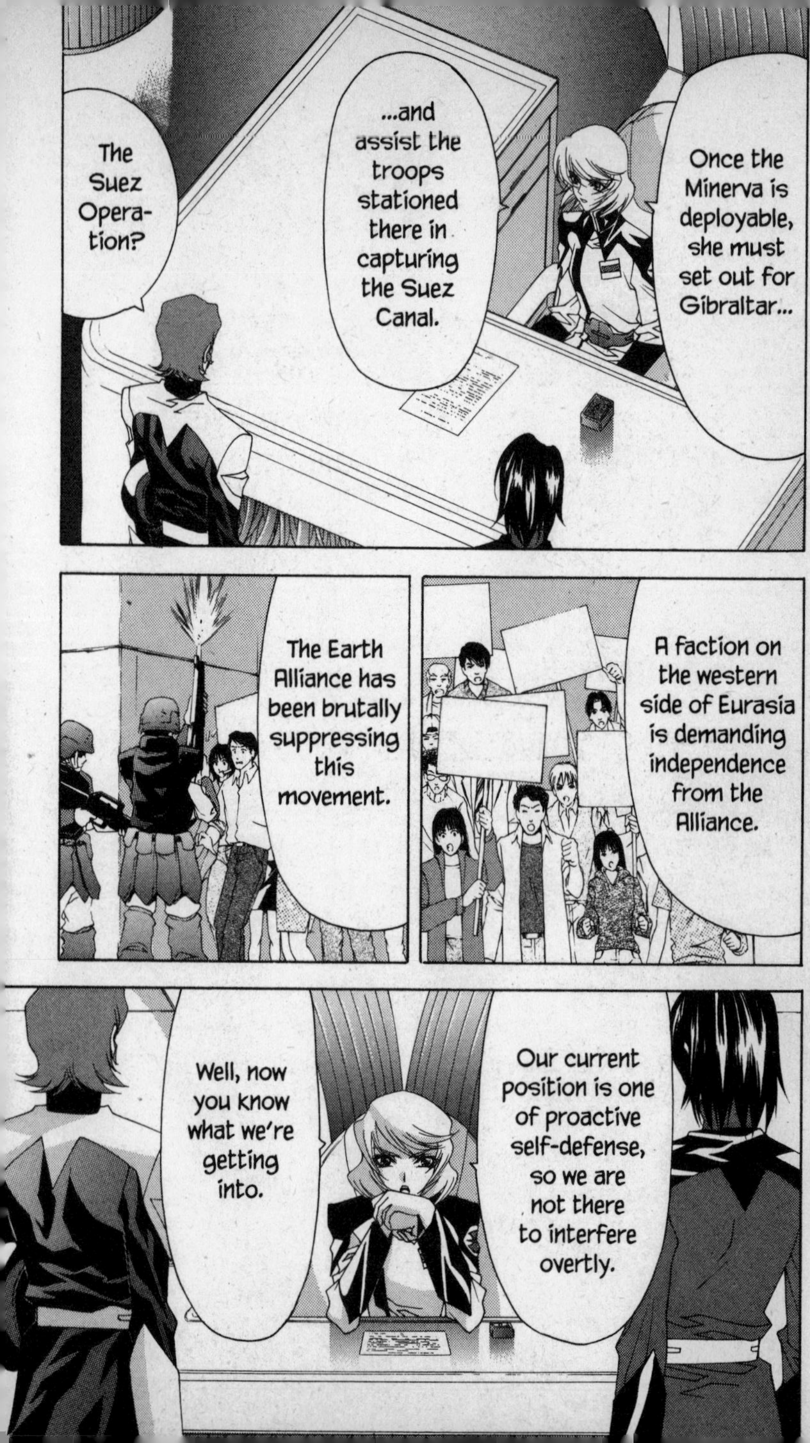

Once the Minerva is deployable, she must set out for Gibraltar...
...and assist the troops stationed there in capturing the Suez Canal.
The Suez Operation?
A faction on the western side of Eurasia is demanding independence from the Alliance.
The Earth Alliance has been brutally suppressing this movement.
Our current position is one of proactive self-defense, so we are not there to interfere overtly.
Well, now you know what we're getting into.

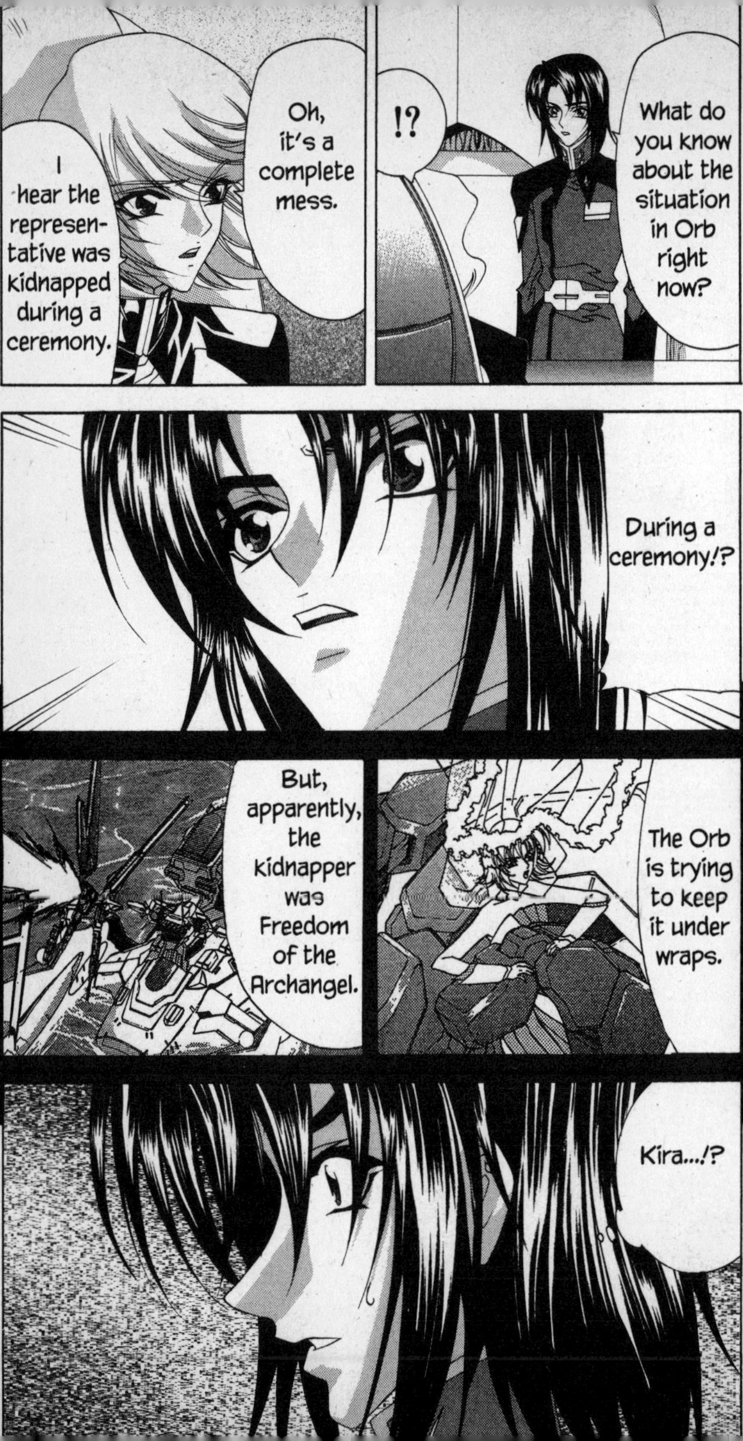
What do you know about the situation in Orb right now?
!?
Oh, it's a complete mess.
I hear the representative was kidnapped during a ceremony.
During a ceremony!?
The Orb is trying to keep it under wraps.
But, apparently, the kidnapper was Freedom of the Archangel.
Kira...!?

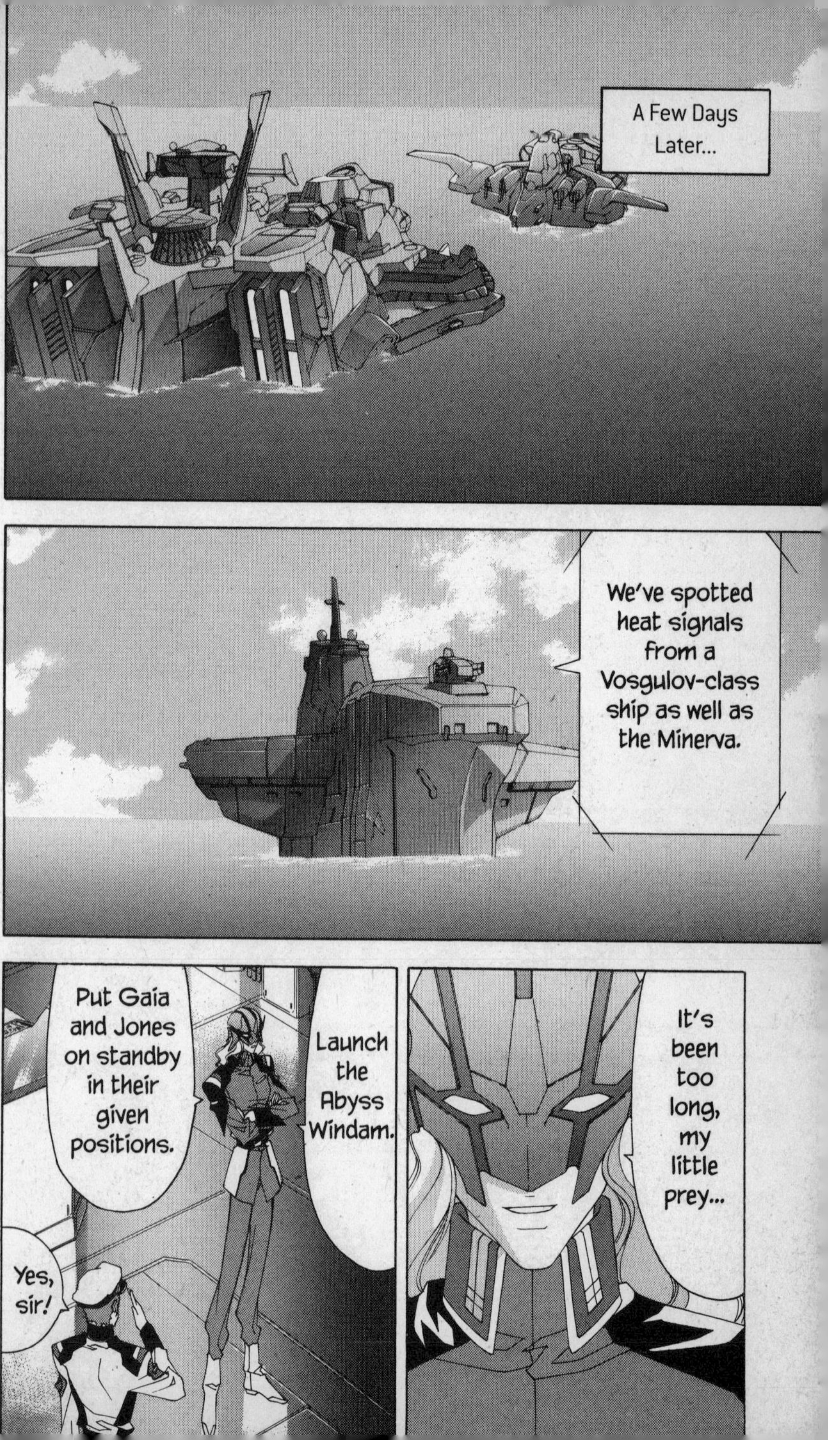
A Few Days Later...
We've spotted heat signals from a Vosgulov-class ship as well as the Minerva.
It's been too long, my little prey...
Launch the Abyss Windam.
Put Gaia and Jones on standby in their given positions.
Yes, sir!

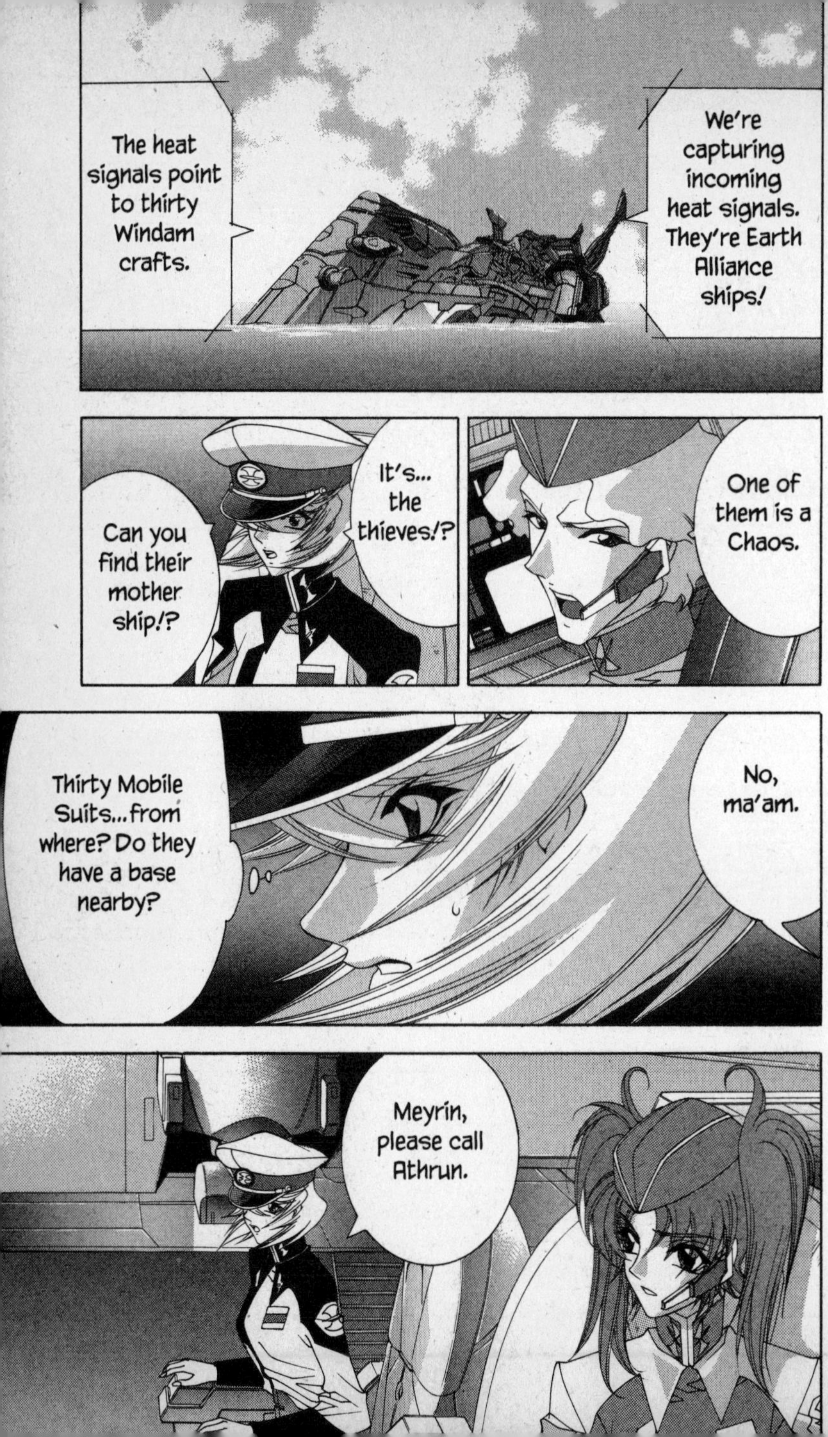
We're capturing incoming heat signals. They're Earth Alliance ships!
The heat signals point to thirty Windam crafts.
One of them is a Chaos.
It's... the thieves!?
Can you find their mother ship!?
No, ma'am.
Thirty Mobile Suits...from where? Do they have a base nearby?
Meyrin, please call Athrun.

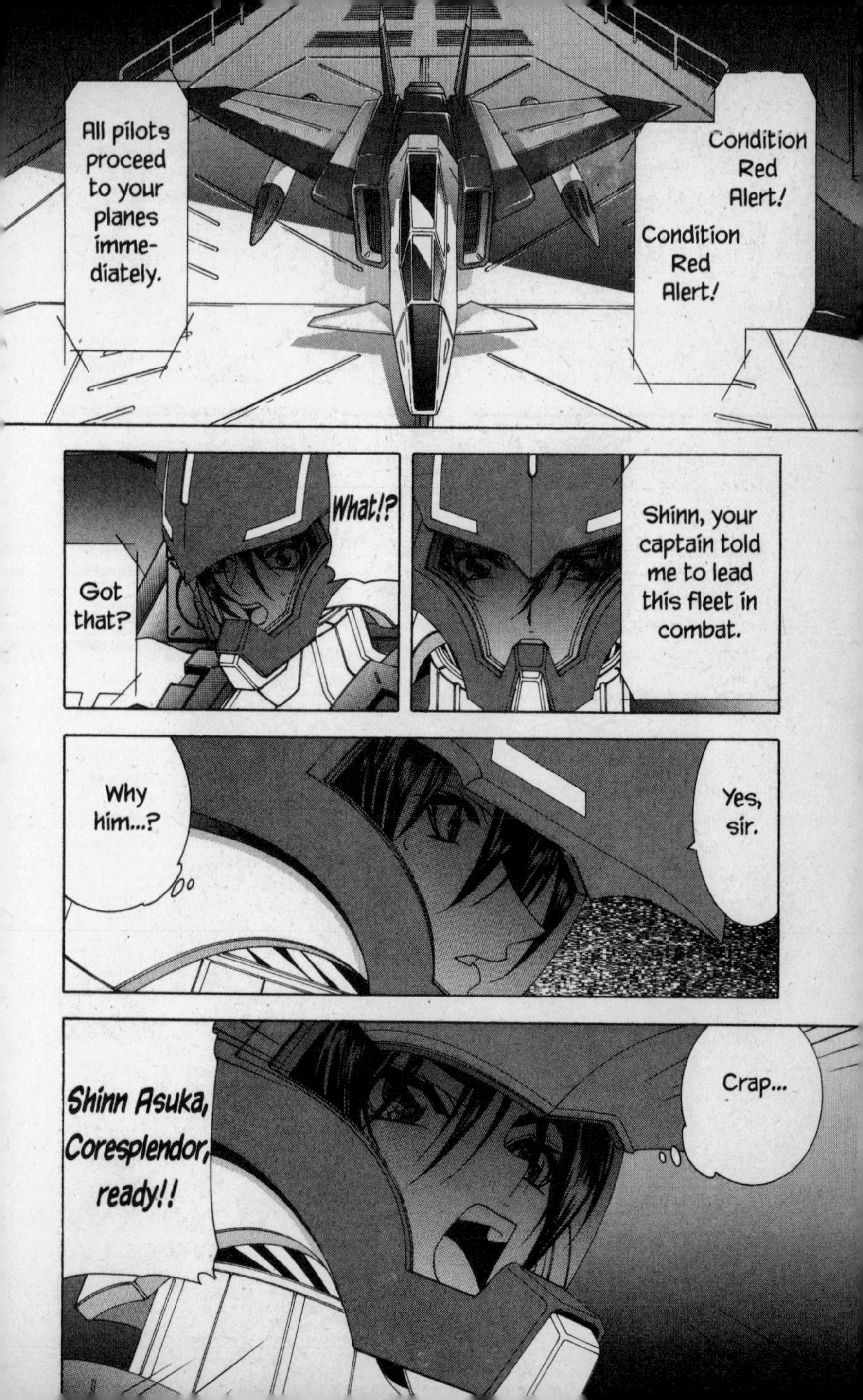
Condition Red Alert!
Condition Red Alert!
All pilots proceed to your planes imme-diately.
Shinn, your captain told me to lead this fleet in combat.
What!?
Got that?
Yes, sir.
Why him...?
Crap...
Shinn Asuka, Coresplendor, ready!!

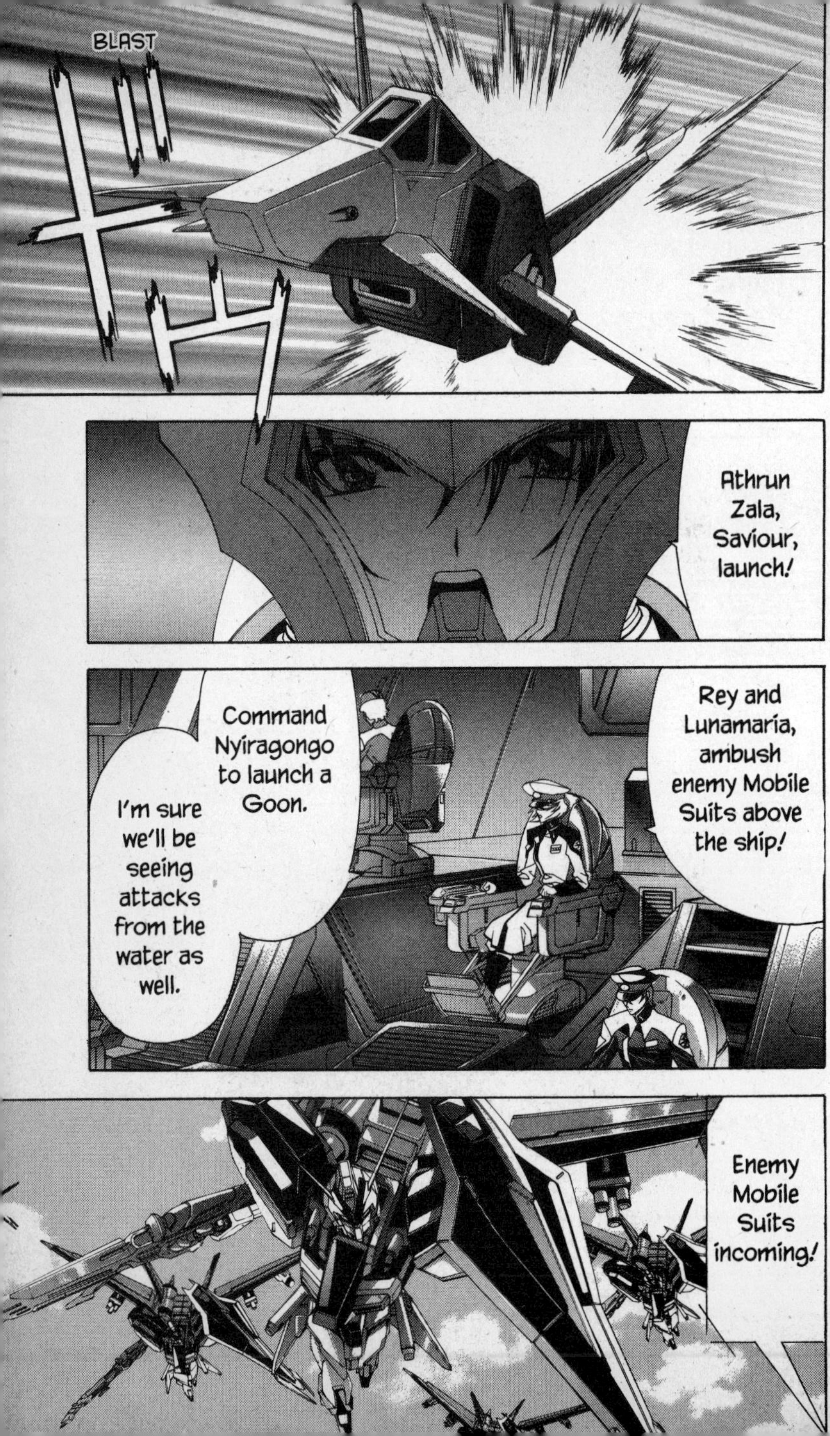
BLAST
Athrun Zala, Saviour, launch!
Rey and Lunamaria, ambush enemy Mobile Suits above the ship!
Command Nyiragongo to launch a Goon.
I'm sure we'll be seeing attacks from the water as well.
Enemy Mobile Suits incoming!

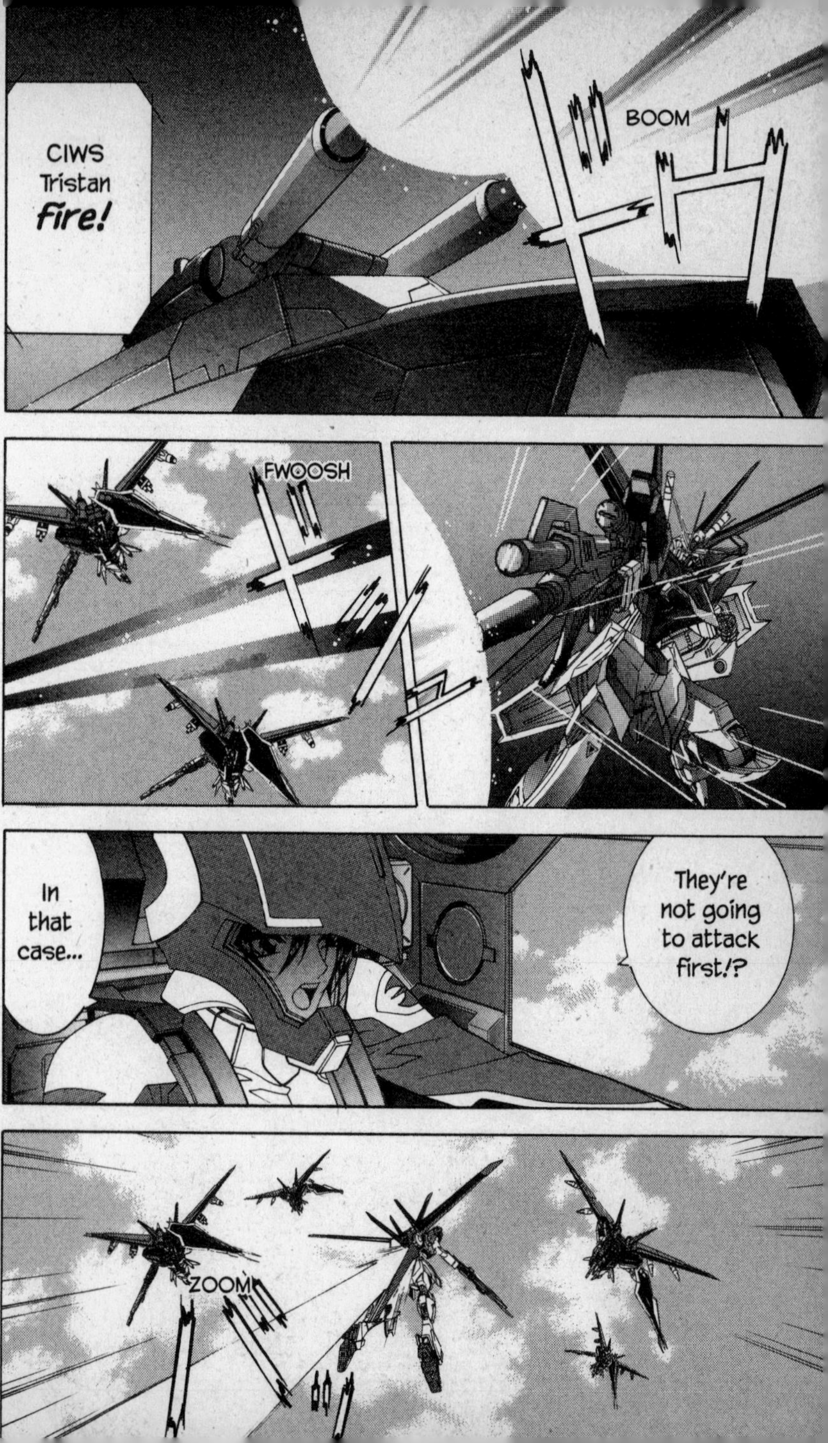
CIWS Tristan *fire!*
BOOM
FWOOSH
They're not going to attack first!?
In that case...
ZOOM

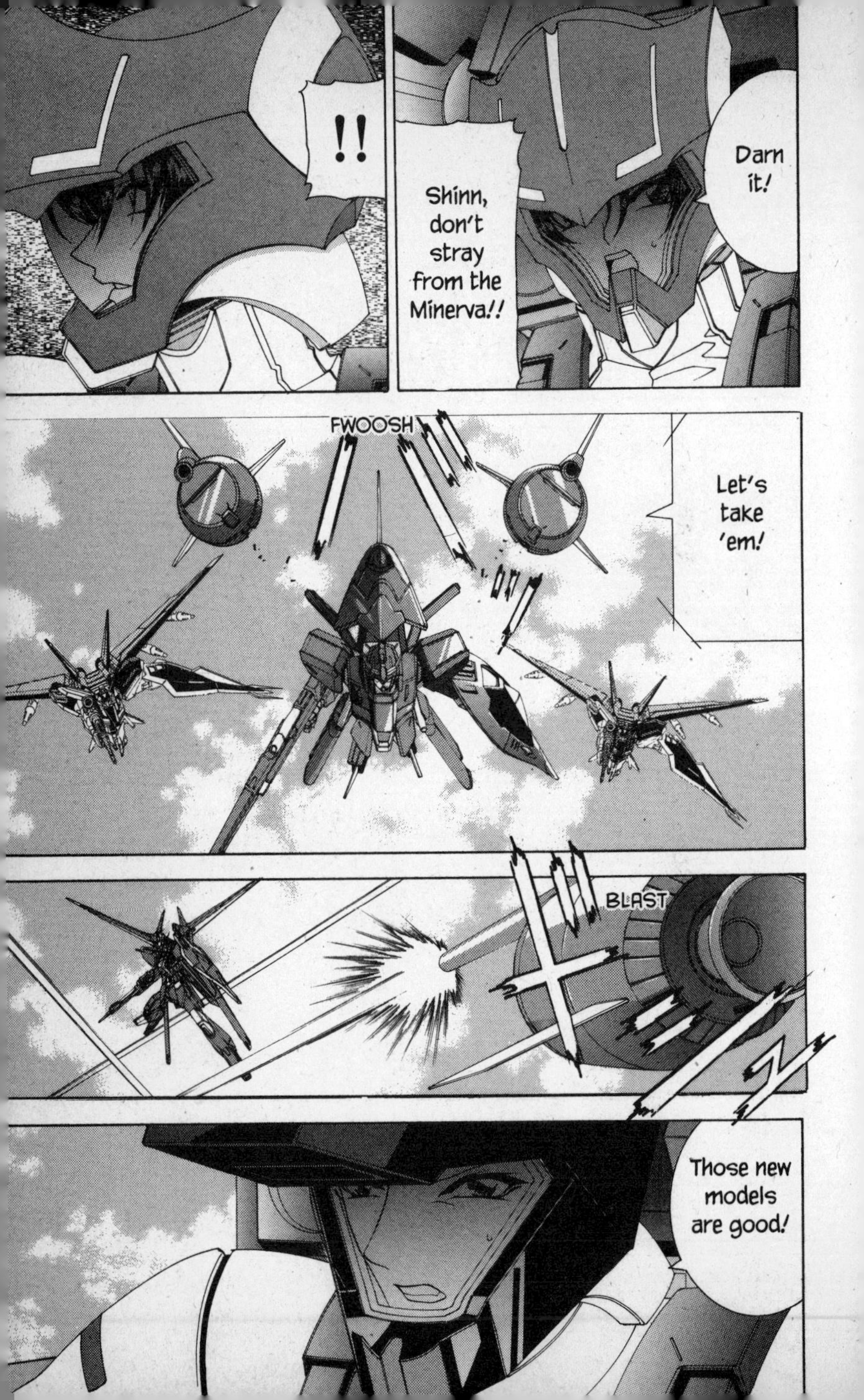
Darn it!
Shinn, don't stray from the Minerva!!
!!
FWOOSH
Let's take 'em!
BLAST
Those new models are good!

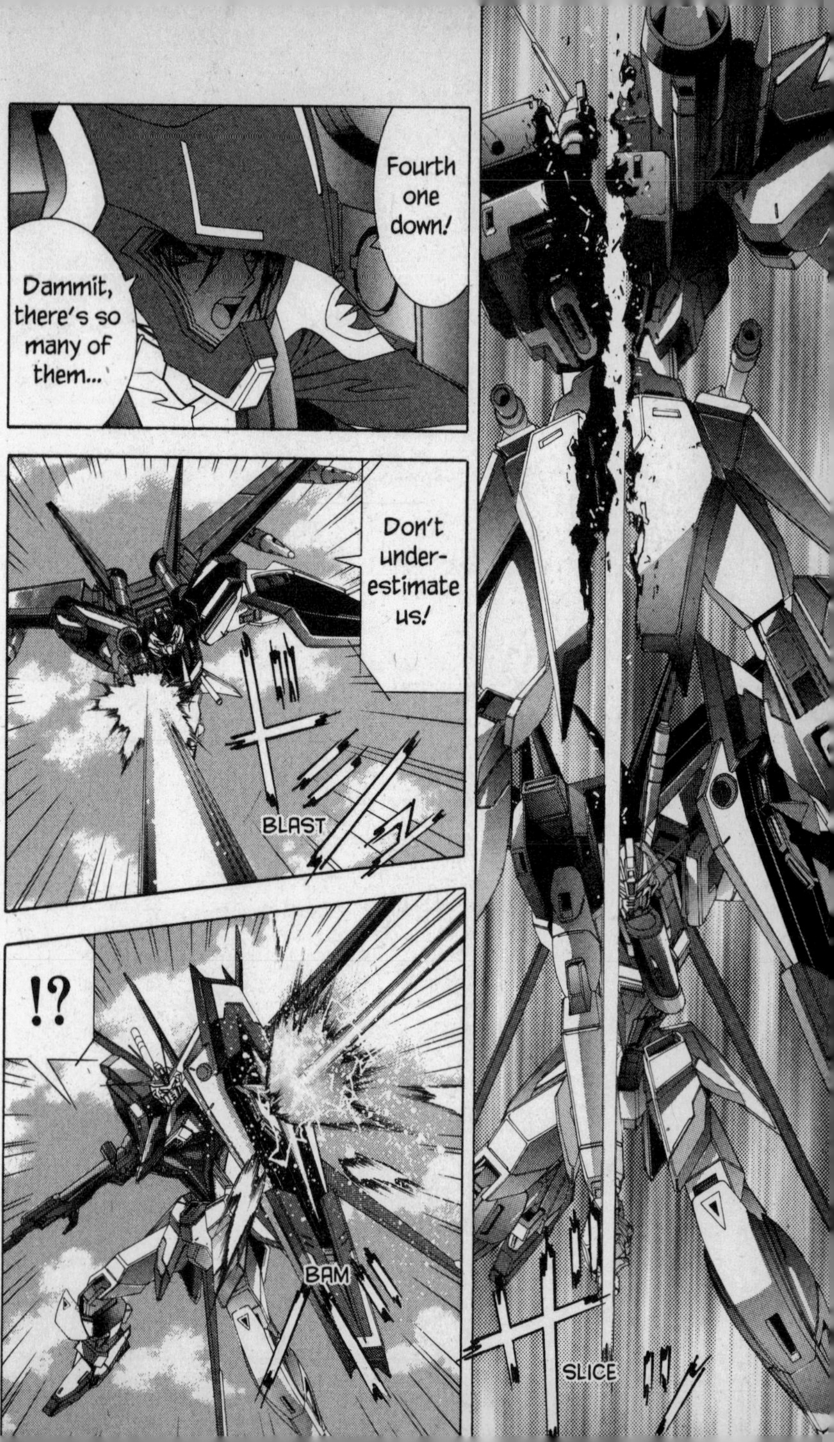
SLICE
Fourth one down!
Dammit, there's so many of them...
Don't under-estimate us!
BLAST
!?
BAM

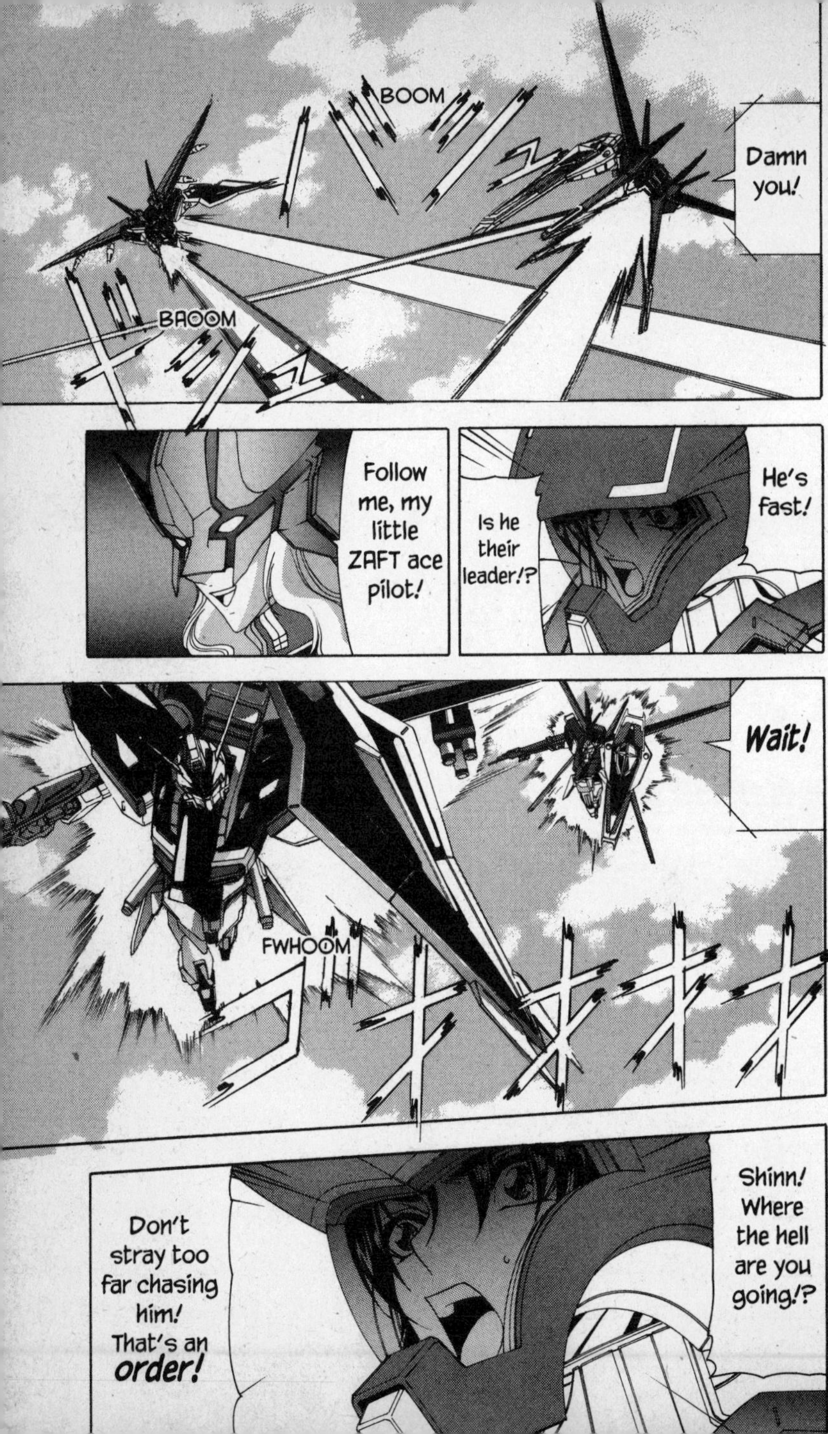
Damn you!
BOOM
BAOOM
He's fast!
Is he their leader!?
Follow me, my little ZAFT ace pilot!
Wait!
FWHOOM
Shinn! Where the hell are you going!?
Don't stray too far chasing him! That's an order!

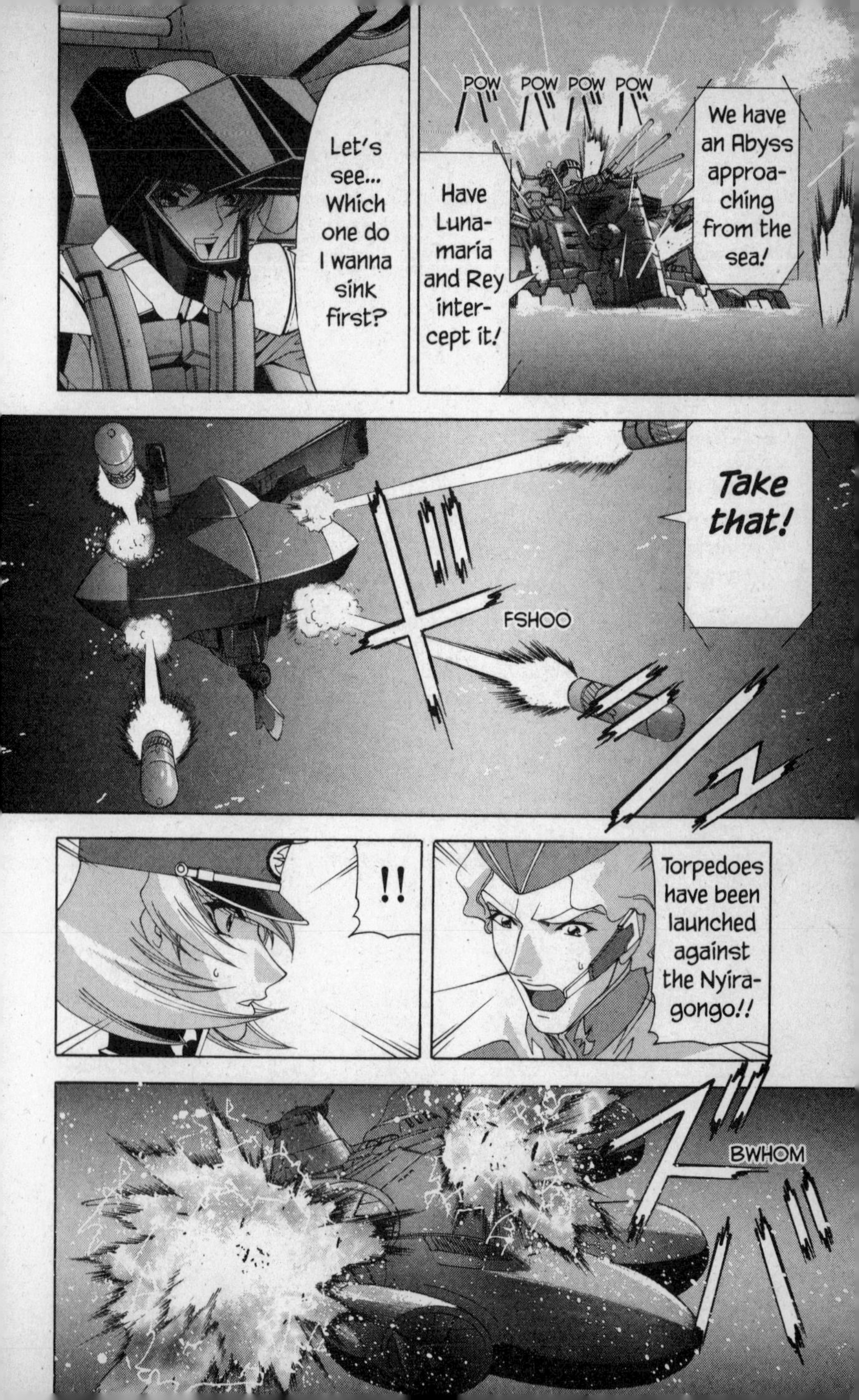

POW POW POW POW
We have an Abyss approaching from the sea!
Have Lunamaria and Rey intercept it!
Let's see... Which one do I wanna sink first?
Take that!
FSHOO
Torpedoes have been launched against the Nyiragongo!!
!!
BWHOM

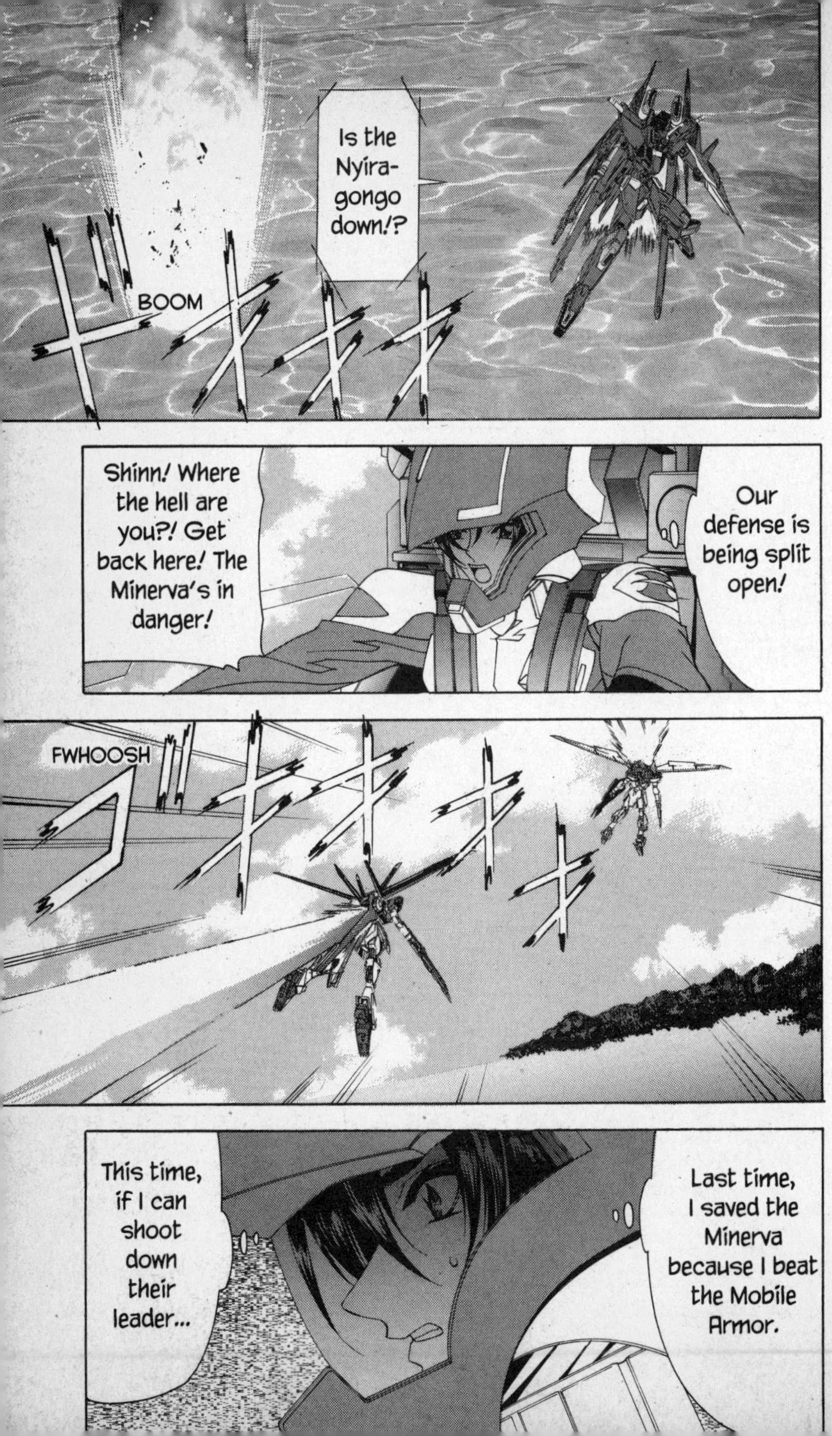
Is the Nyira-gongo down!?
BOOM
Our defense is being split open!
Shinn! Where the hell are you?! Get back here! The Minerva's in danger!
FWHOOSH
Last time, I saved the Minerva because I beat the Mobile Armor.
This time, if I can shoot down their leader...

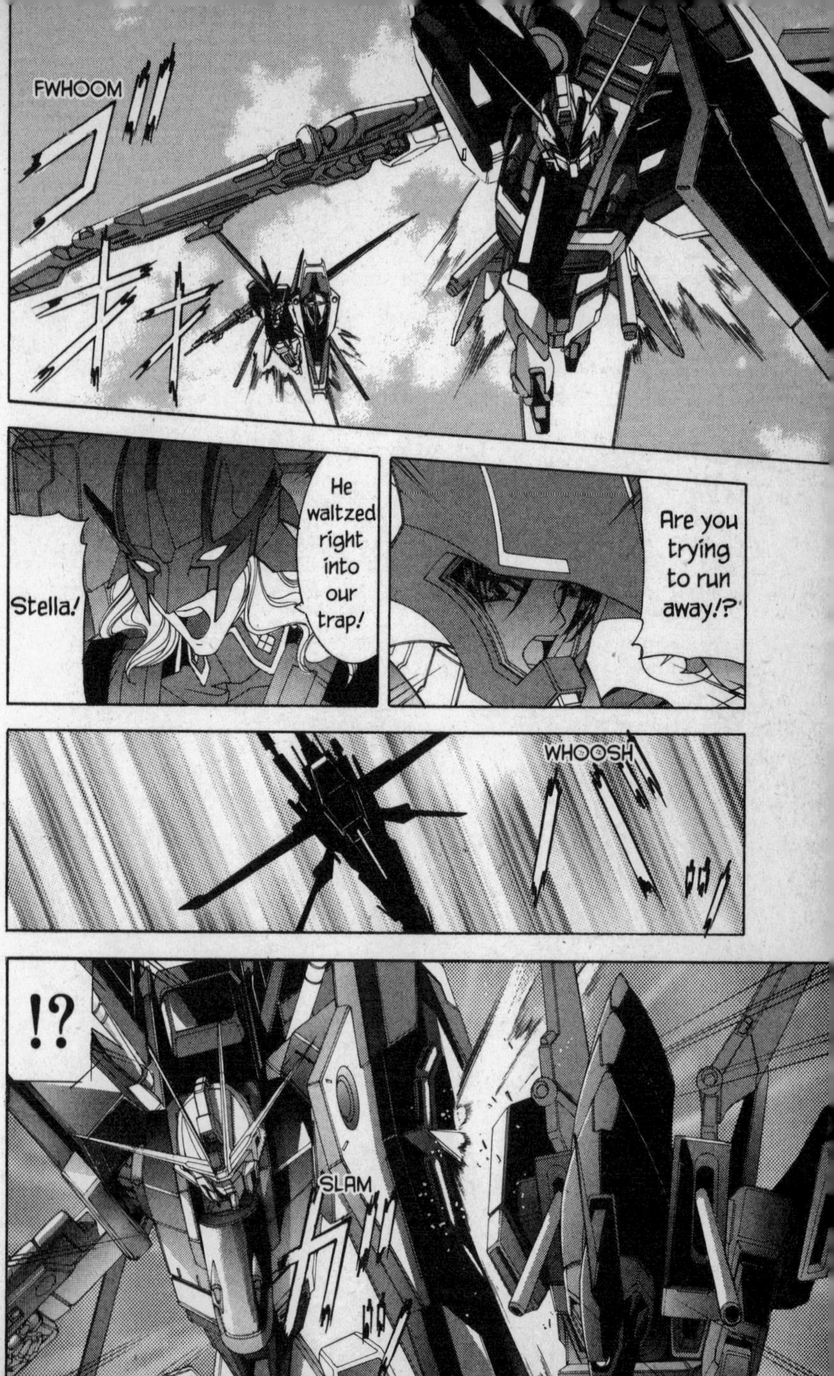
FWHOOM
Are you trying to run away!?
He waltzed right into our trap!
Stella!
WHOOSH
!?
SLAM

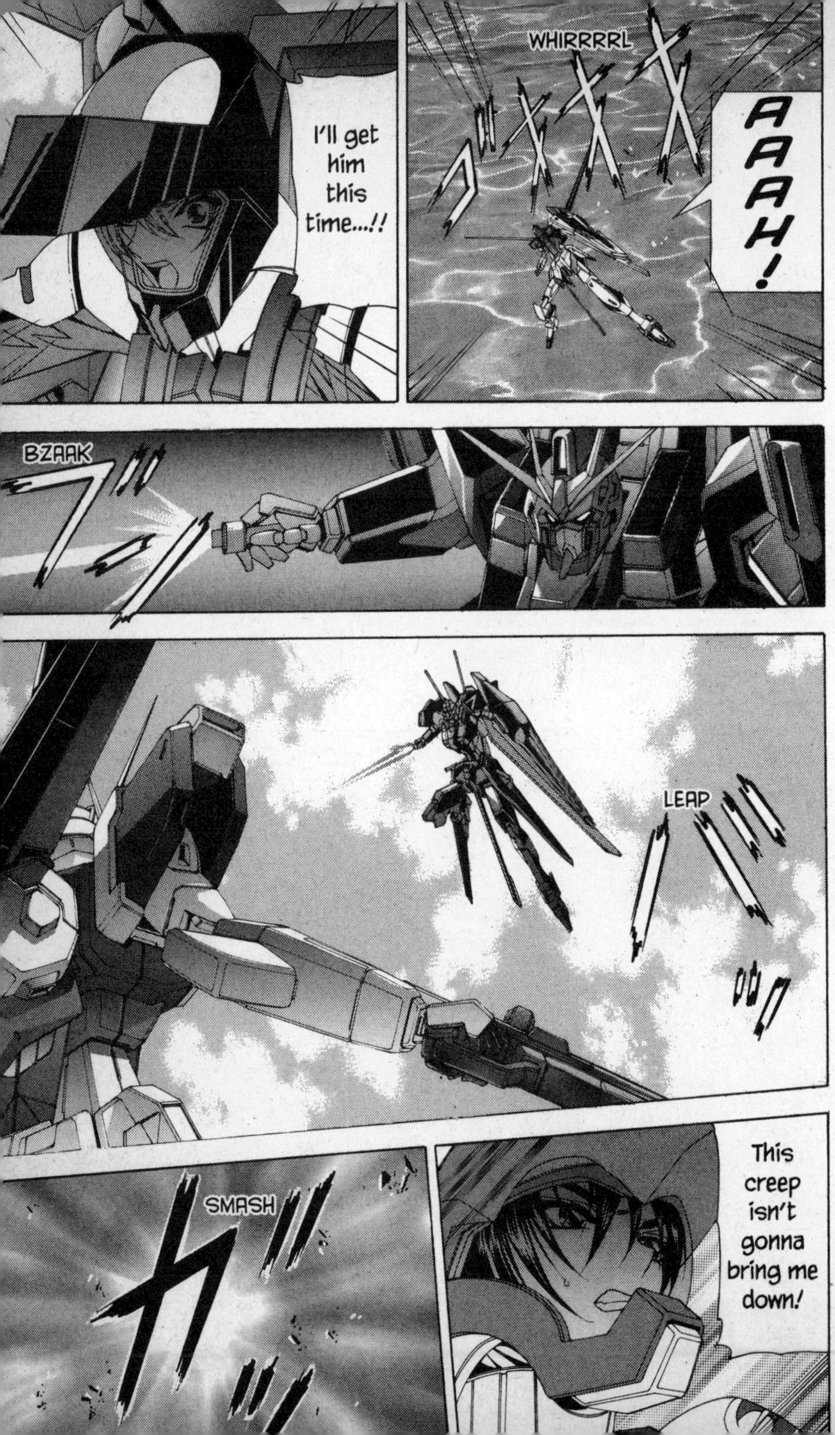
WHIRRRRL
AAAAH!
I'll get him this time...!!
BZAAK
LEAP
This creep isn't gonna bring me down!
SMASH

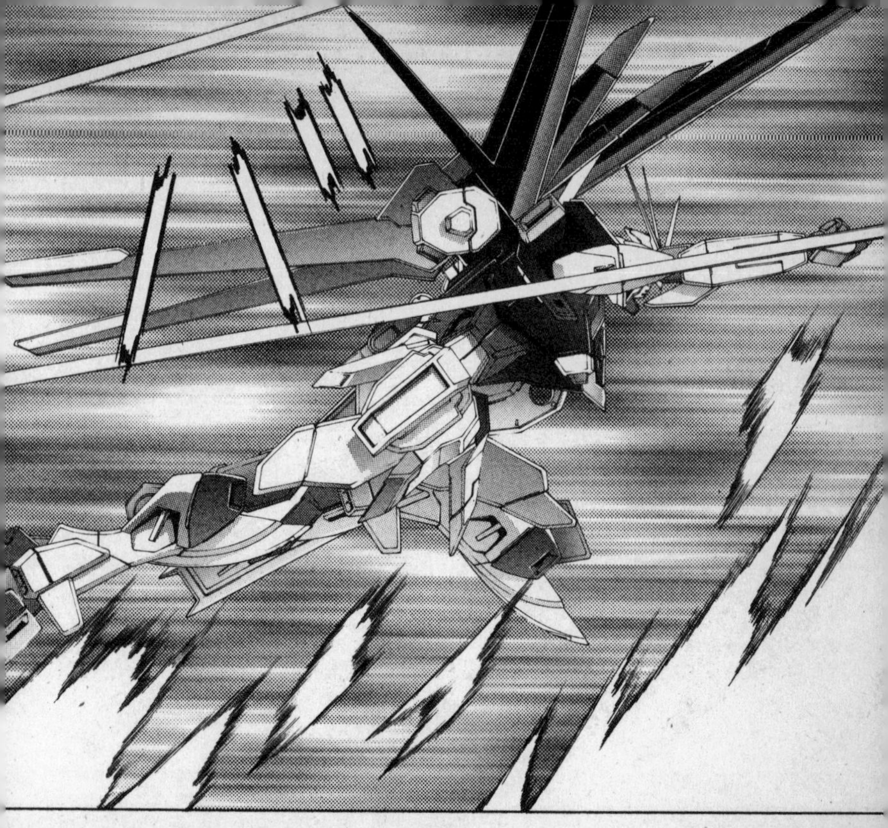
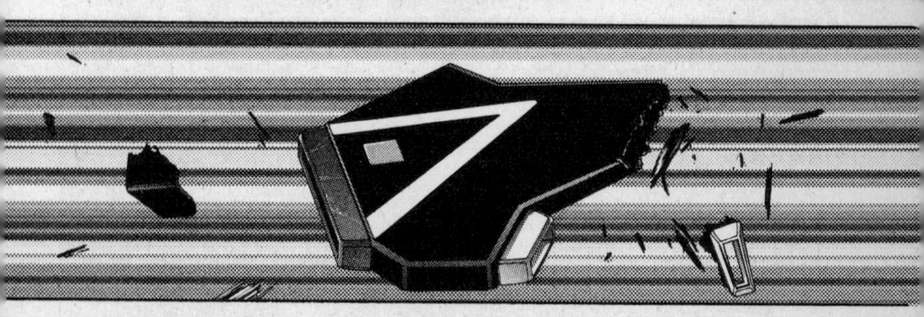
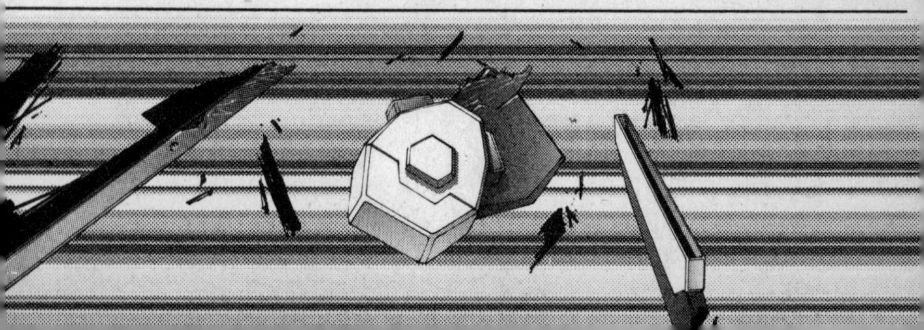

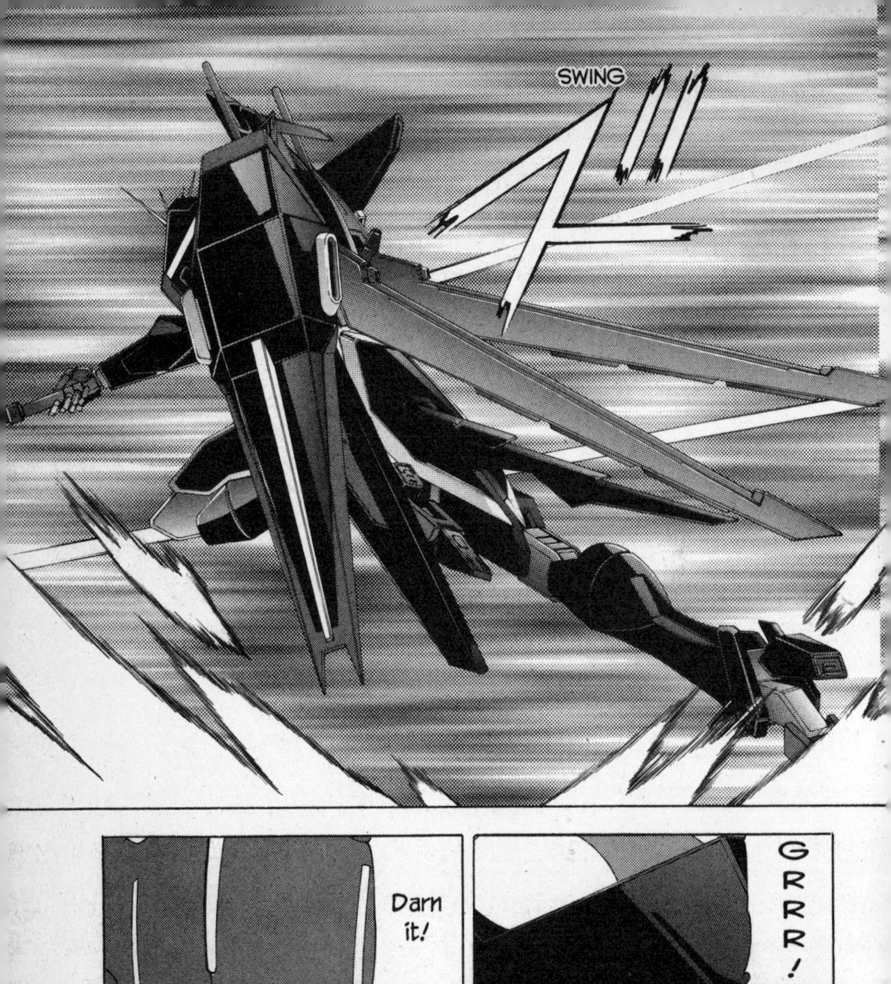
SWING
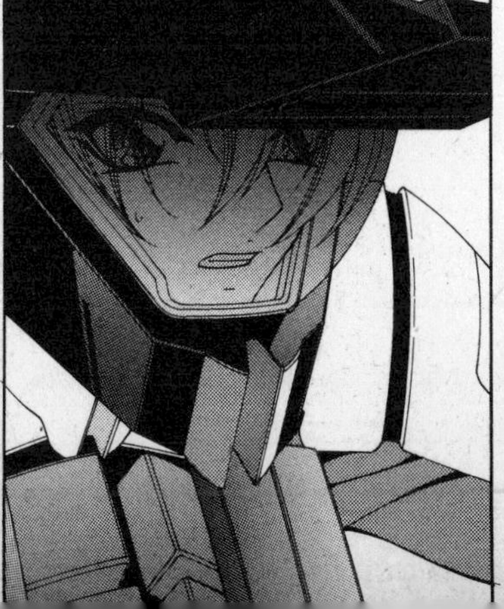
GRRR!
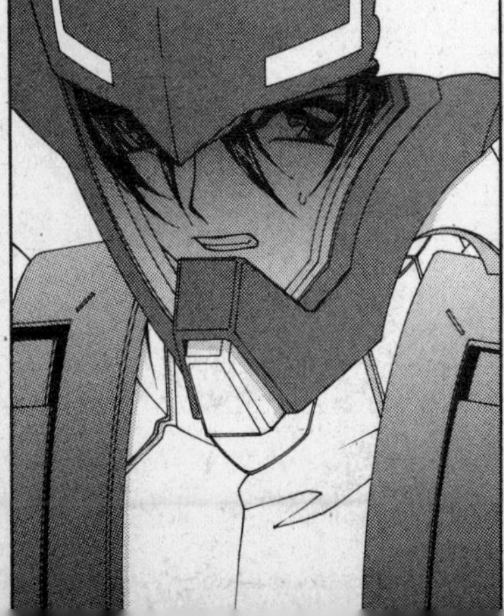
Darn it!

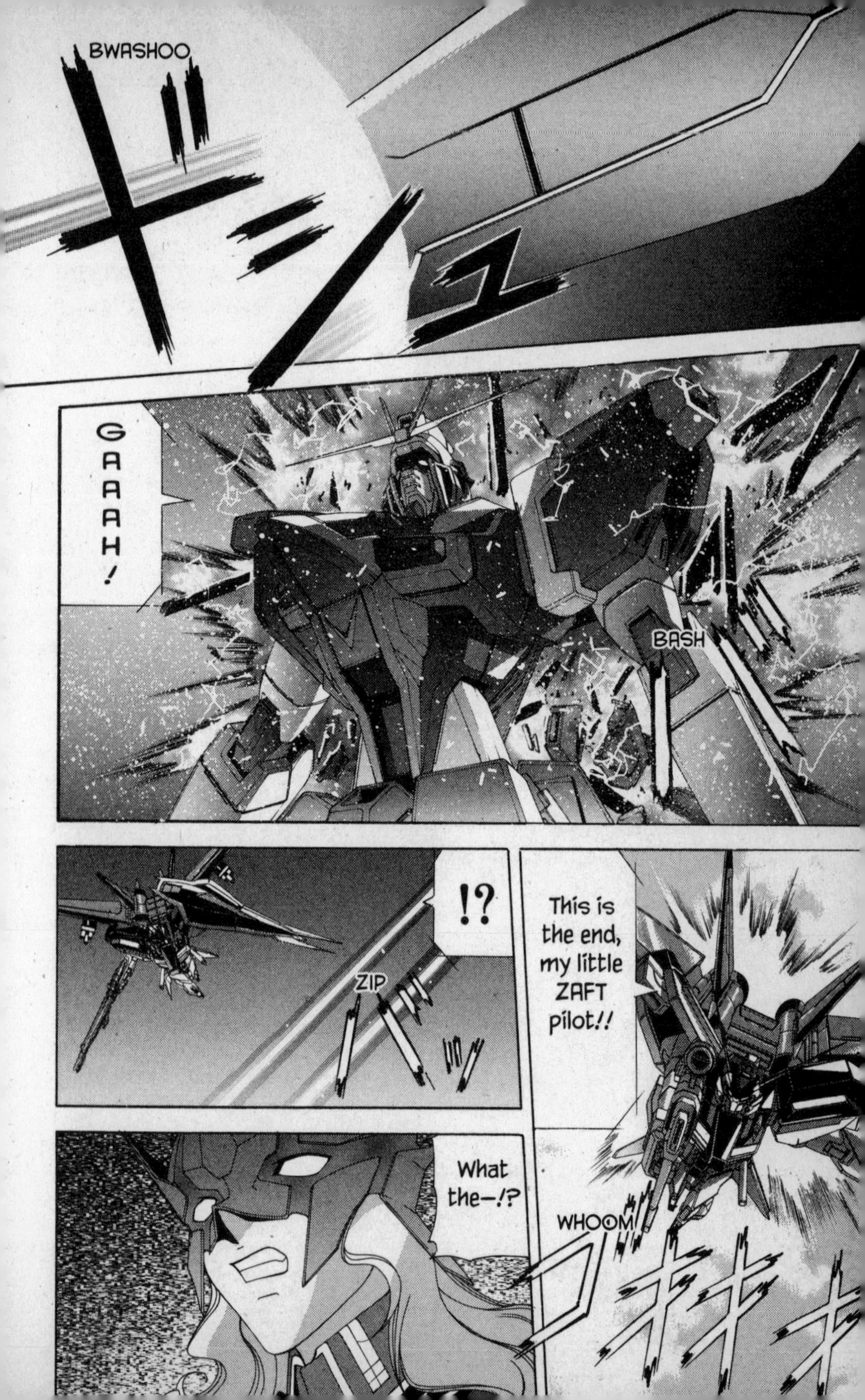
BWASHOO
GAAAAH!
BASH
This is the end, my little ZAFT pilot!!
WHOOM
!?
ZIP
What the–!?

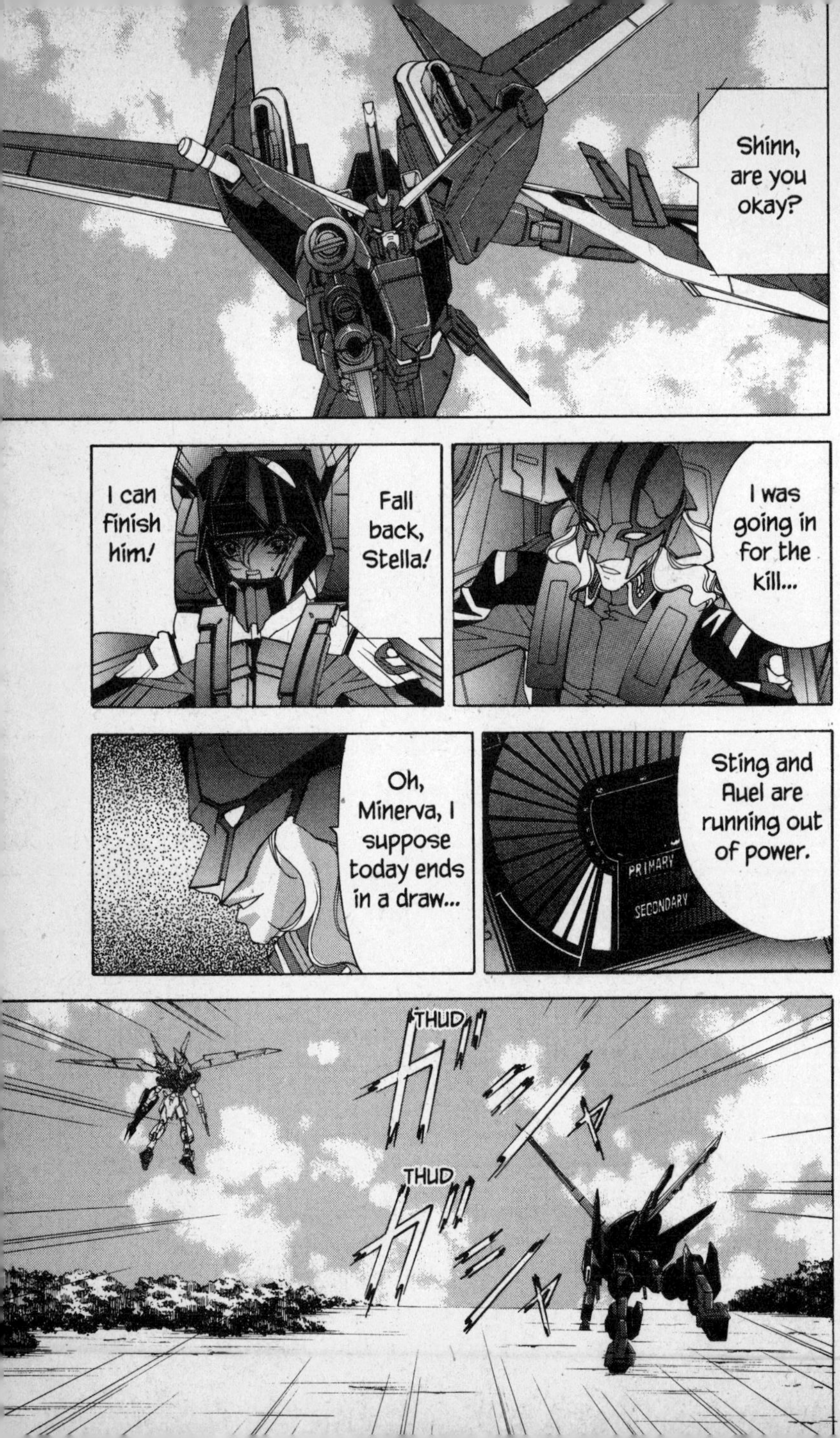
Shinn, are you okay?
I was going in for the kill...
Fall back, Stella!
I can finish him!
Sting and Auel are running out of power.
PRIMARY
SECONDARY
Oh, Minerva, I suppose today ends in a draw...
THUD
THUD

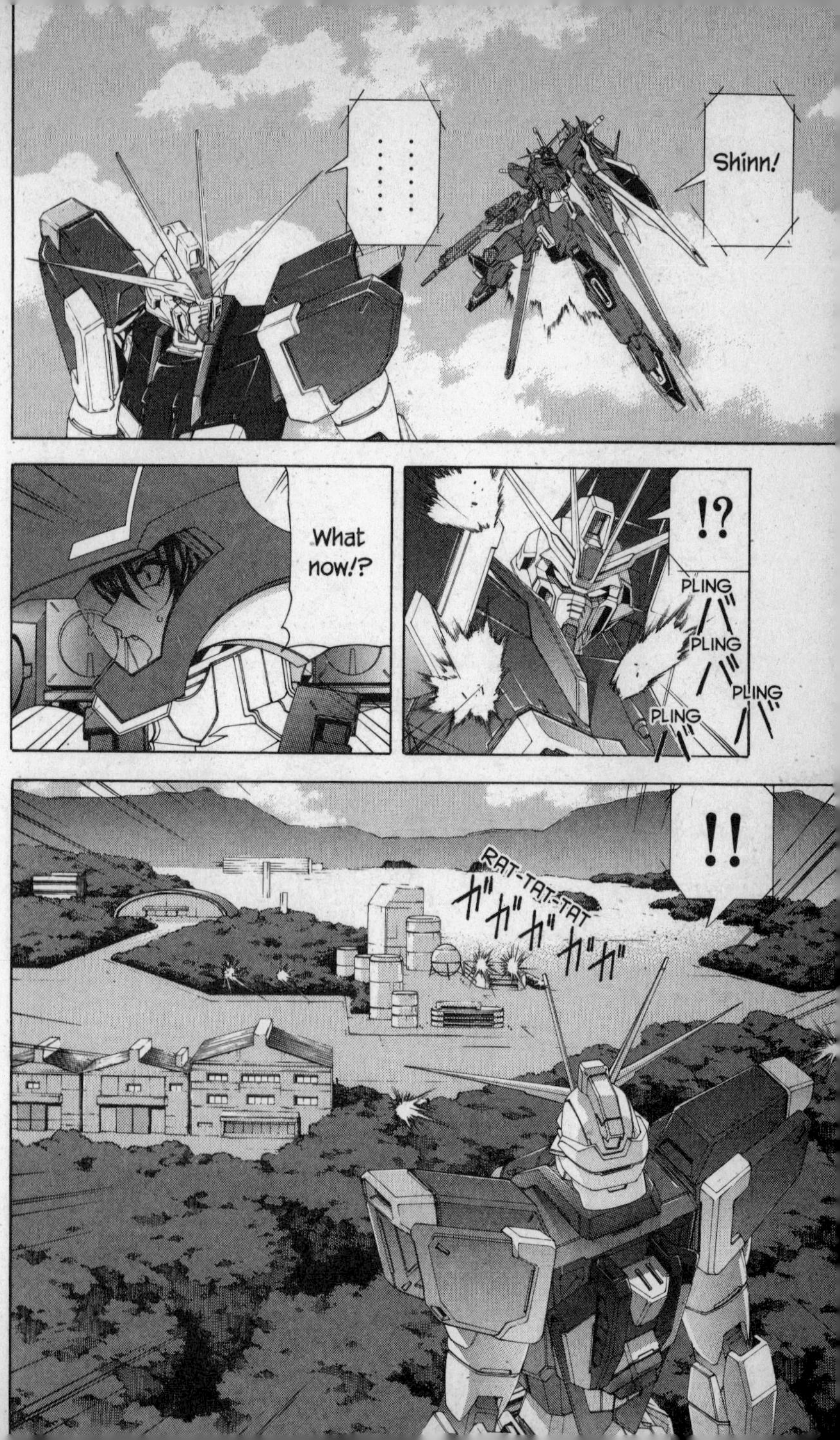
Shinn!
......
!?
PLING
PLING
PLING
PLING
What now!?
!!
RAT-TAT-TAT

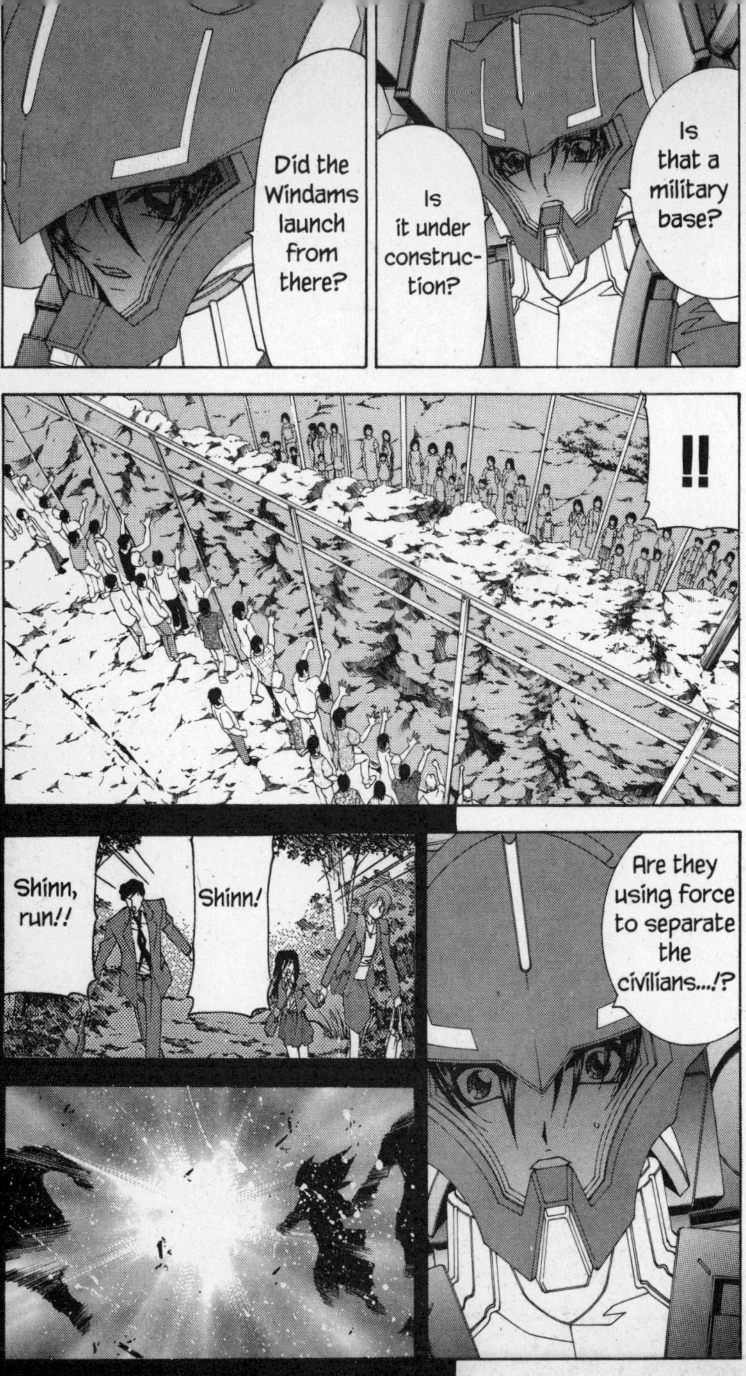
Is that a military base?
Is it under construction?
Did the Windams launch from there?
!!
Are they using force to separate the civilians...!?
Shinn!
Shinn, run!!

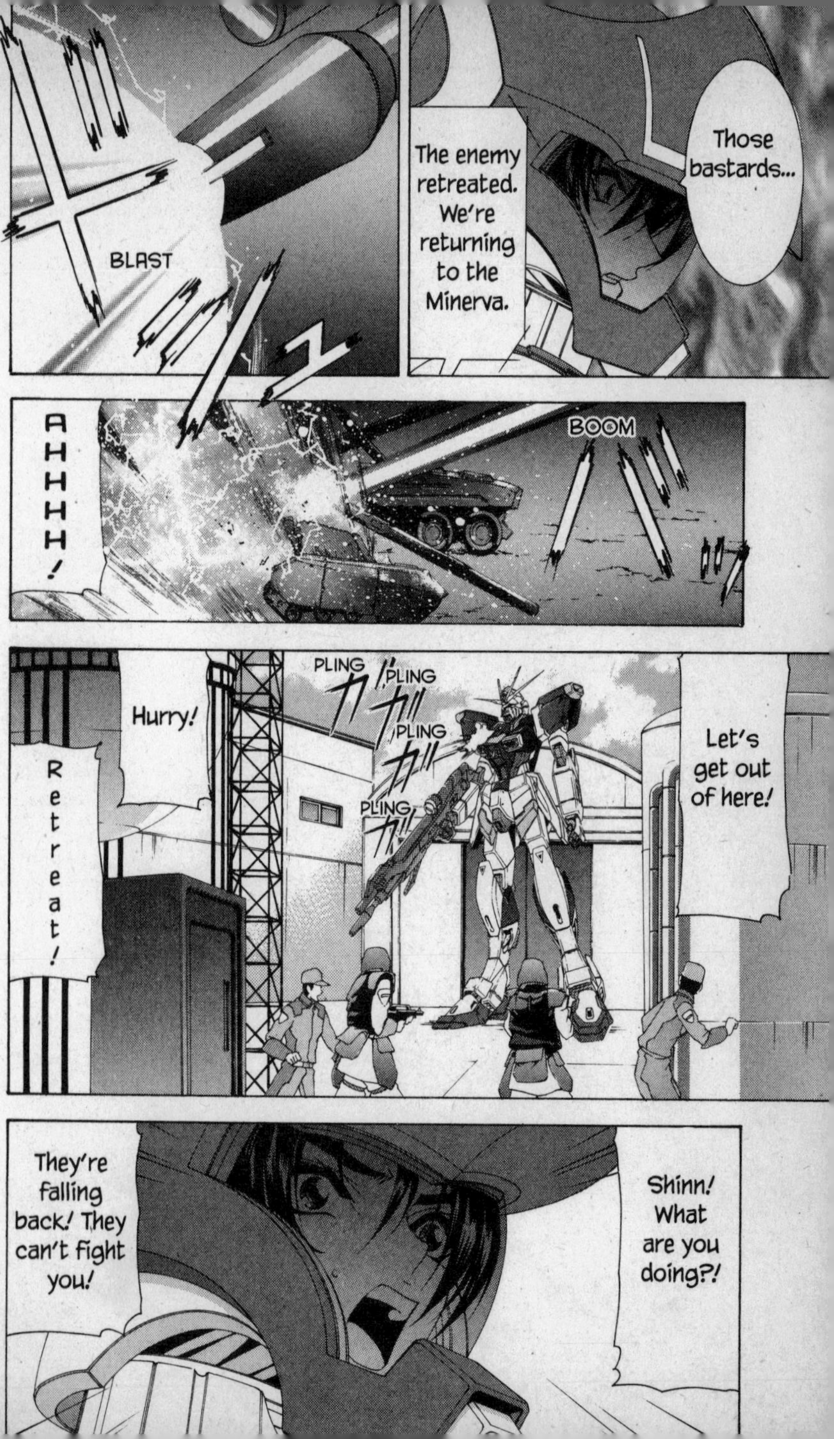
Those bastards...
The enemy retreated. We're returning to the Minerva.
BLAST
BOOM
AHHHHH!
Let's get out of here!
PLING
PLING
PLING
PLING
Hurry!
Retreat!
Shinn! What are you doing?!
They're falling back! They can't fight you!

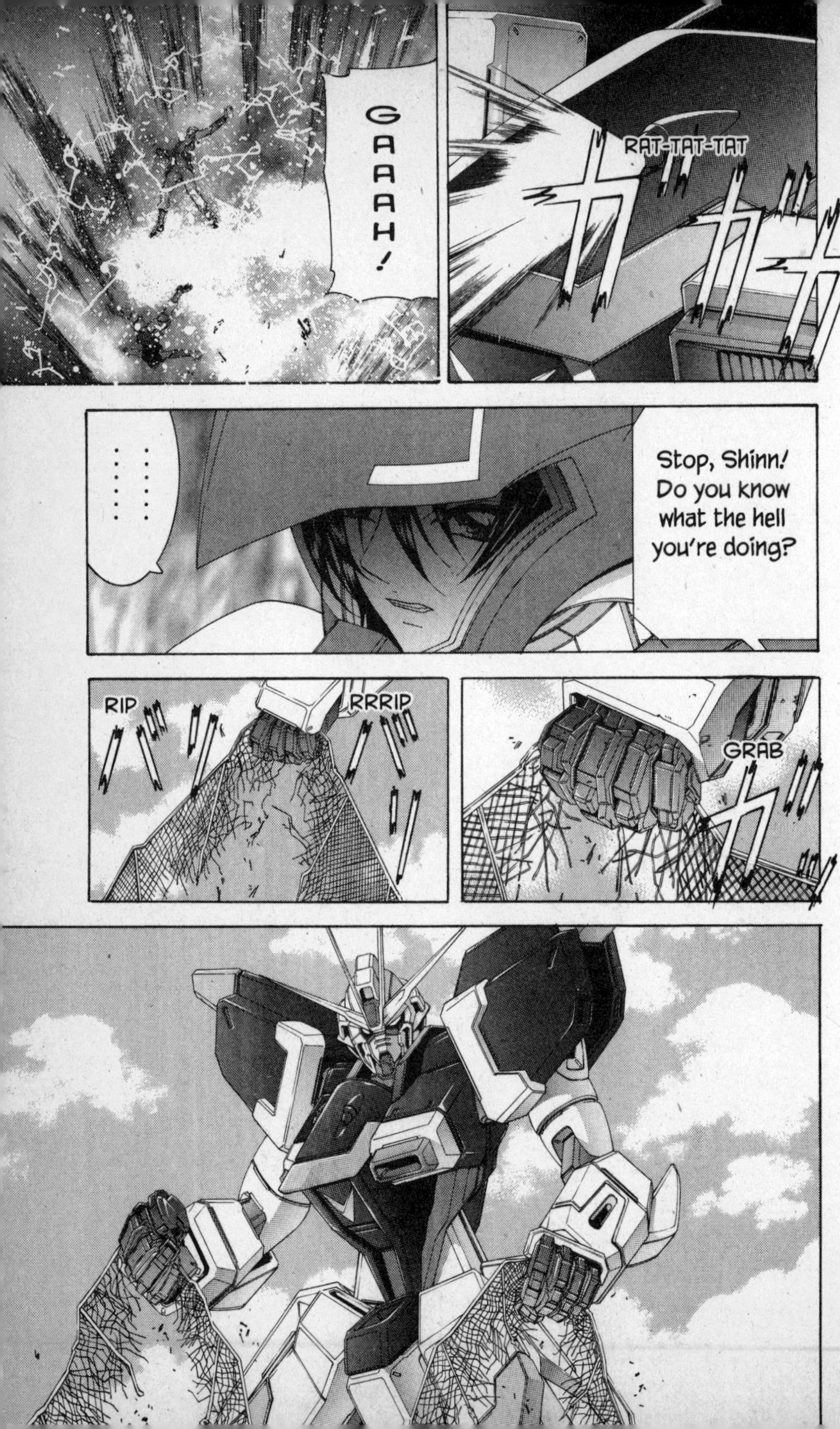
RAT-TAT-TAT
GAAAAH!
Stop, Shinn! Do you know what the hell you're doing?
......
GRAB
RIP
RRRIP

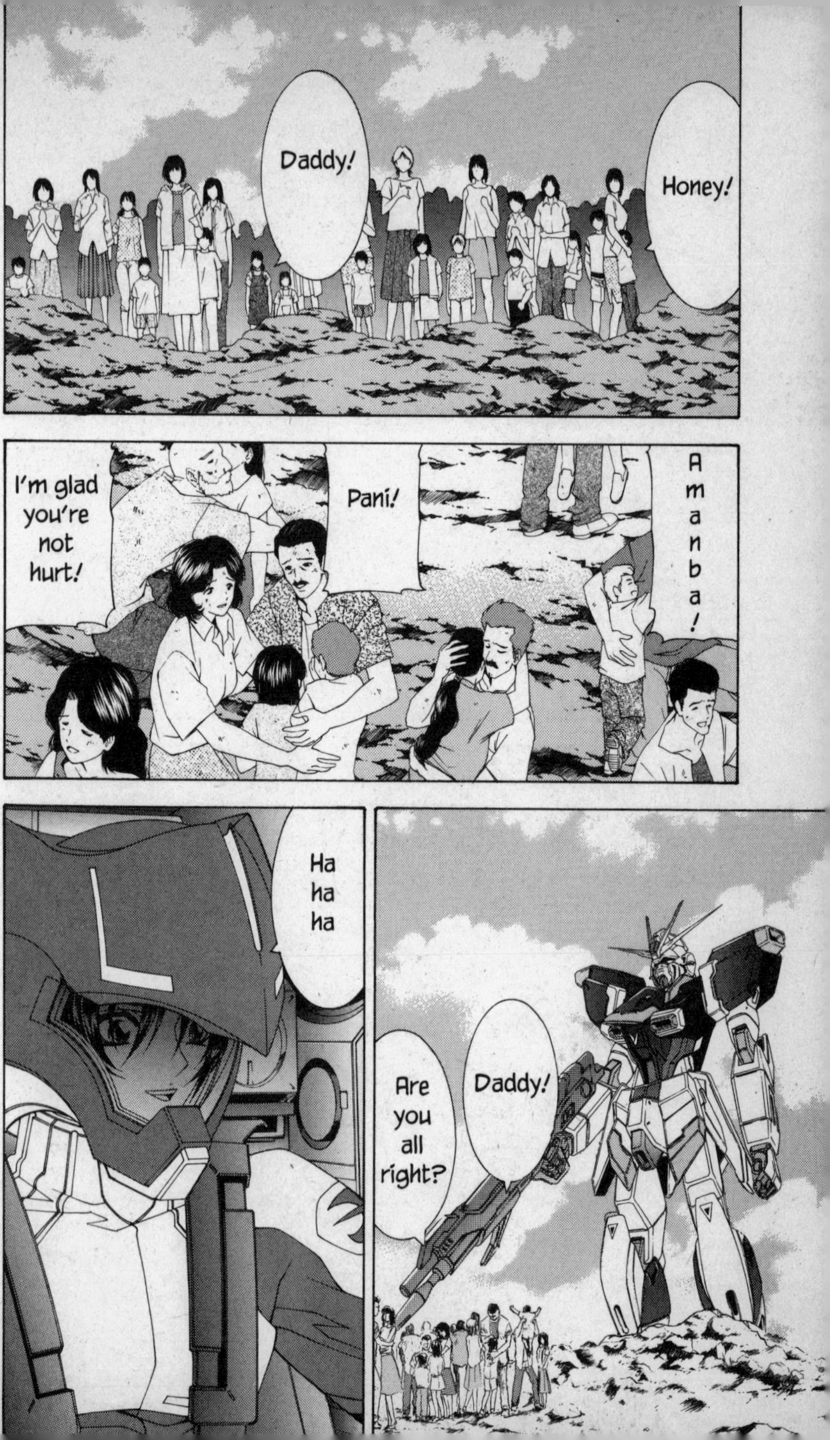
Honey!
Daddy!
Amanba!
Pani!
I'm glad you're not hurt!
Daddy!
Are you all right?
Ha ha ha

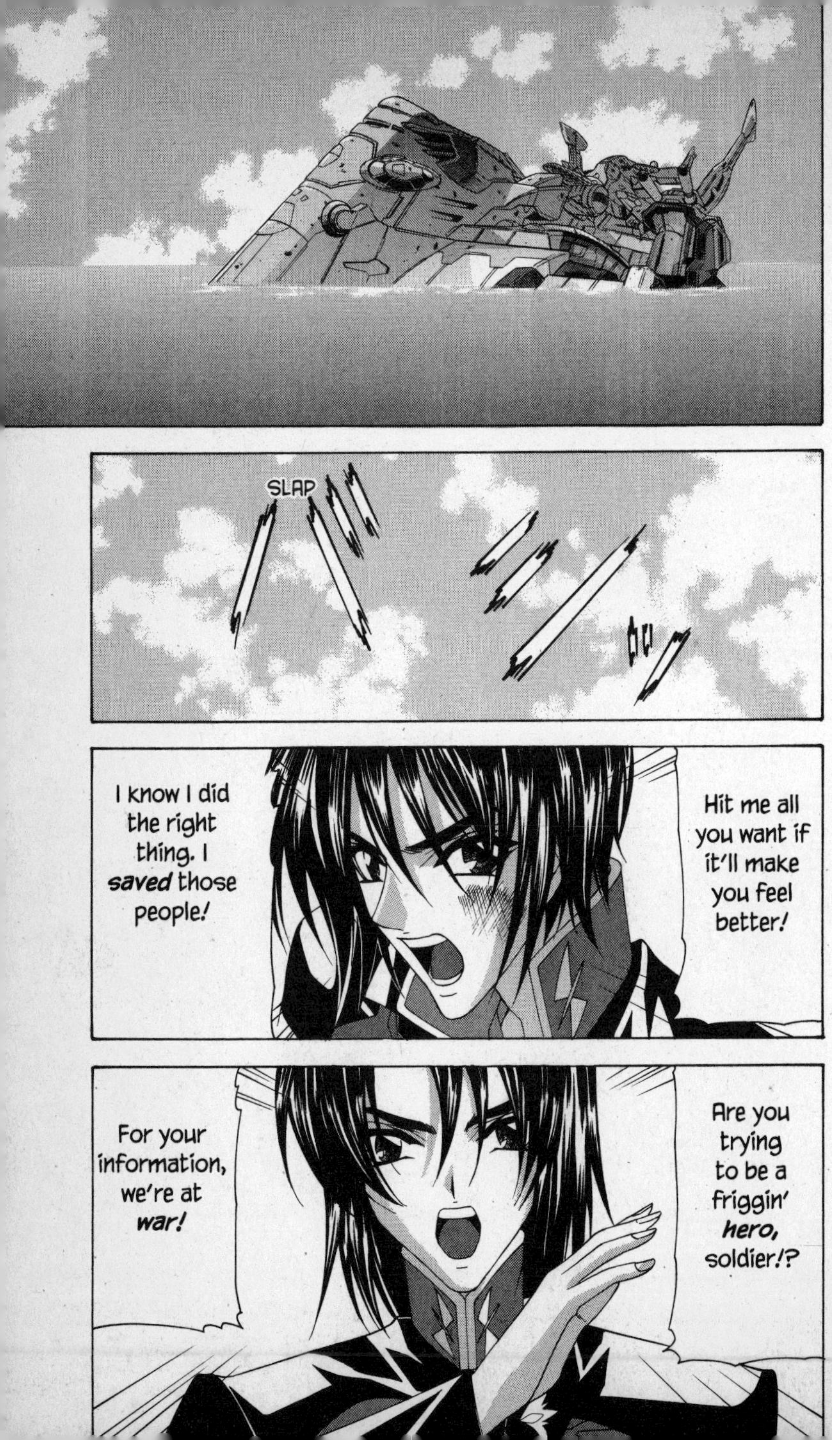
SLAP
Hit me all you want if it'll make you feel better!
I know I did the right thing. I *saved* those people!
Are you trying to be a friggin' *hero,* soldier!?
For your information, we're at *war!*

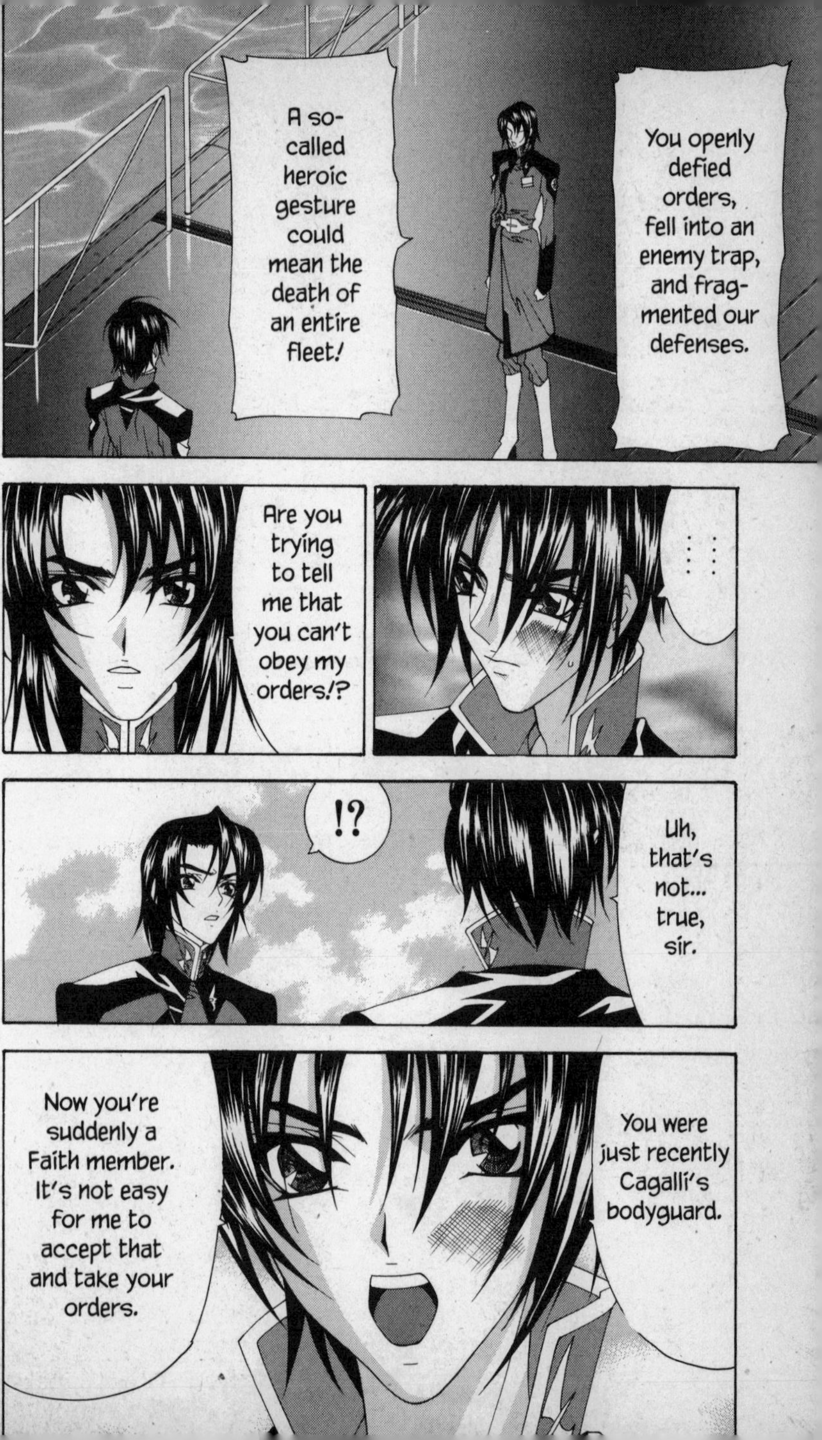
You openly defied orders, fell into an enemy trap, and fragmented our defenses.
A so-called heroic gesture could mean the death of an entire fleet!
......
Are you trying to tell me that you can't obey my orders!?
Uh, that's not... true, sir.
!?
You were just recently Cagalli's bodyguard.
Now you're suddenly a Faith member. It's not easy for me to accept that and take your orders.

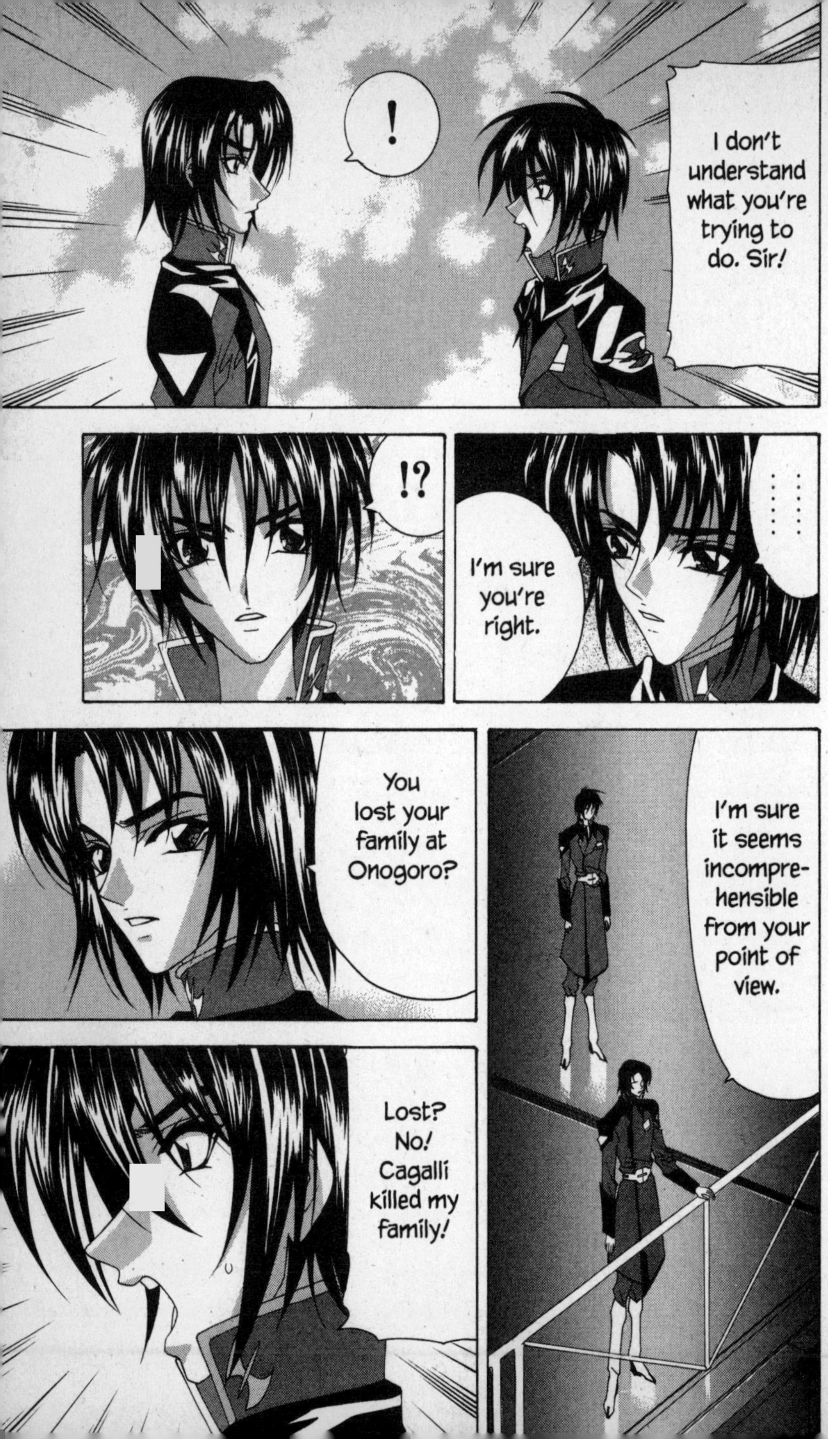
I don't understand what you're trying to do. Sir!
!
......
I'm sure you're right.
!?
I'm sure it seems incompre-hensible from your point of view.
You lost your family at Onogoro?
Lost? No! Cagalli killed my family!

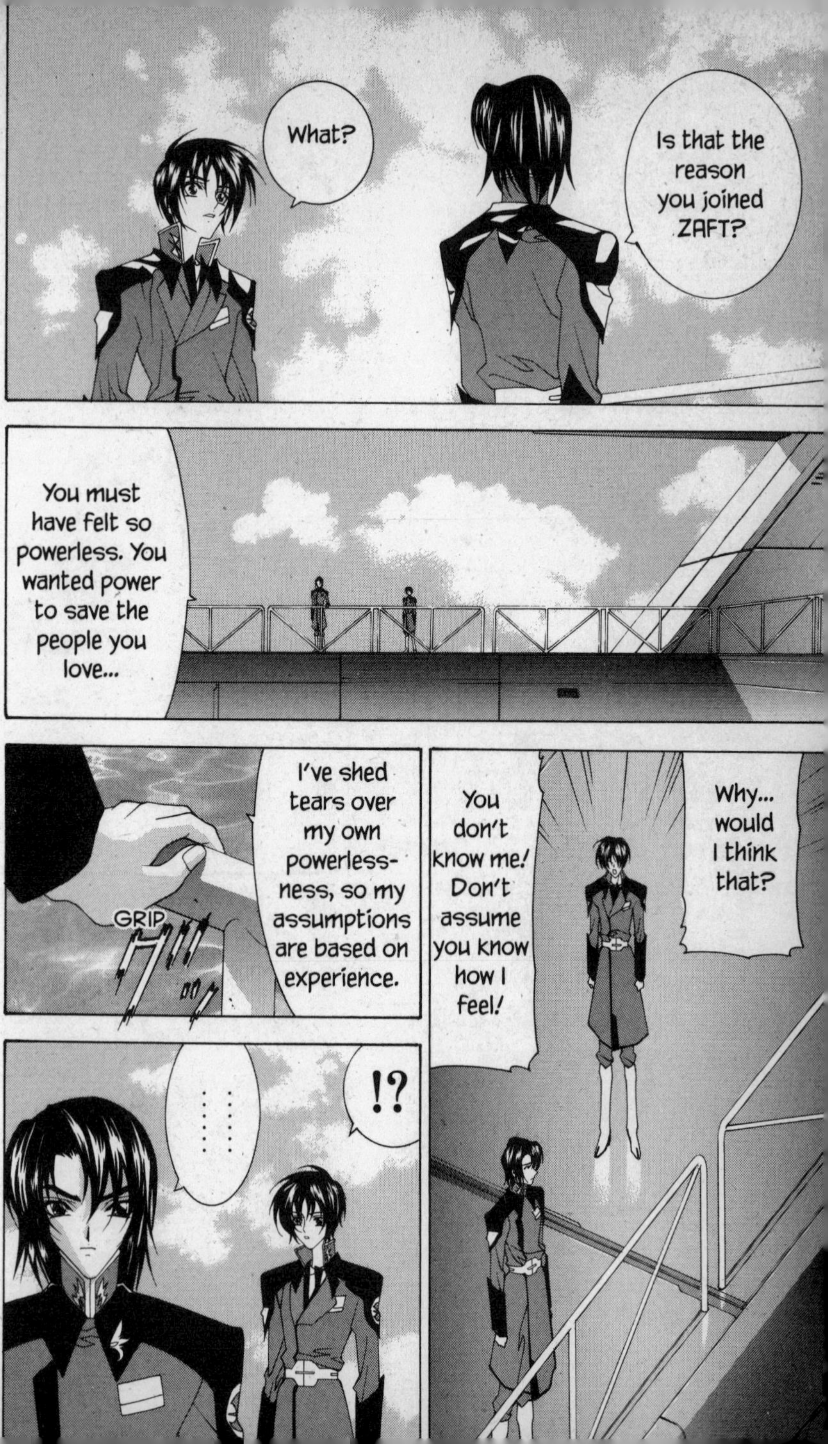
Is that the reason you joined ZAFT?
What?
You must have felt so powerless. You wanted power to save the people you love...
Why... would I think that?
You don't know me! Don't assume you know how I feel!
I've shed tears over my own powerless-ness, so my assumptions are based on experience.
GRIP
!?
......

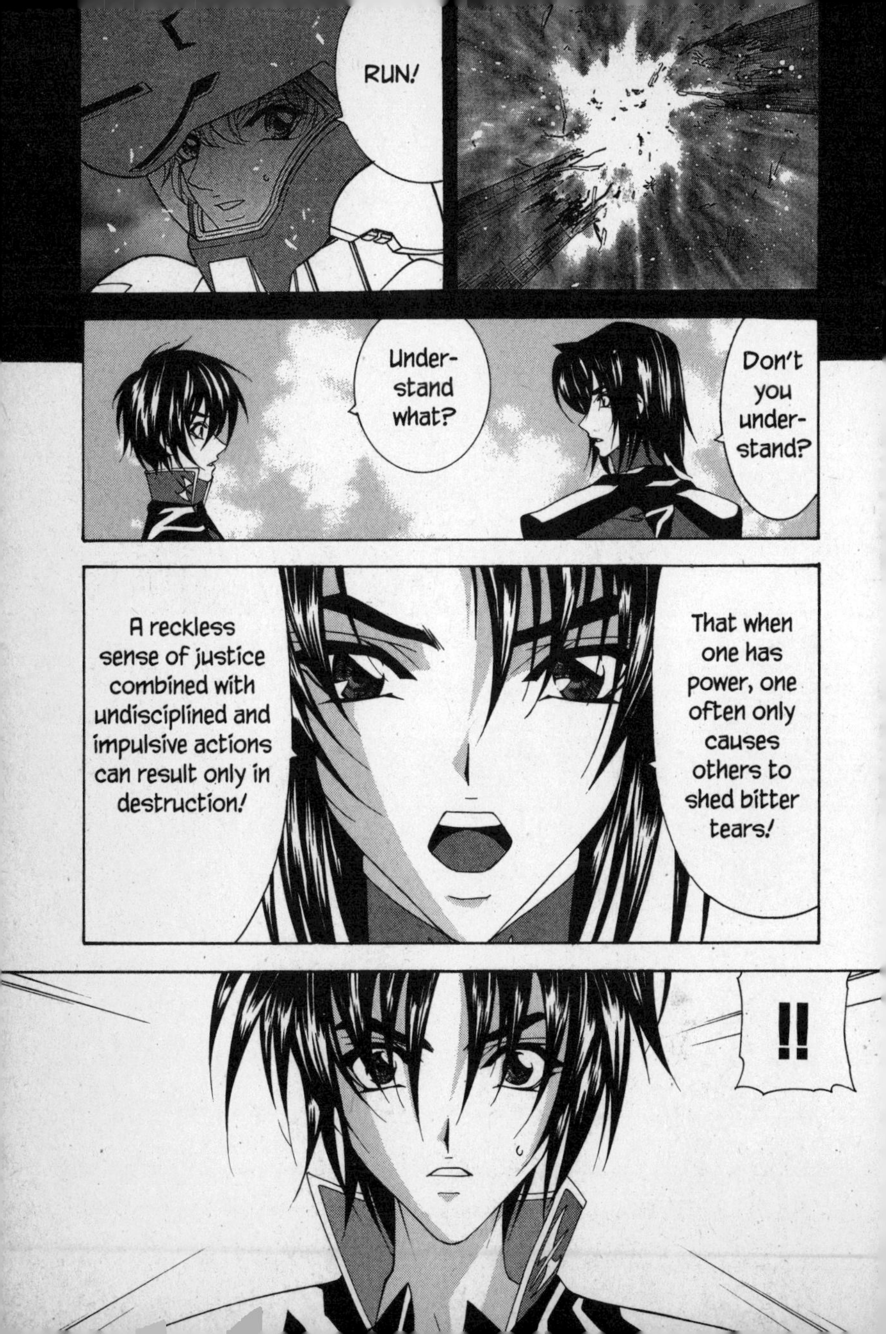
RUN!
Don't you understand?
Understand what?
That when one has power, one often only causes others to shed bitter tears!
A reckless sense of justice combined with undisciplined and impulsive actions can result only in destruction!
!!

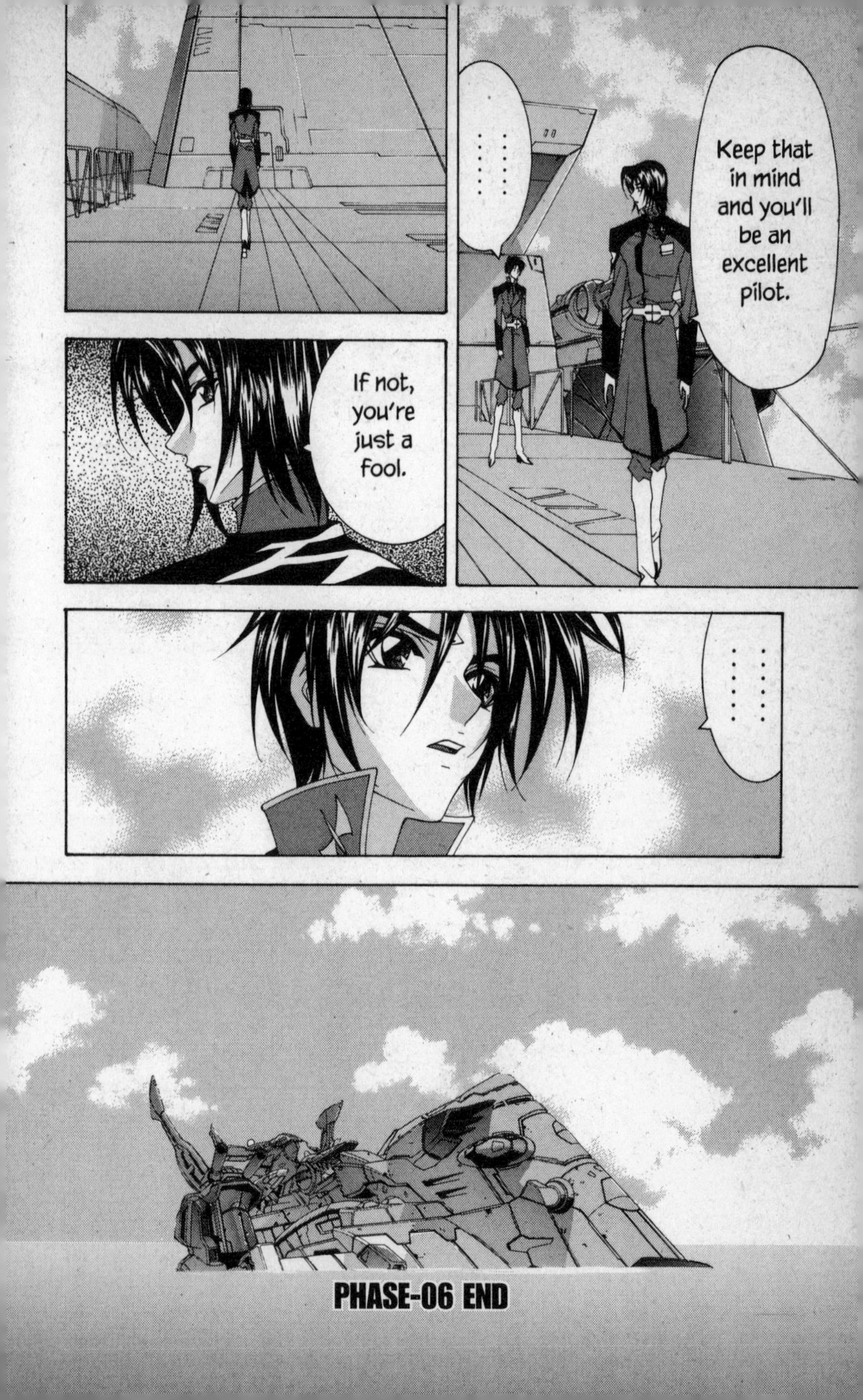
Keep that in mind and you'll be an excellent pilot.
......
If not, you're just a fool.
......
PHASE-06 END

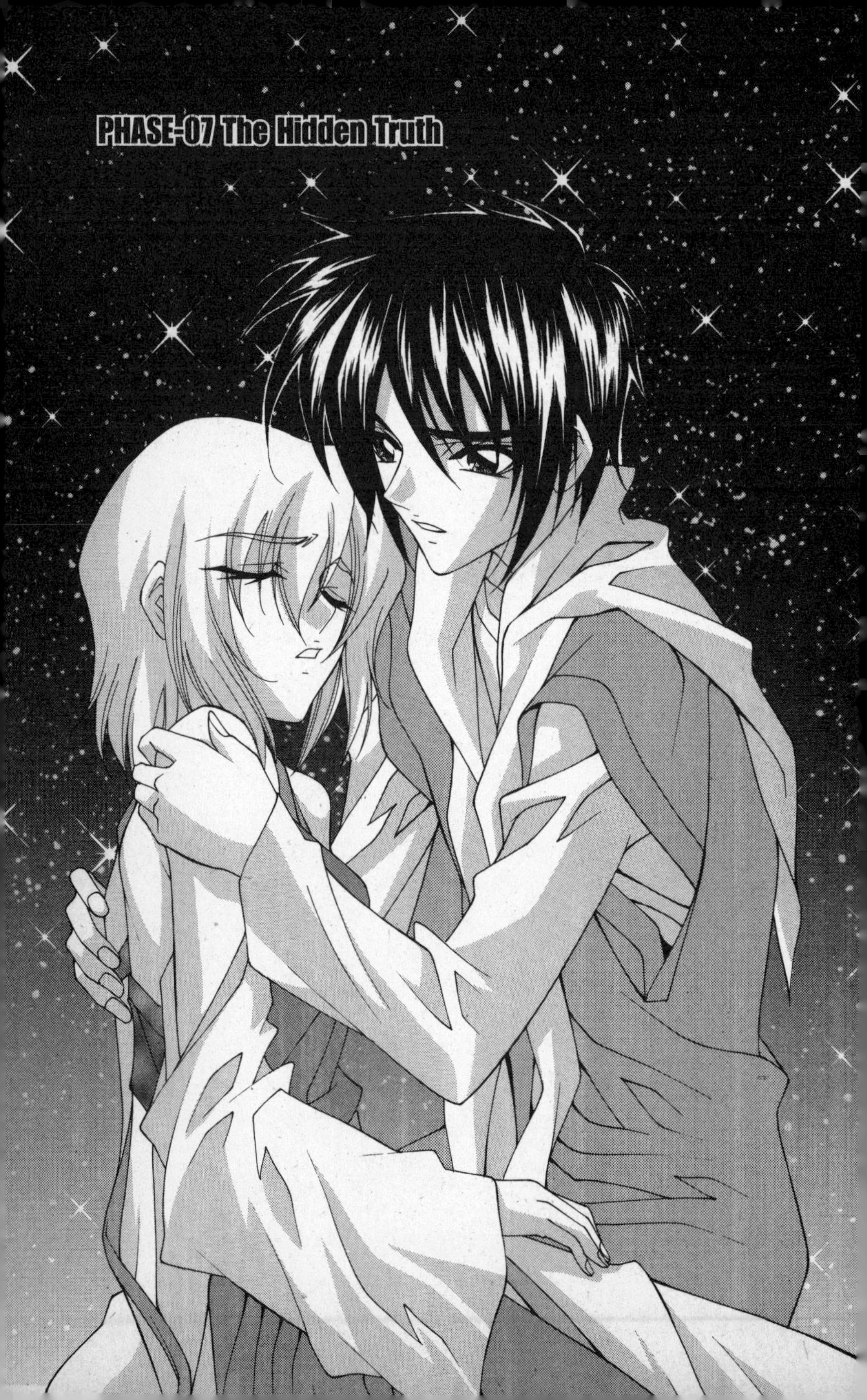
PHASE-07 The Hidden Truth

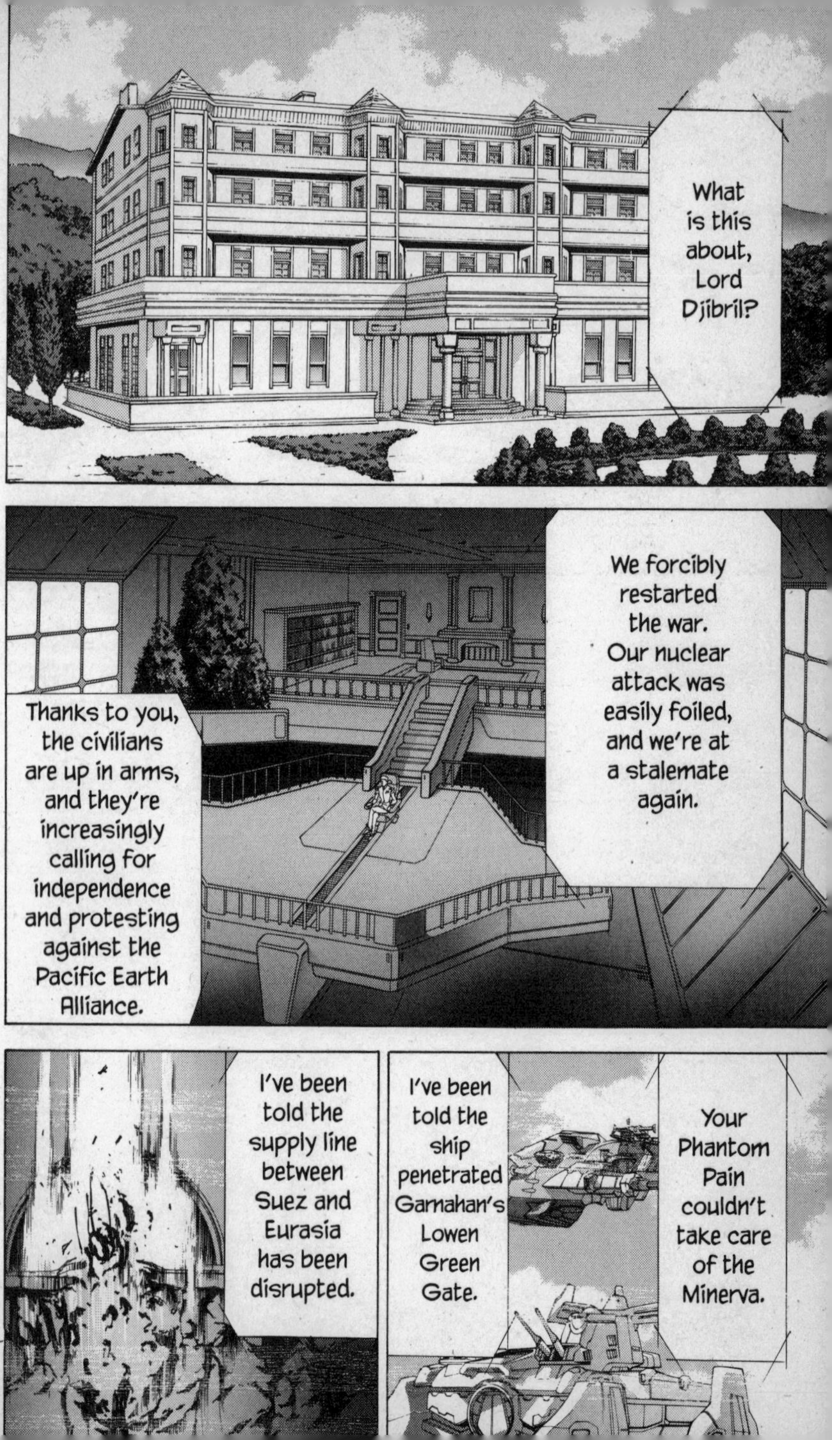
What is this about, Lord Djibril?
We forcibly restarted the war. Our nuclear attack was easily foiled, and we're at a stalemate again.
Thanks to you, the civilians are up in arms, and they're increasingly calling for independence and protesting against the Pacific Earth Alliance.
Your Phantom Pain couldn't take care of the Minerva.
I've been told the ship penetrated Garnahan's Lowen Green Gate.
I've been told the supply line between Suez and Eurasia has been disrupted.

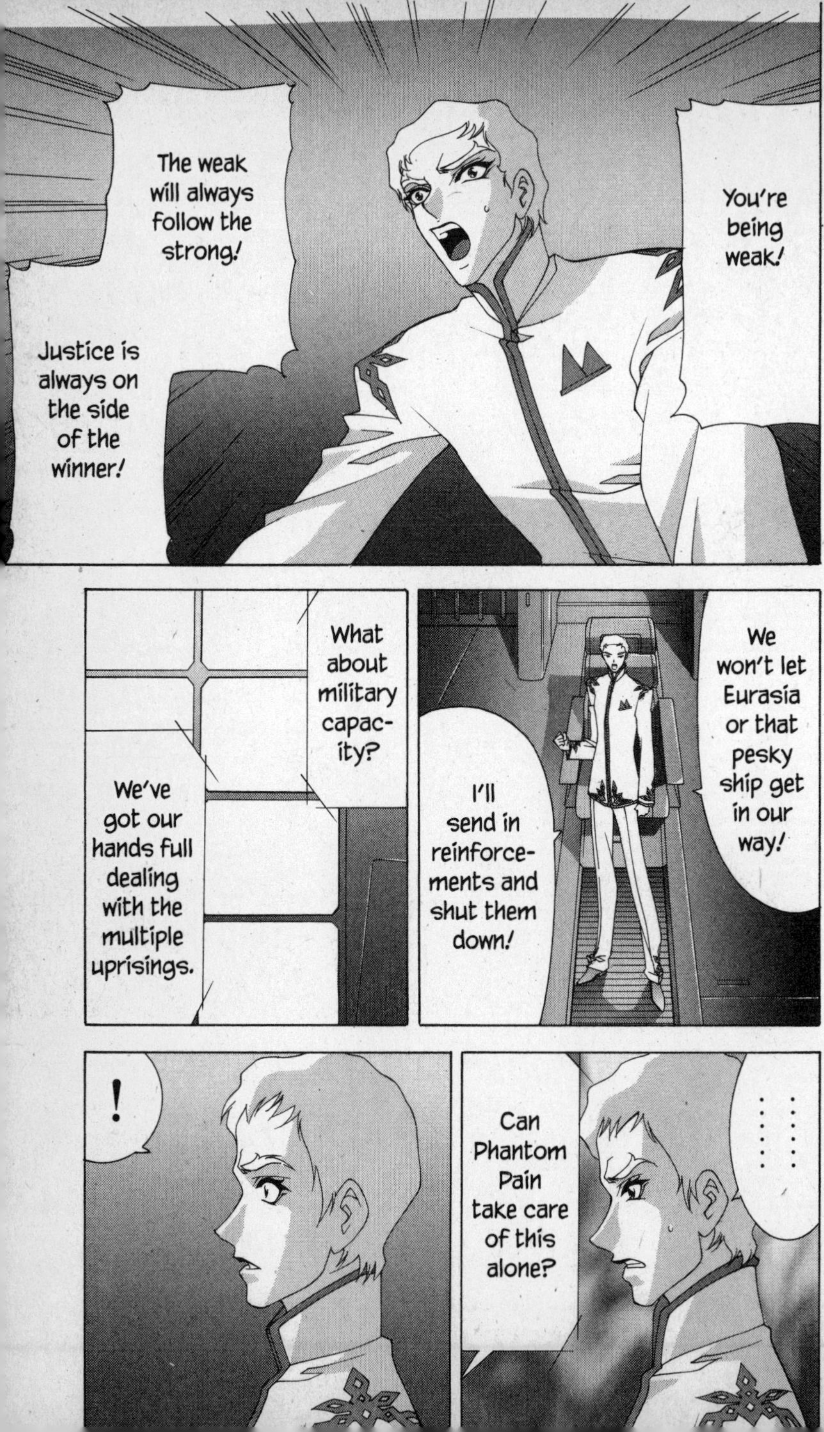
You're being weak!
The weak will always follow the strong!
Justice is always on the side of the winner!
We won't let Eurasia or that pesky ship get in our way!
I'll send in reinforcements and shut them down!
What about military capacity?
We've got our hands full dealing with the multiple uprisings.
......
Can Phantom Pain take care of this alone?
!

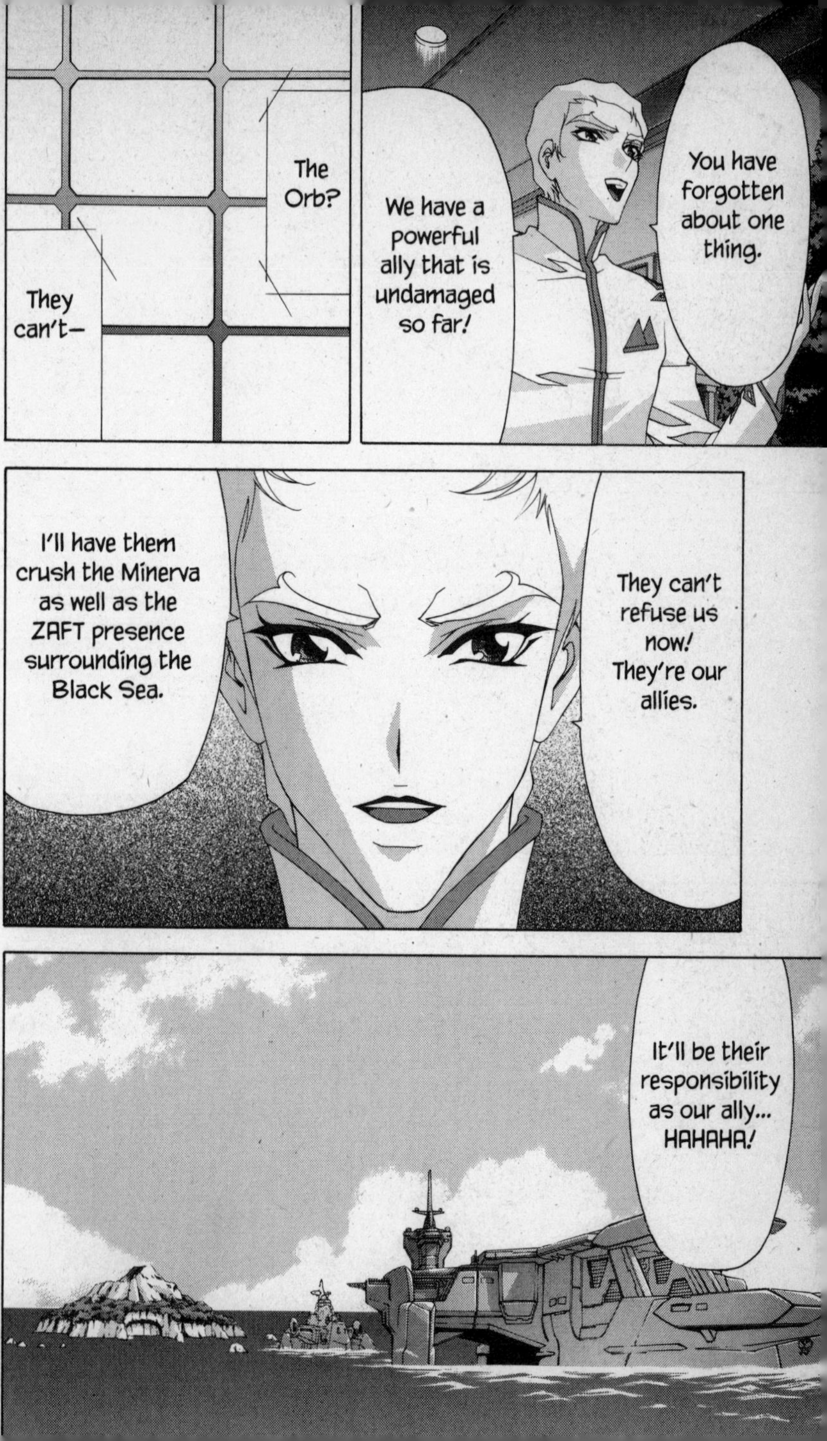
You have forgotten about one thing.
We have a powerful ally that is undamaged so far!
The Orb?
They can't—
They can't refuse us now! They're our allies.
I'll have them crush the Minerva as well as the ZAFT presence surrounding the Black Sea.
It'll be their responsibility as our ally... HAHAHA!

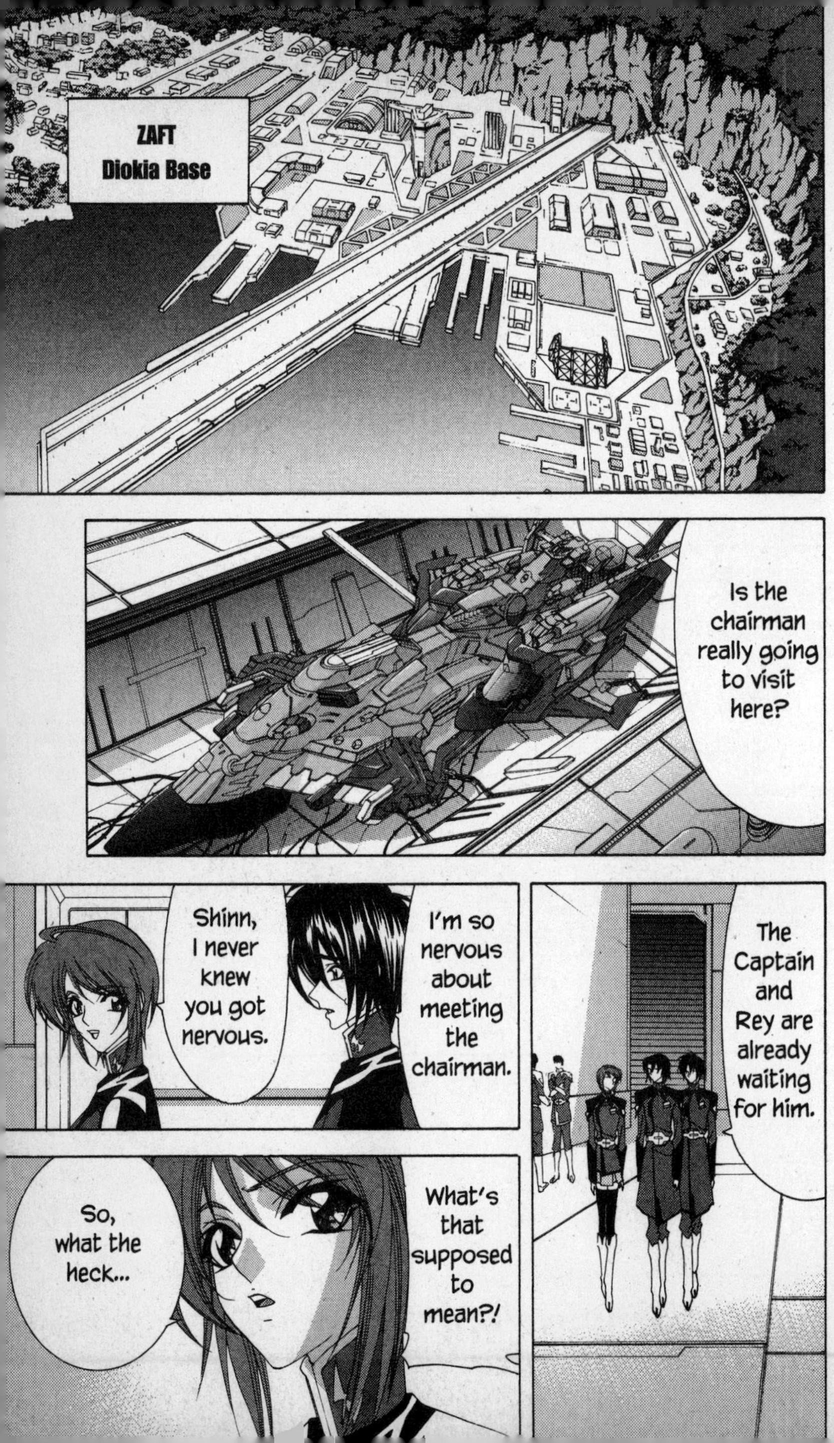
ZAFT
Diokia Base
Is the chairman really going to visit here?
The Captain and Rey are already waiting for him.
I'm so nervous about meeting the chairman.
Shinn, I never knew you got nervous.
What's that supposed to mean?!
So, what the heck...

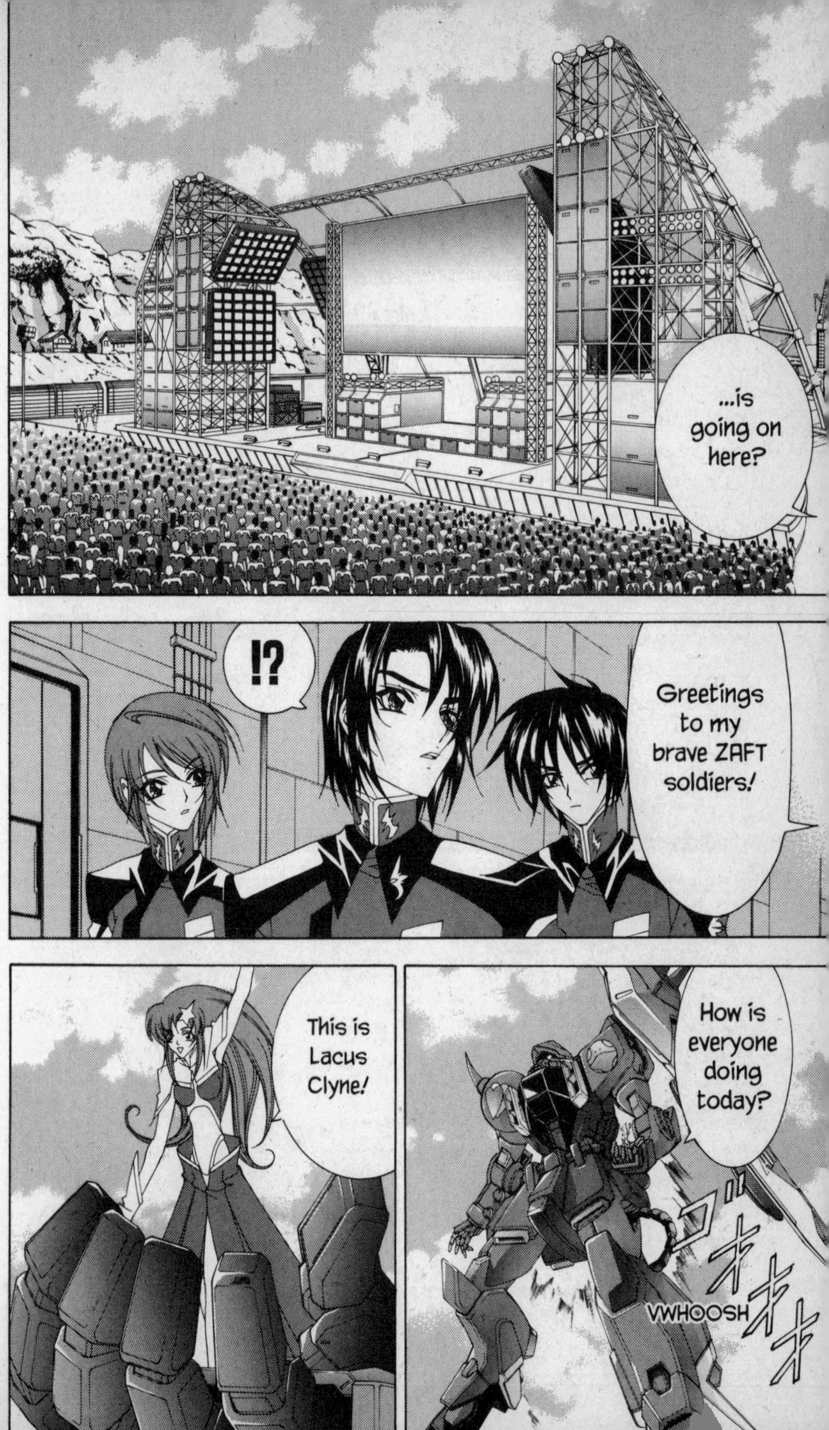
...is going on here?
Greetings to my brave ZAFT soldiers!
!?
How is everyone doing today?
VWHOOSH
This is Lacus Clyne!

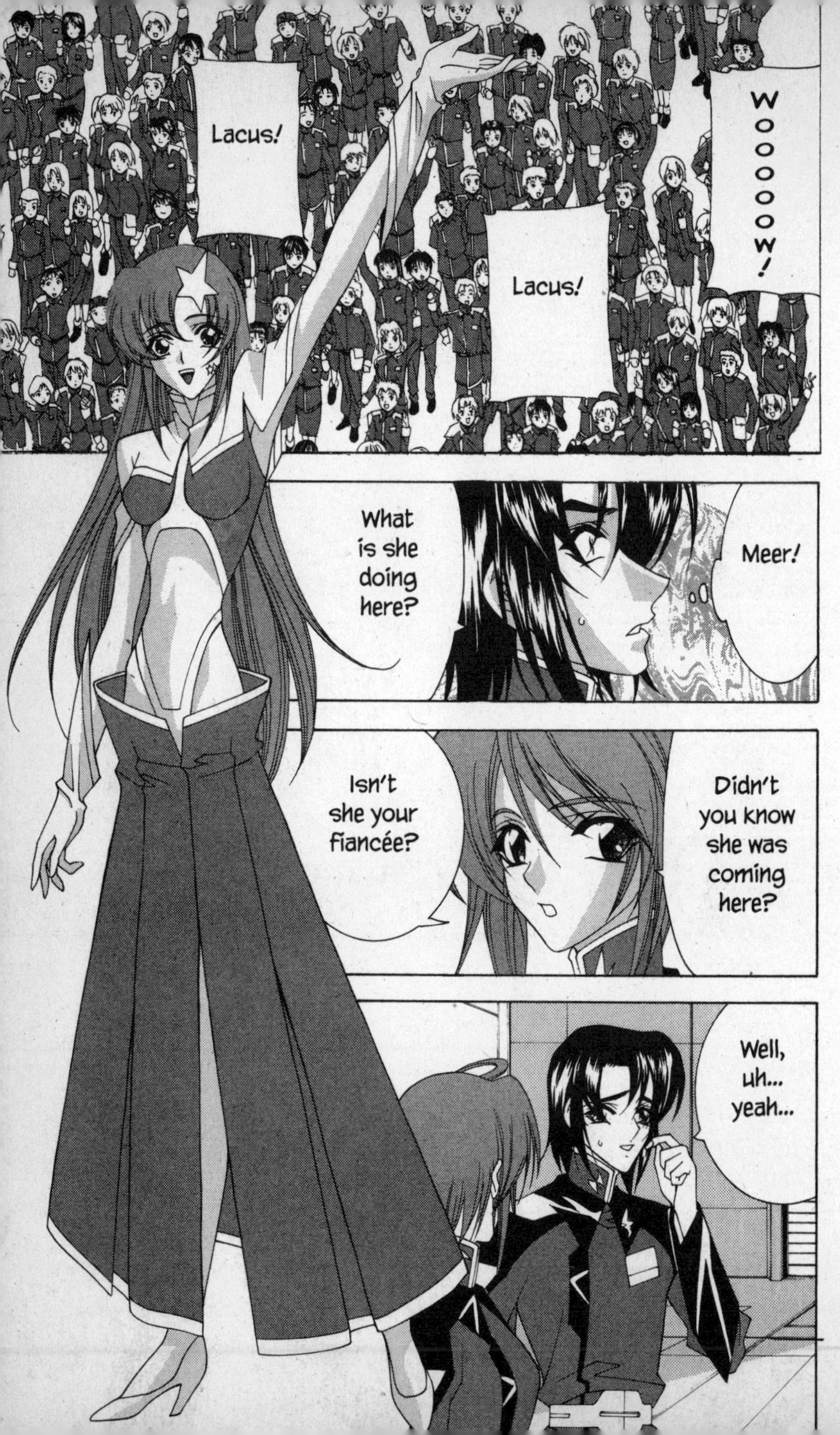
WOOOOOW!
Lacus!
Lacus!
Meer!
What is she doing here?
Didn't you know she was coming here?
Isn't she your fiancée?
Well, uh... yeah...

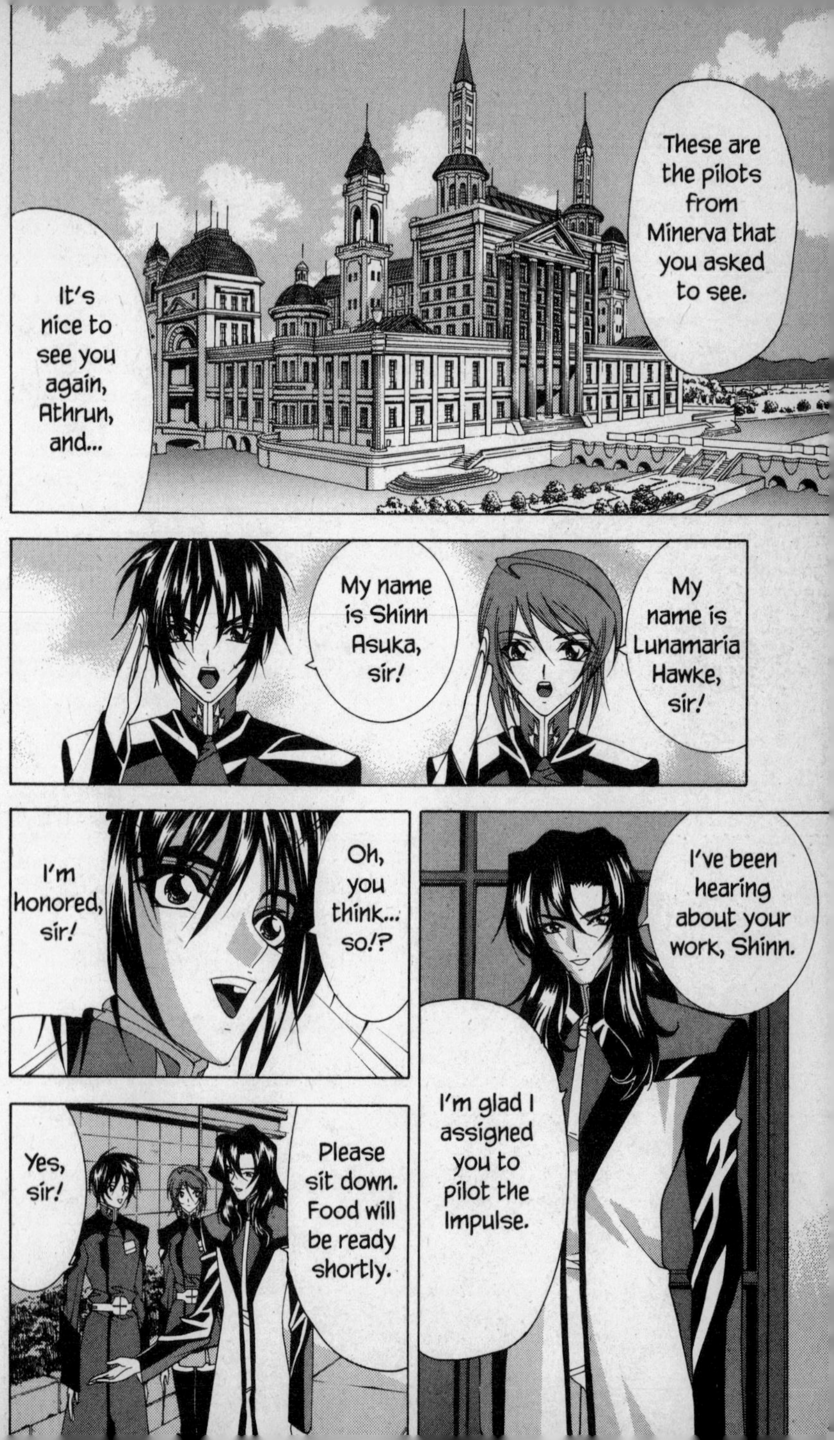
These are the pilots from Minerva that you asked to see.
It's nice to see you again, Athrun, and...
My name is Lunamaria Hawke, sir!
My name is Shinn Asuka, sir!
I've been hearing about your work, Shinn.
I'm glad I assigned you to pilot the Impulse.
Oh, you think... so!?
I'm honored, sir!
Please sit down. Food will be ready shortly.
Yes, sir!

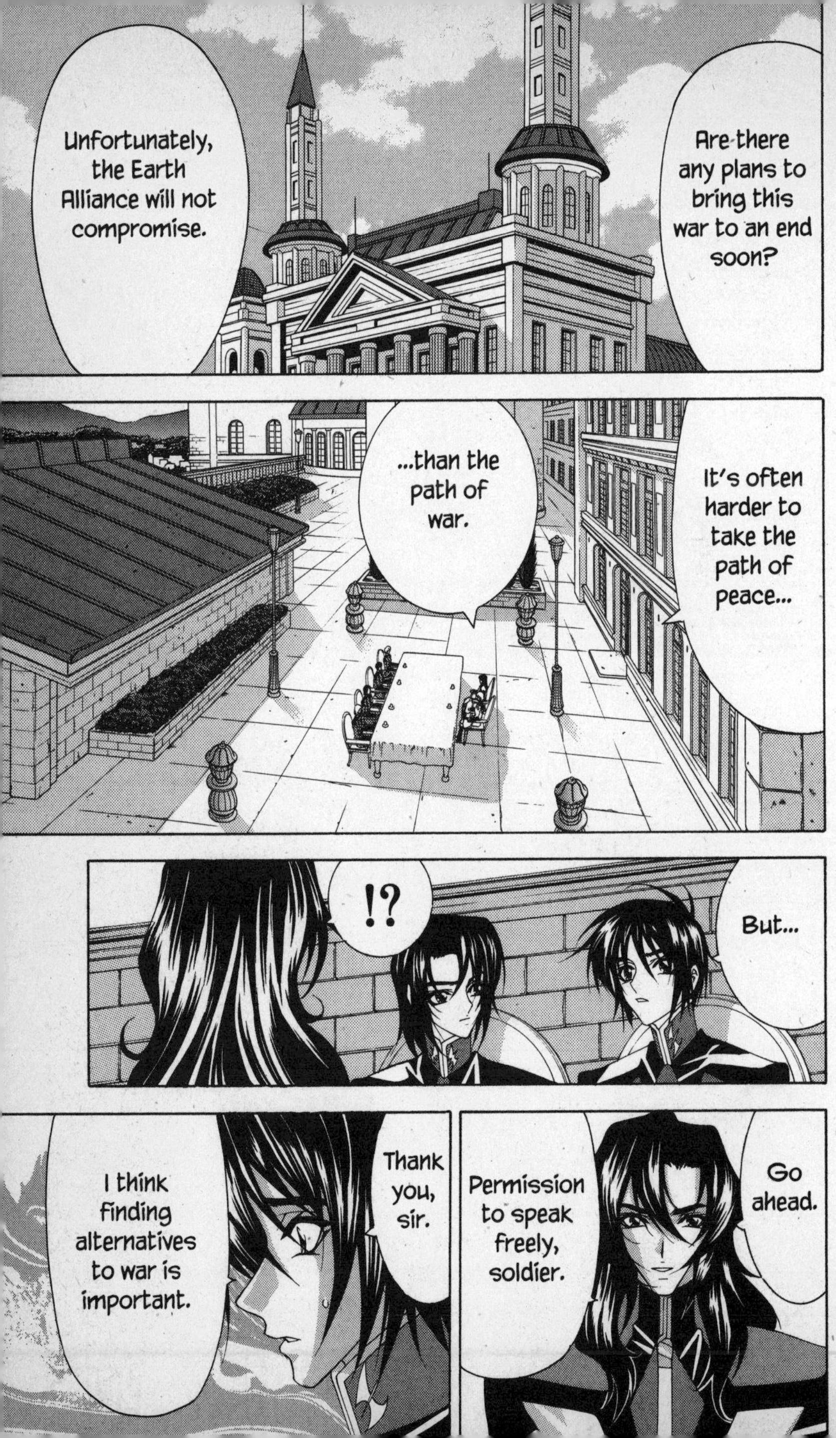
Are there any plans to bring this war to an end soon?
Unfortunately, the Earth Alliance will not compromise.
It's often harder to take the path of peace...
...than the path of war.
But...
!?
Go ahead.
Permission to speak freely, soldier.
Thank you, sir.
I think finding alternatives to war is important.

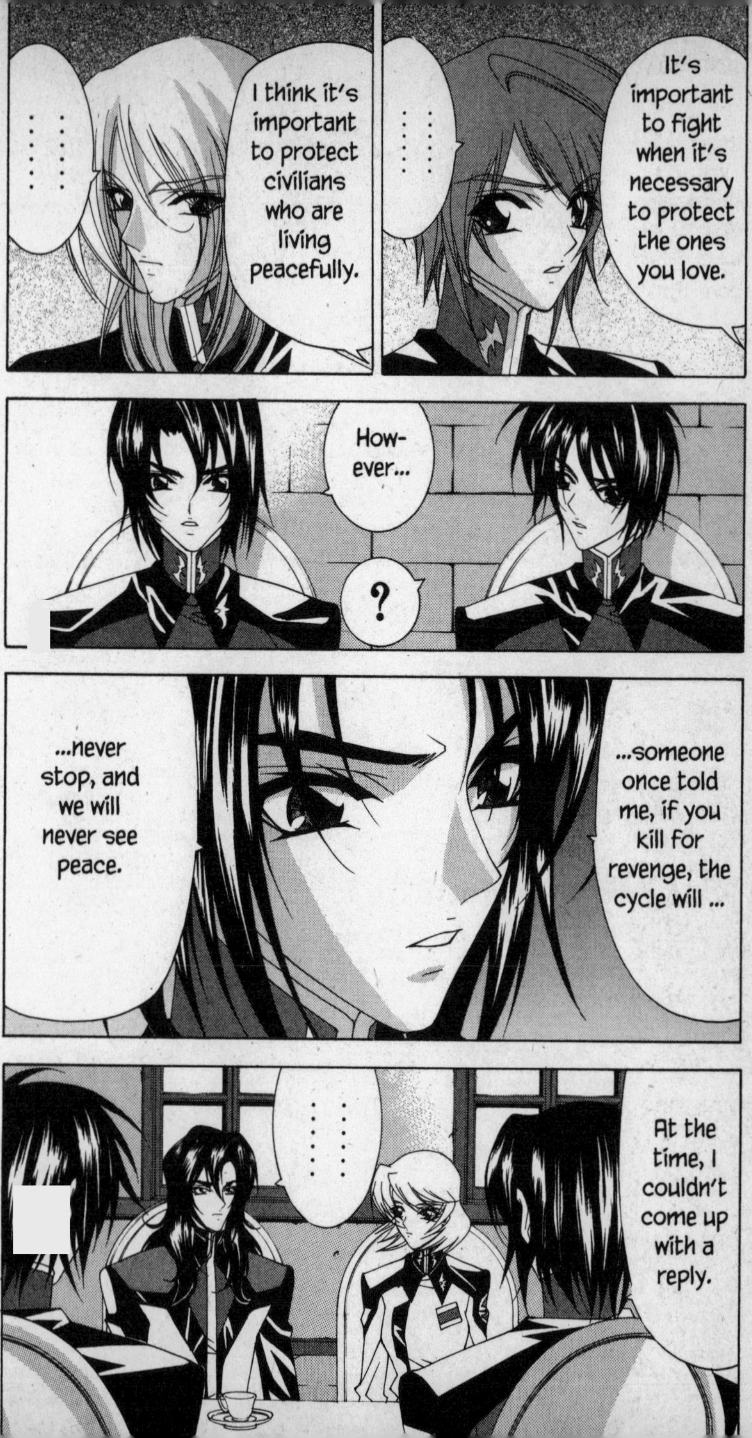
It's important to fight when it's necessary to protect the ones you love.
......
I think it's important to protect civilians who are living peacefully.
......
How-ever...
?
...someone once told me, if you kill for revenge, the cycle will ...
...never stop, and we will never see peace.
At the time, I couldn't come up with a reply.
......

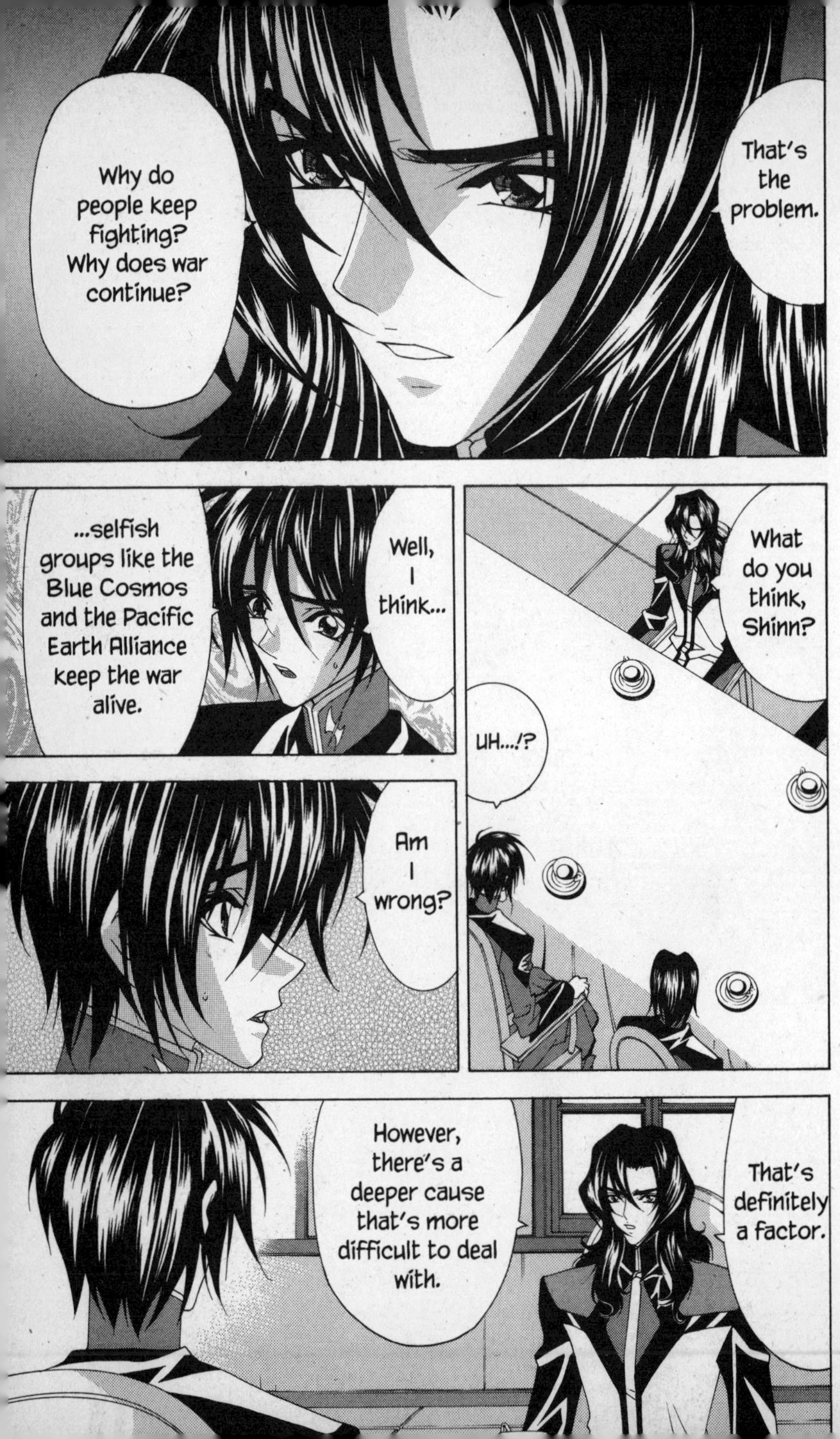
That's the problem.
Why do people keep fighting? Why does war continue?
What do you think, Shinn?
UH...!?
Well, I think...
...selfish groups like the Blue Cosmos and the Pacific Earth Alliance keep the war alive.
Am I wrong?
That's definitely a factor.
However, there's a deeper cause that's more difficult to deal with.

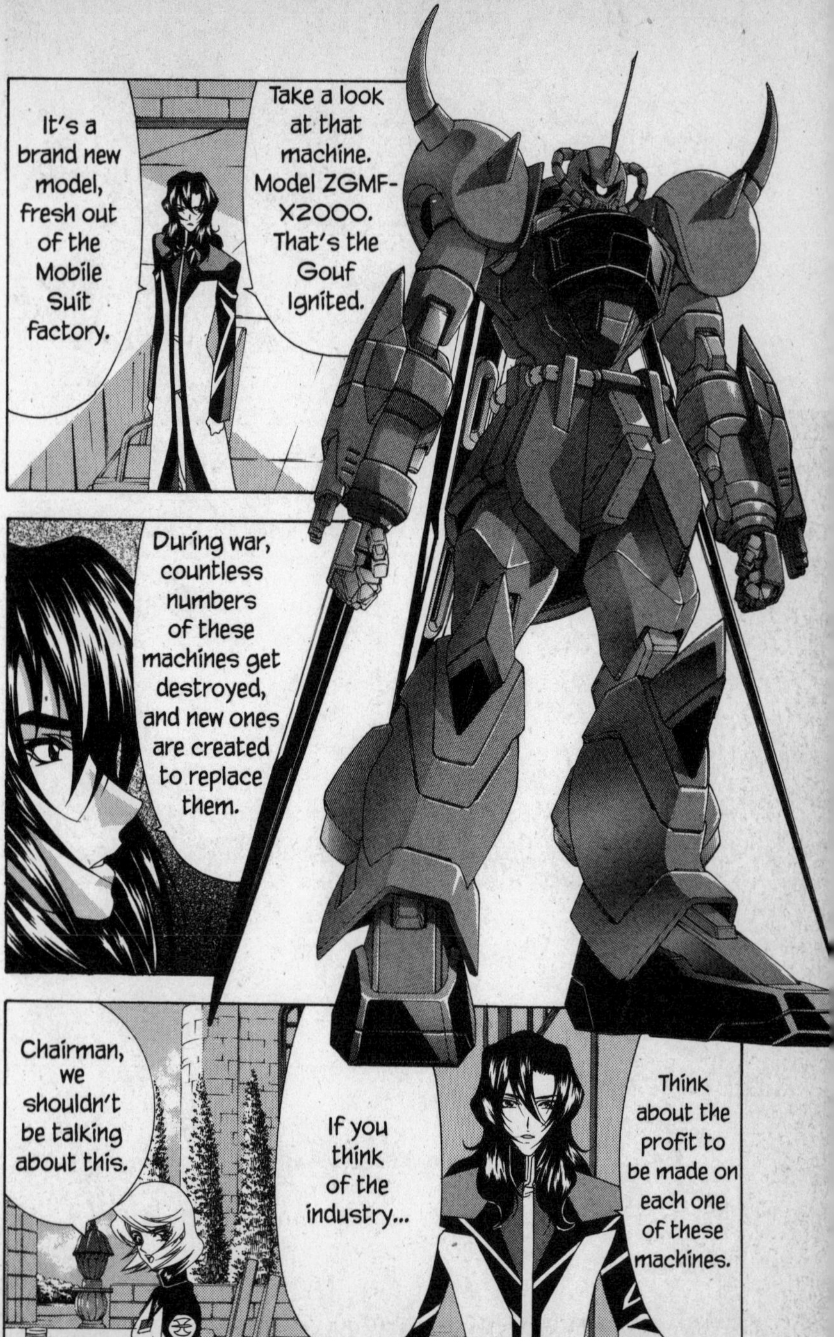
Take a look at that machine. Model ZGMF-X2000. That's the Gouf Ignited.
It's a brand new model, fresh out of the Mobile Suit factory.
During war, countless numbers of these machines get destroyed, and new ones are created to replace them.
Think about the profit to be made on each one of these machines.
If you think of the industry...
Chairman, we shouldn't be talking about this.

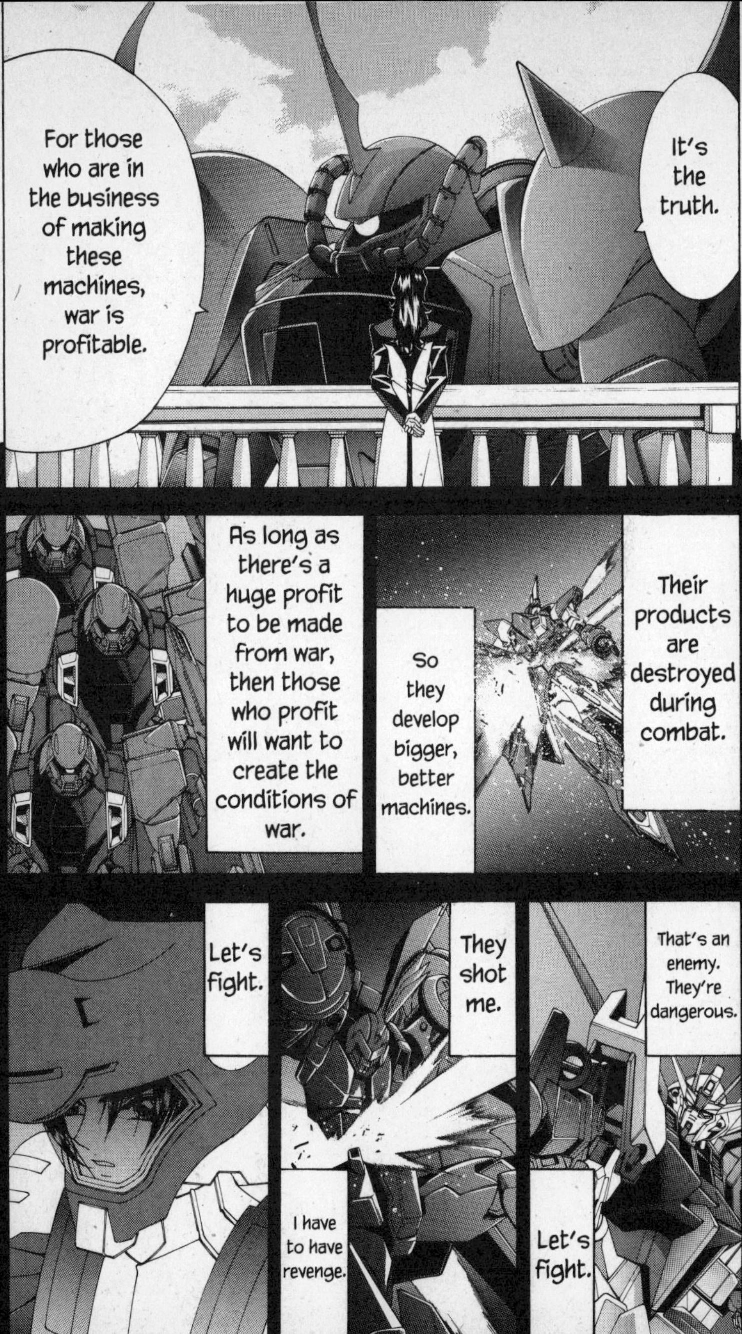
It's the truth.
For those who are in the business of making these machines, war is profitable.
Their products are destroyed during combat.
So they develop bigger, better machines.
As long as there's a huge profit to be made from war, then those who profit will want to create the conditions of war.
That's an enemy. They're dangerous.
Let's fight.
They shot me.
I have to have revenge.
Let's fight.

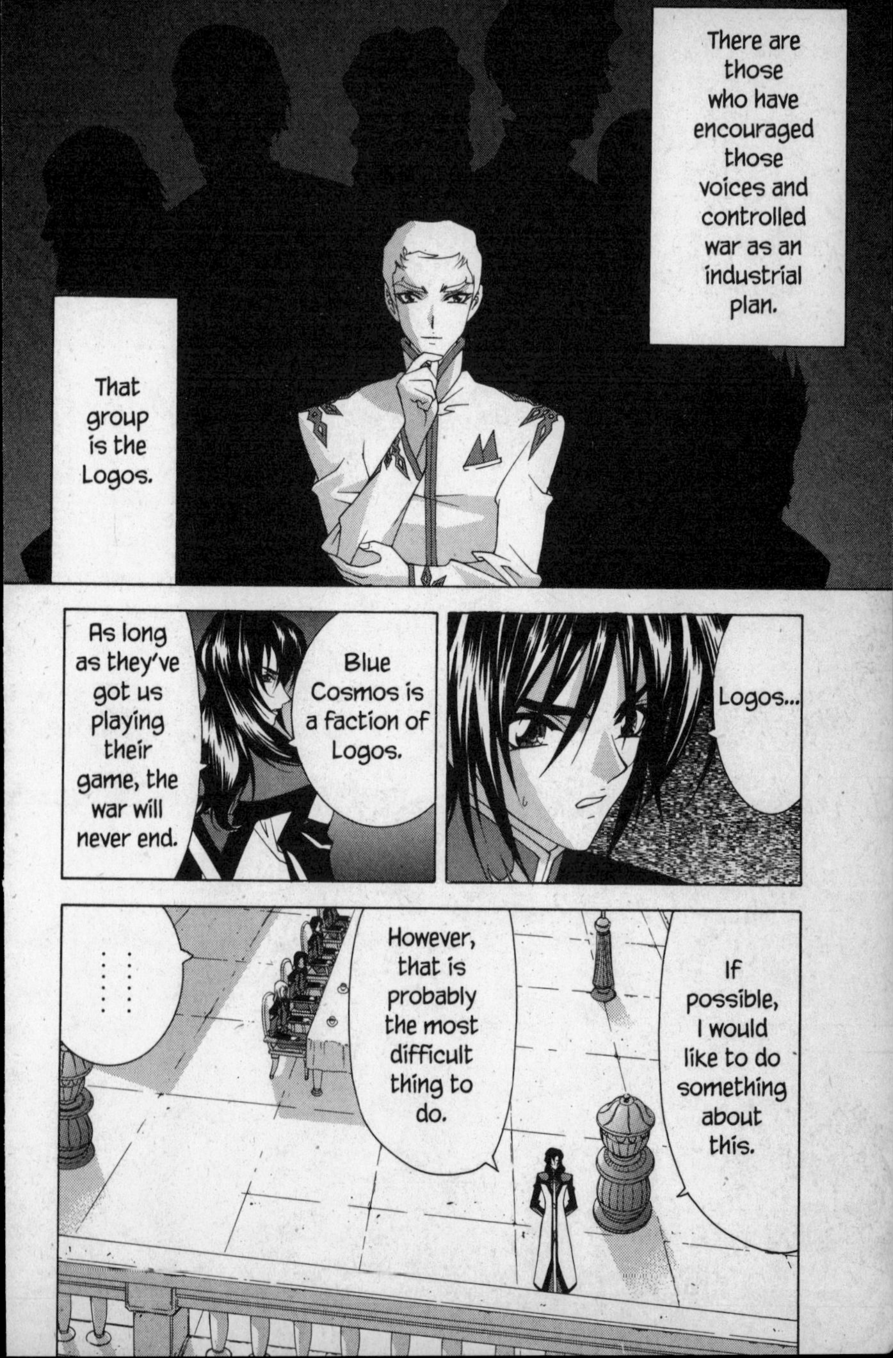
There are those who have encouraged those voices and controlled war as an industrial plan.
That group is the Logos.
Logos...
Blue Cosmos is a faction of Logos.
As long as they've got us playing their game, the war will never end.
If possible, I would like to do something about this.
However, that is probably the most difficult thing to do.
......

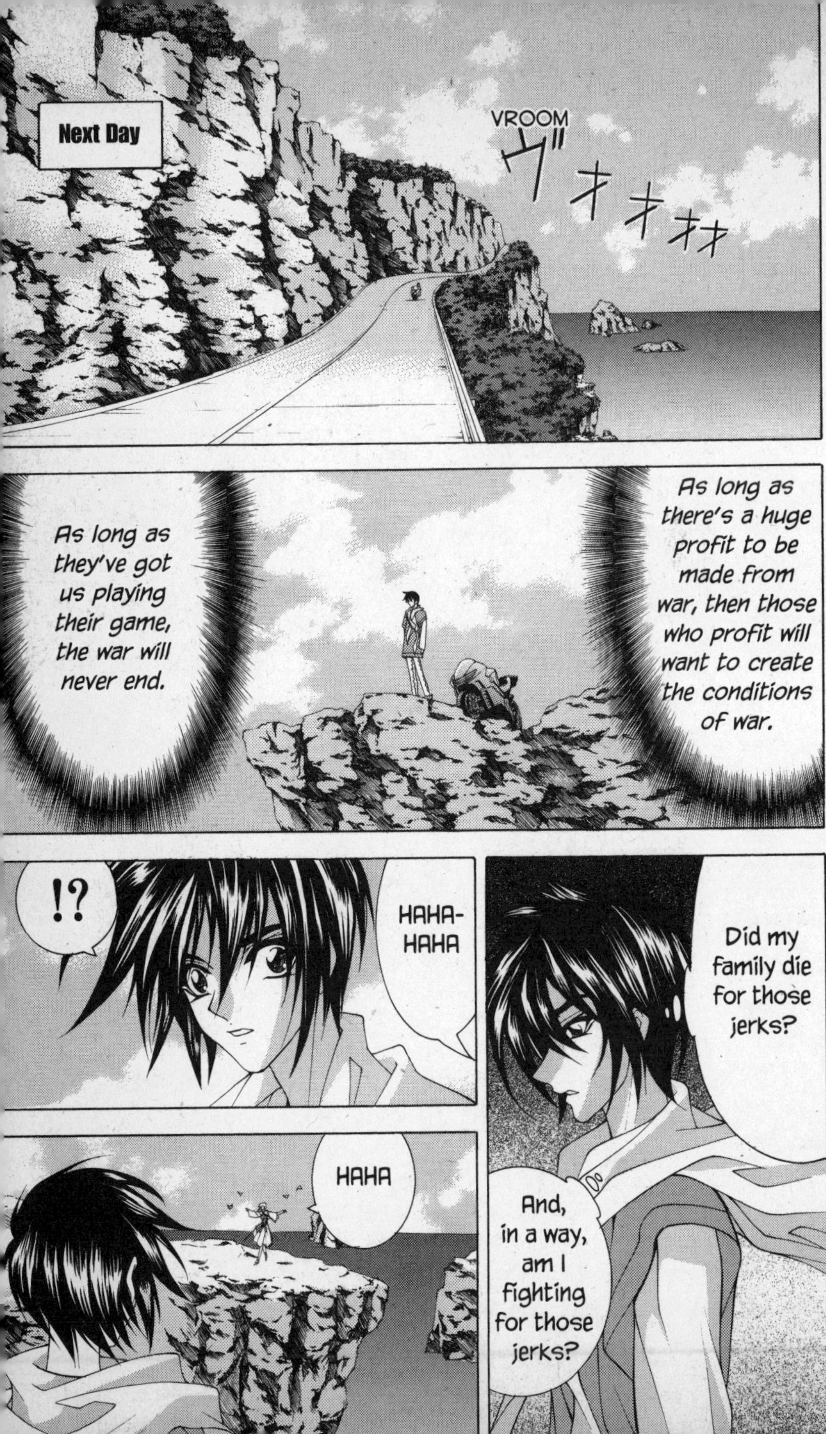

Next Day
VROOM
ヴオオオオ
As long as there's a huge profit to be made from war, then those who profit will want to create the conditions of war.
As long as they've got us playing their game, the war will never end.
Did my family die for those jerks?
And, in a way, am I fighting for those jerks?
HAHA-HAHA
!?
HAHA

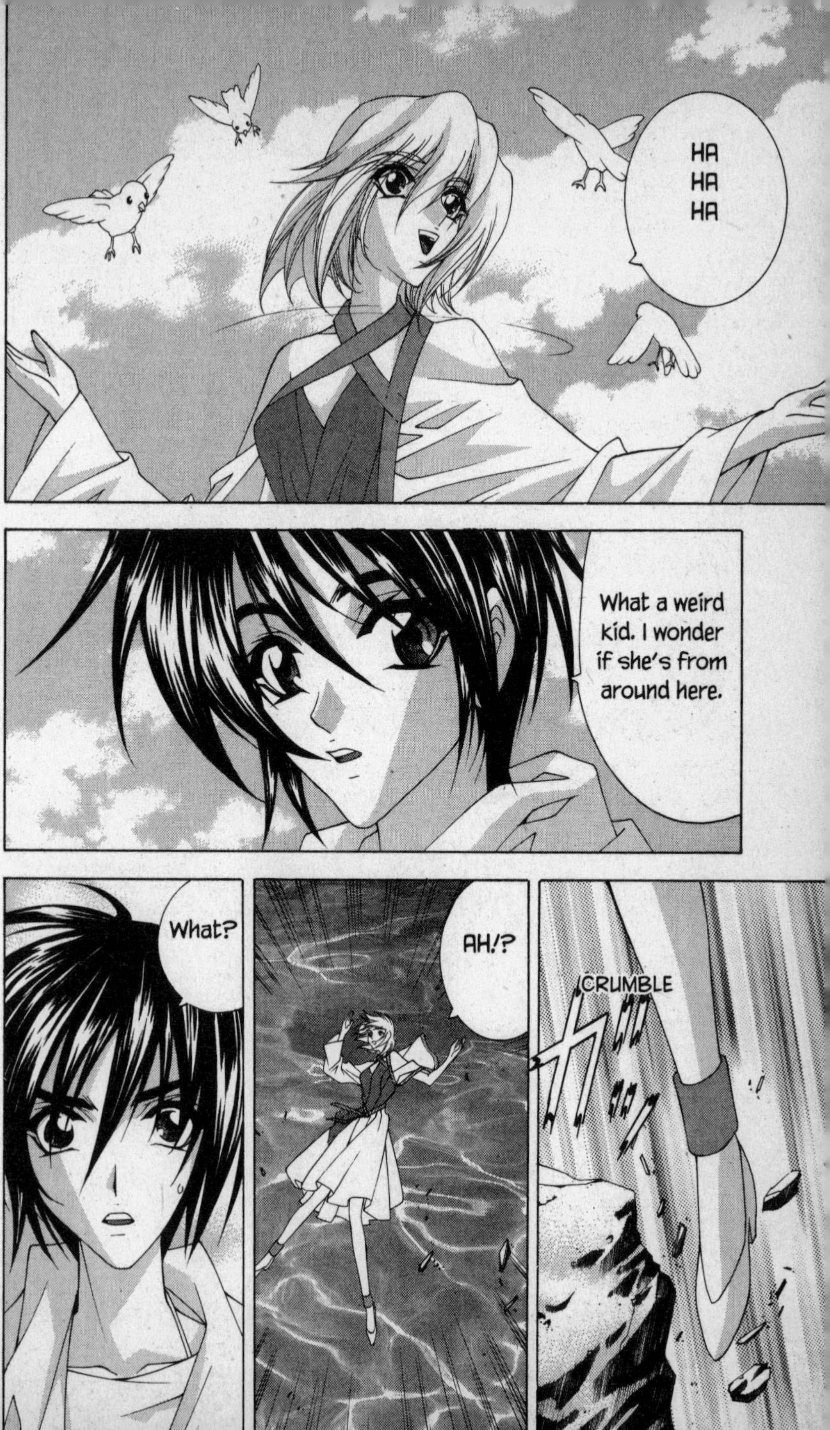
HA
HA
HA
What a weird kid. I wonder if she's from around here.
CRUMBLE
AH!?
What?

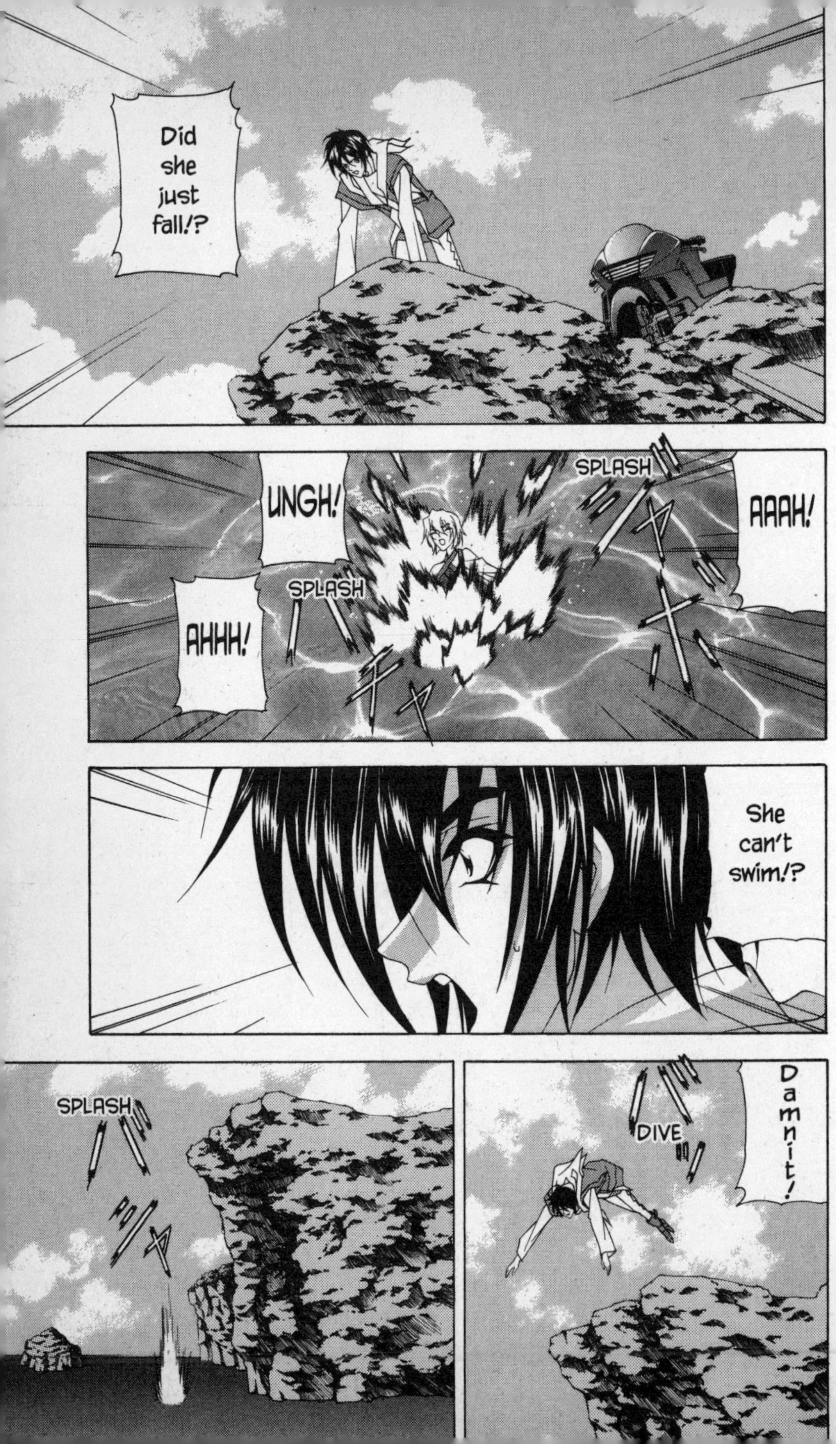
Did she just fall!?
SPLASH
AAAH!
UNGH!
SPLASH
AHHH!
She can't swim!?
Damnit!
DIVE
SPLASH

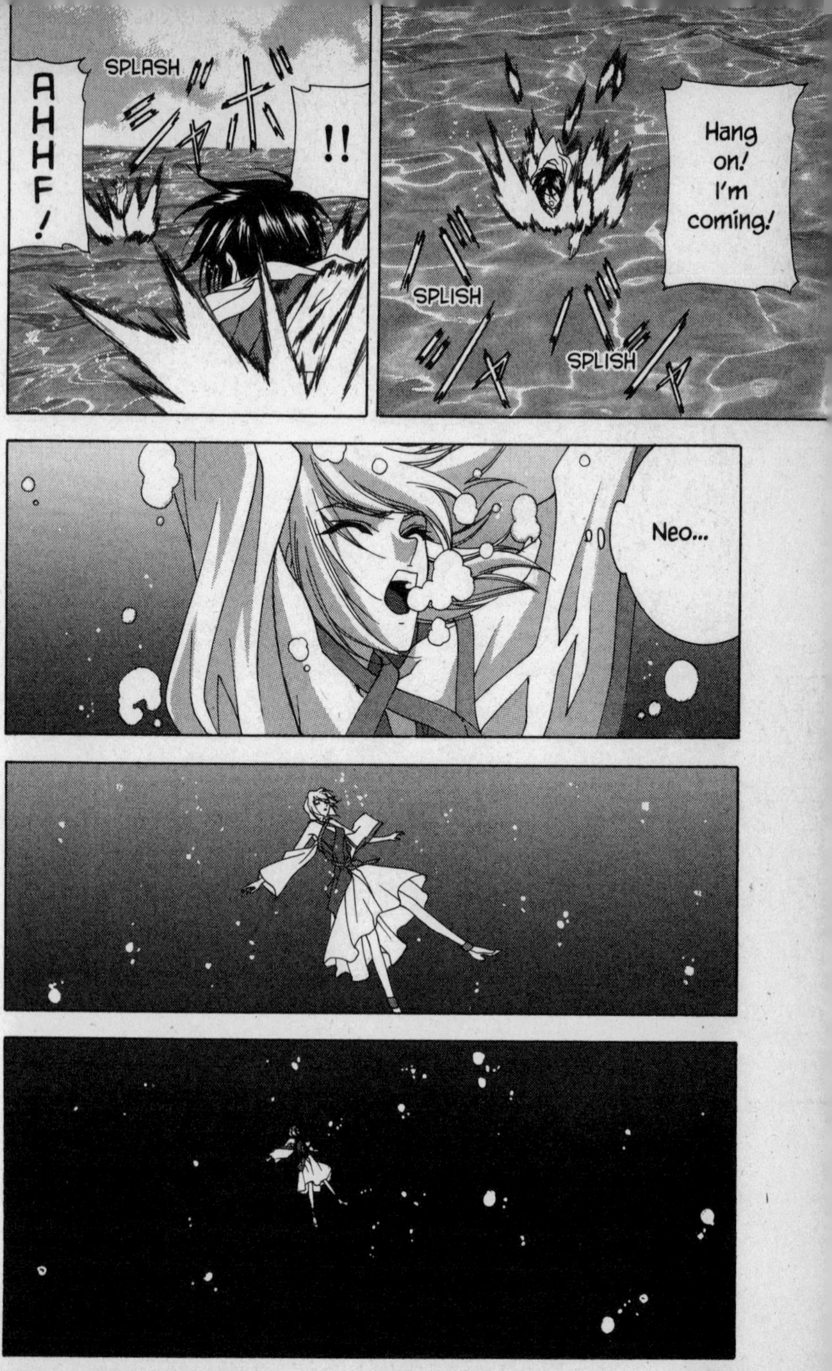
Hang on! I'm coming!
SPLISH
SPLISH
SPLASH
AHHF!
!!
Neo...

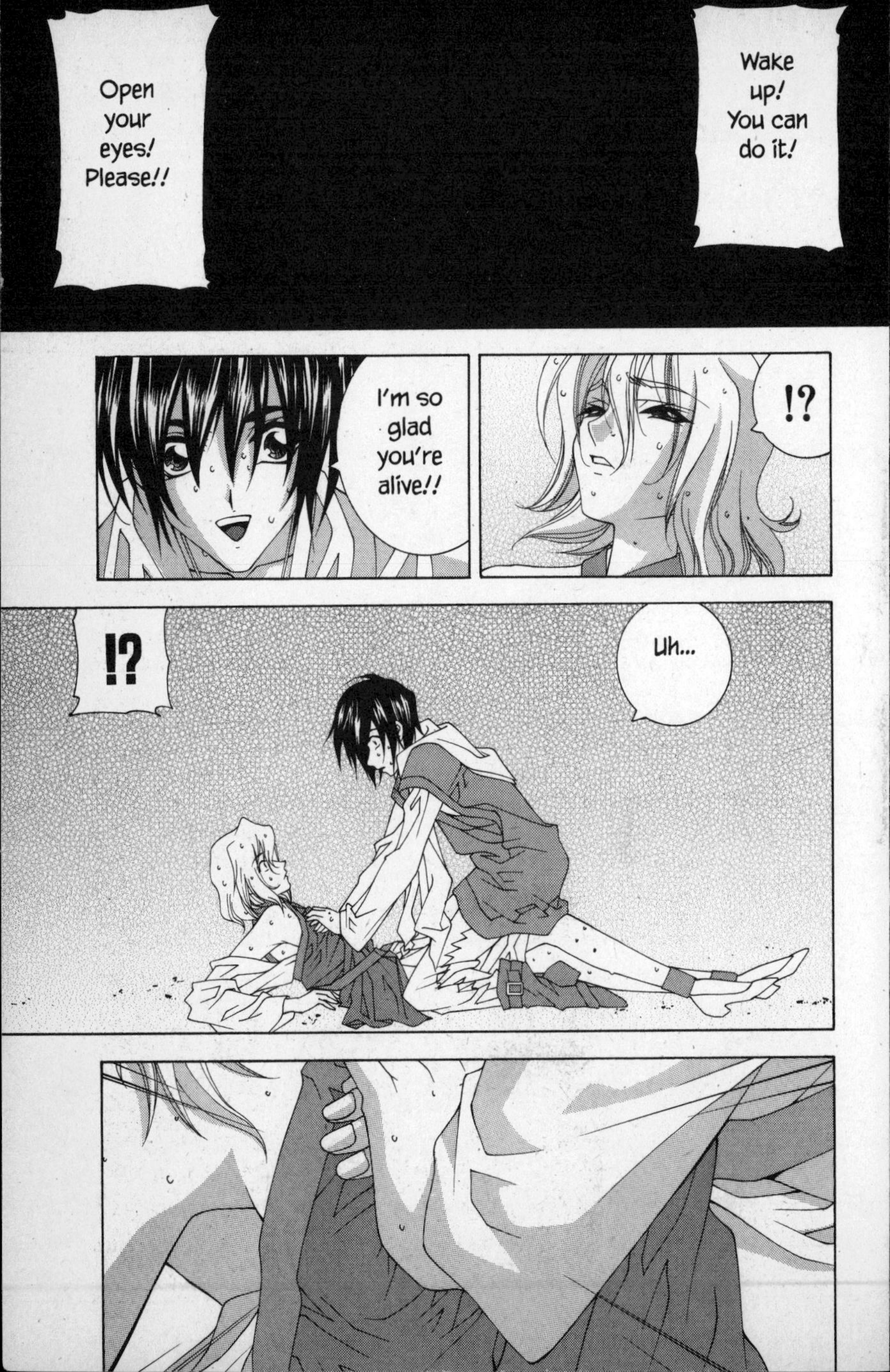
Wake up! You can do it!
Open your eyes! Please!!
!?
I'm so glad you're alive!!
Uh...
!?

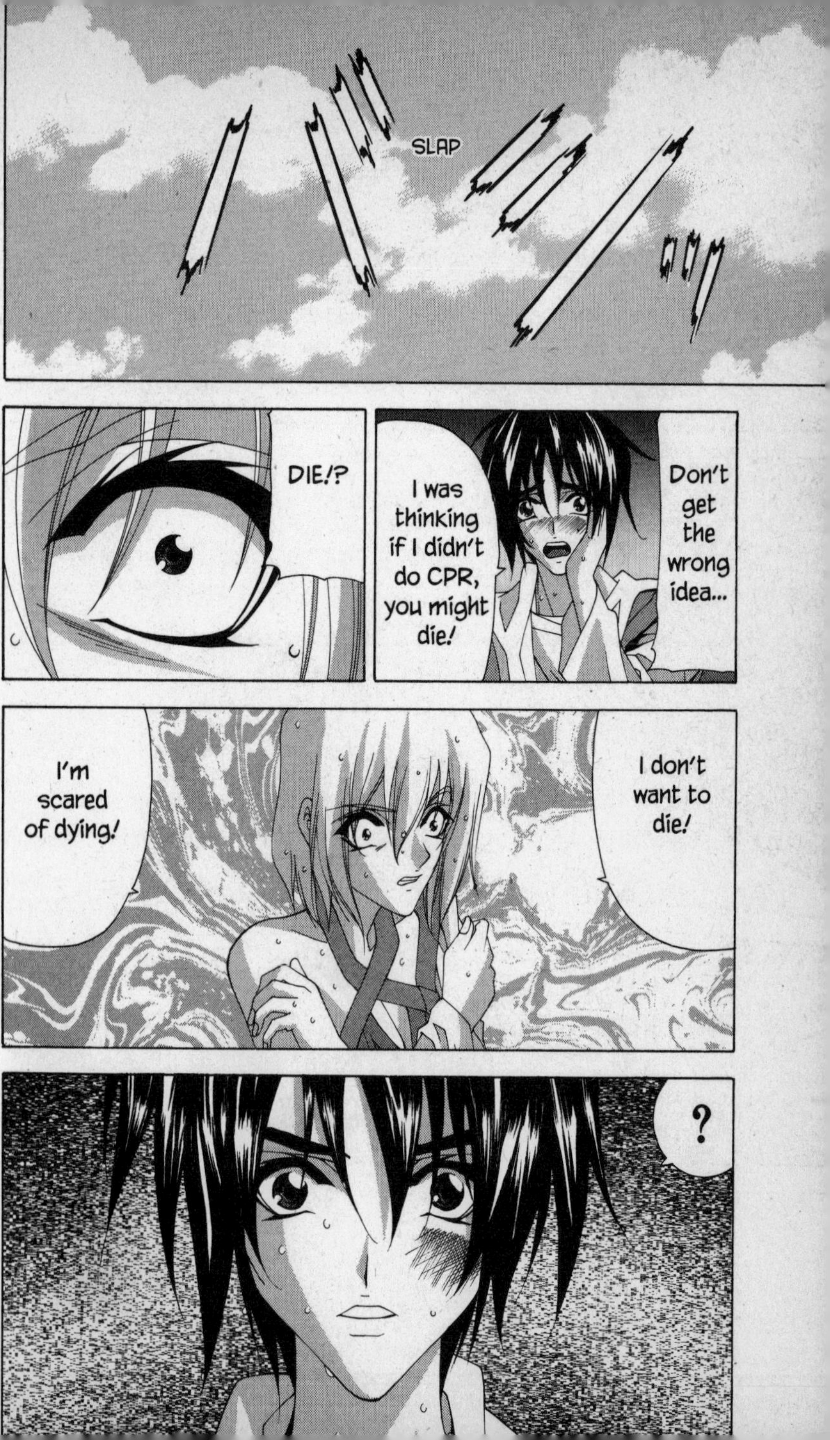
SLAP
Don't get the wrong idea...
I was thinking if I didn't do CPR, you might die!
DIE!?
I don't want to die!
I'm scared of dying!
?

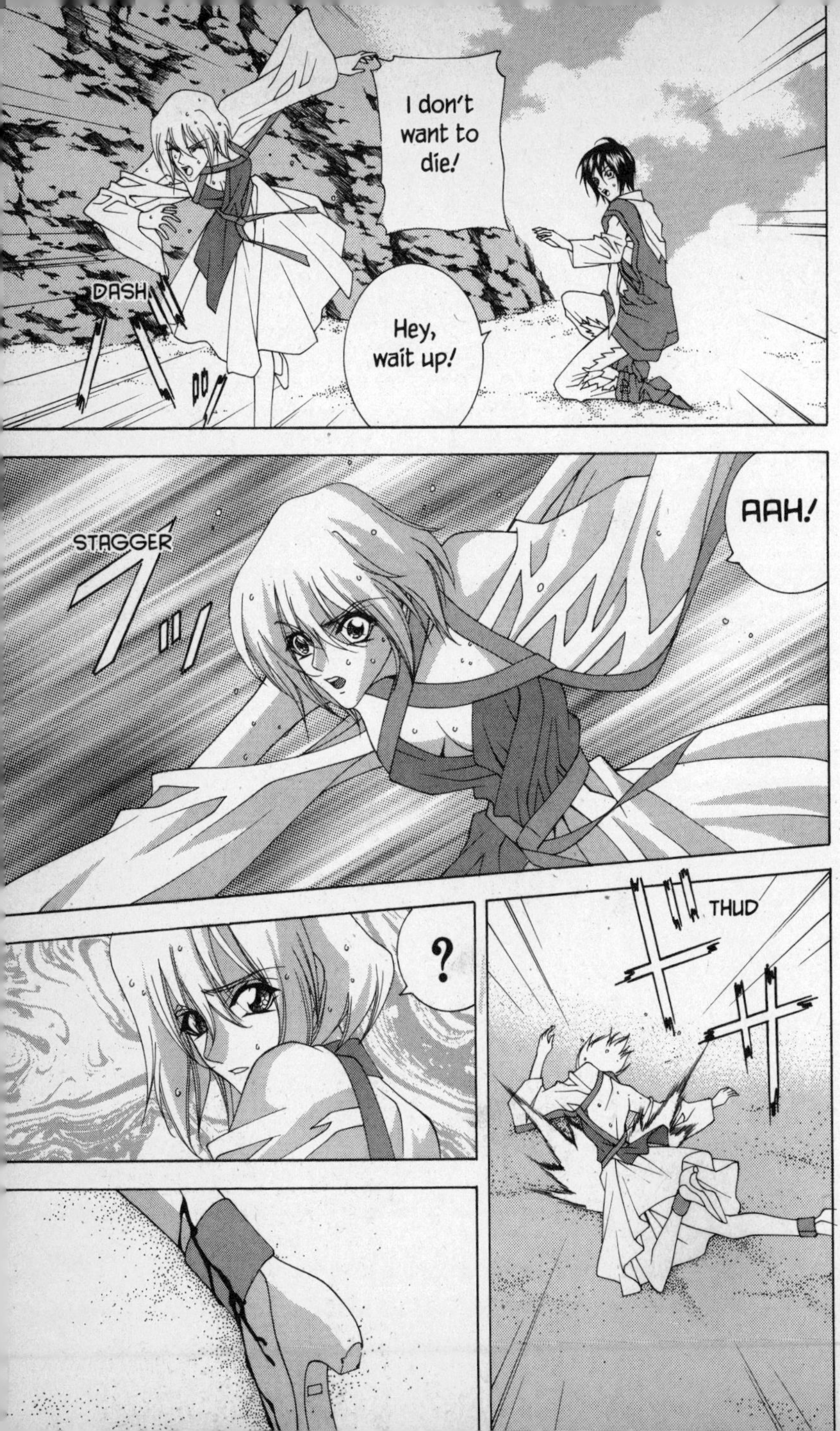
I don't want to die!
Hey, wait up!
DASH
AAH!
STAGGER
THUD
?

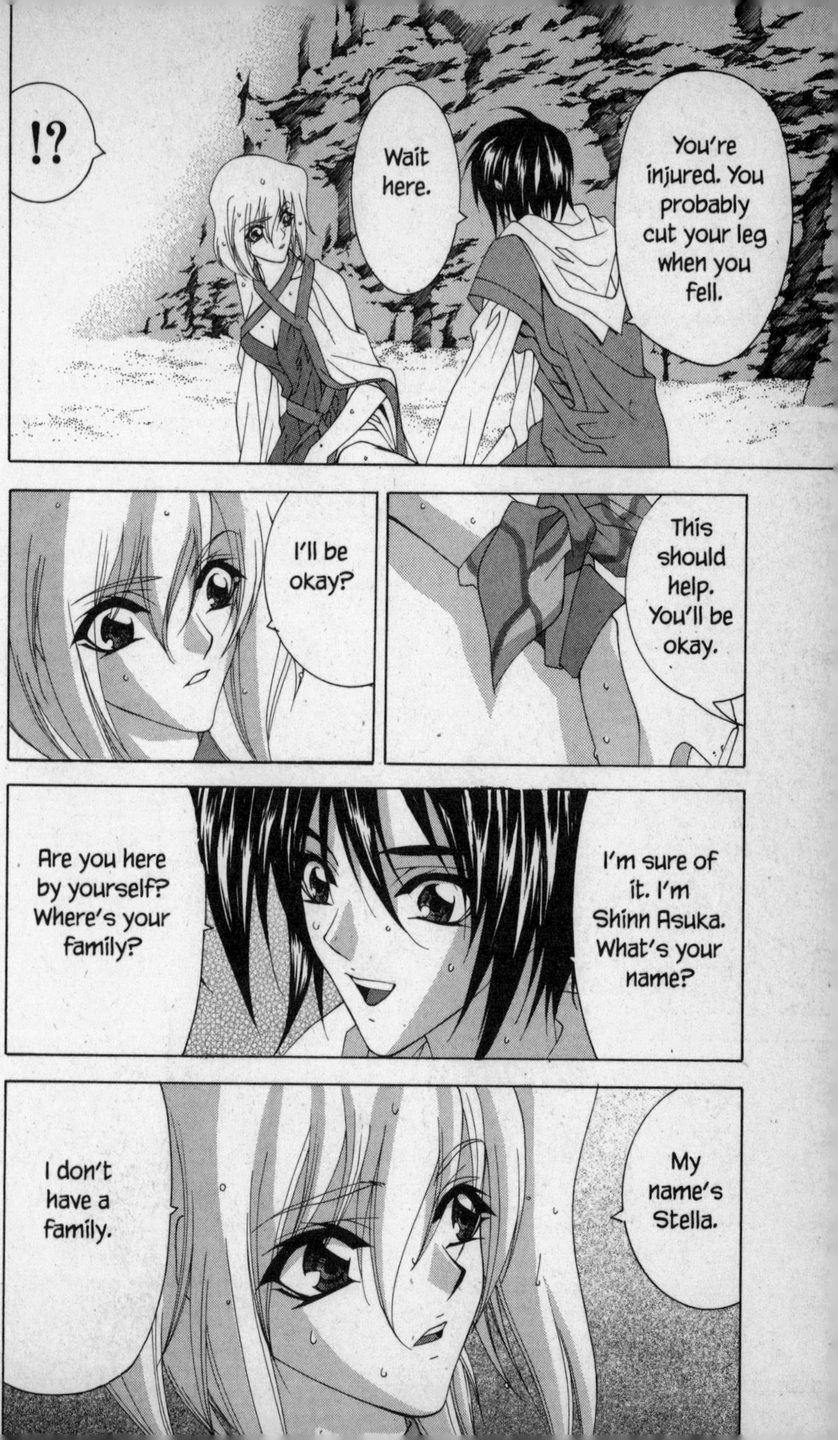
You're injured. You probably cut your leg when you fell.
Wait here.
!?
This should help. You'll be okay.
I'll be okay?
I'm sure of it. I'm Shinn Asuka. What's your name?
Are you here by yourself? Where's your family?
My name's Stella.
I don't have a family.

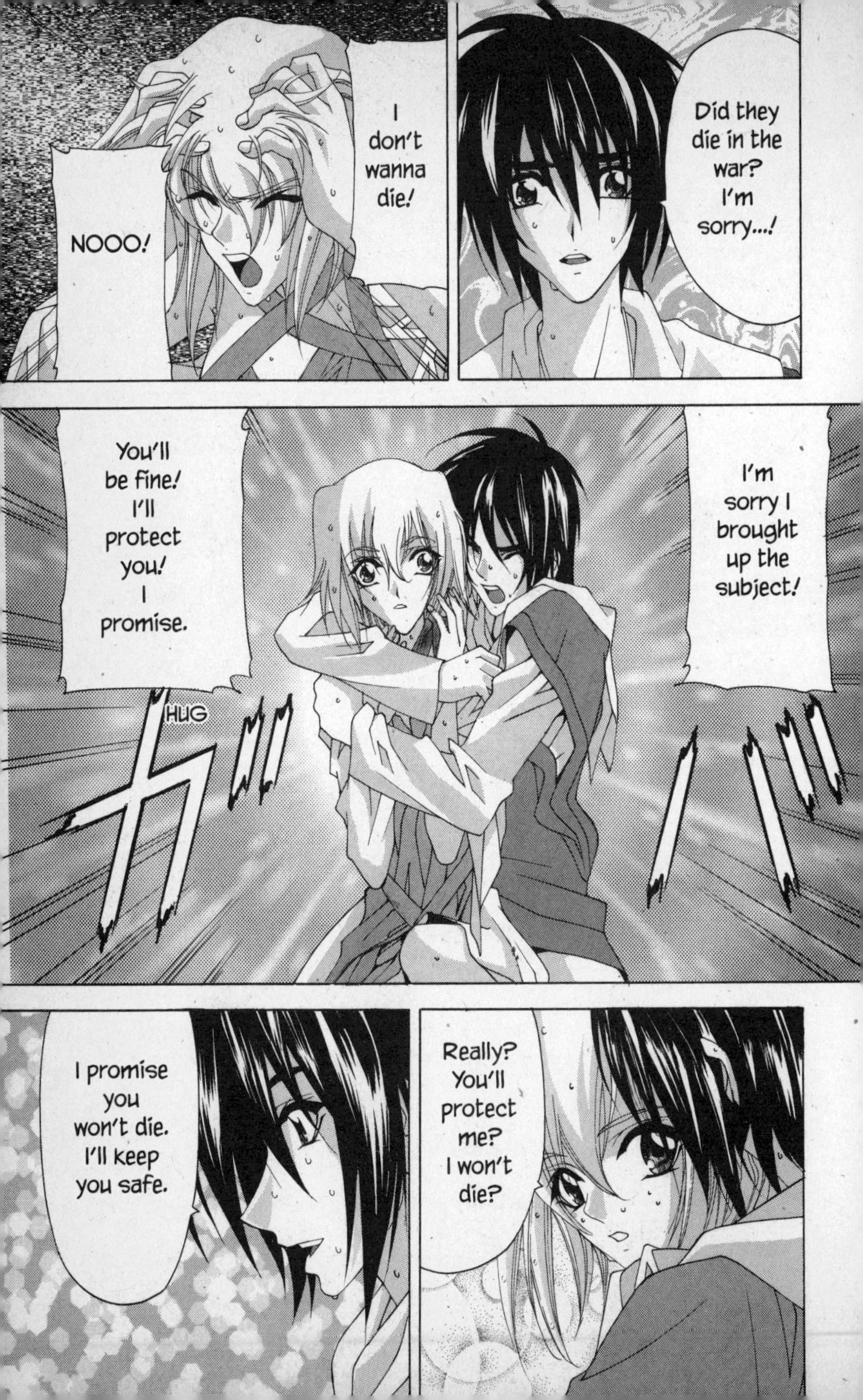
Did they die in the war? I'm sorry...!
I don't wanna die!
NOOO!
I'm sorry I brought up the subject!
You'll be fine! I'll protect you! I promise.
HUG
Really? You'll protect me? I won't die?
I promise you won't die. I'll keep you safe.

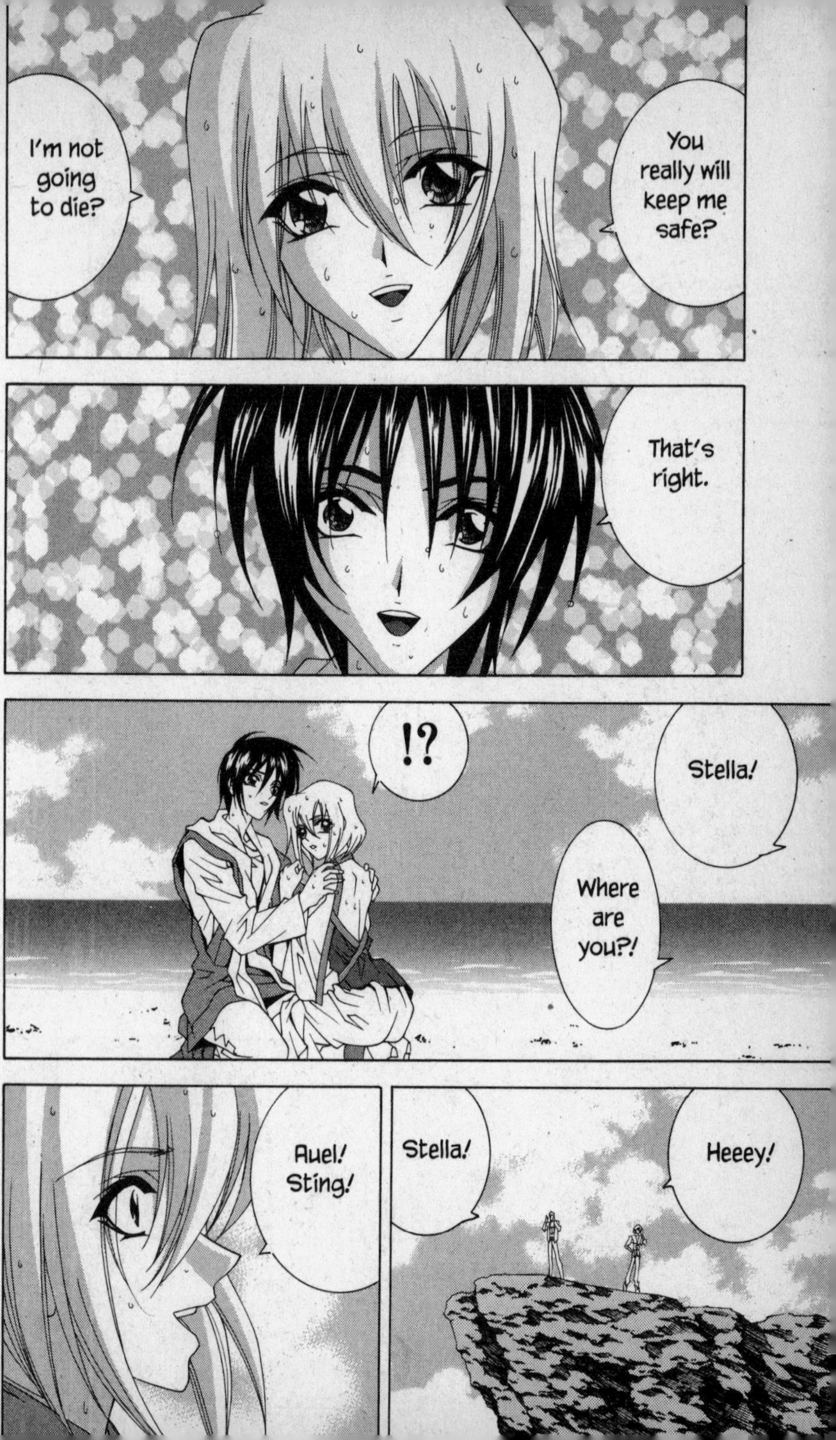
You really will keep me safe?
I'm not going to die?
That's right.
Stella!
Where are you?!
!?
Heeey!
Stella!
Auel! Sting!

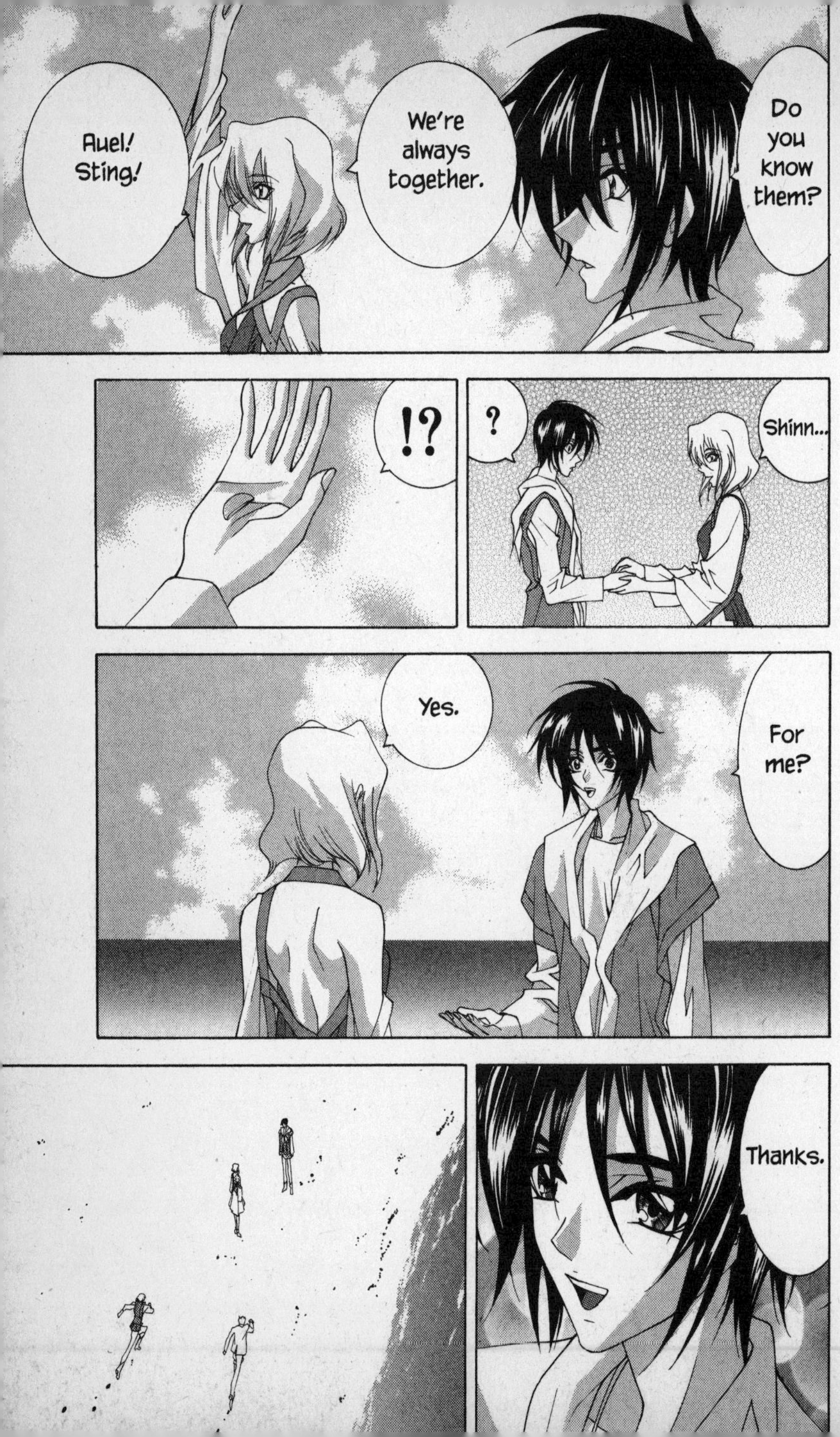
Do you know them?
We're always together.
Auel! Sting!
Shinn...
?
!?
For me?
Yes.
Thanks.

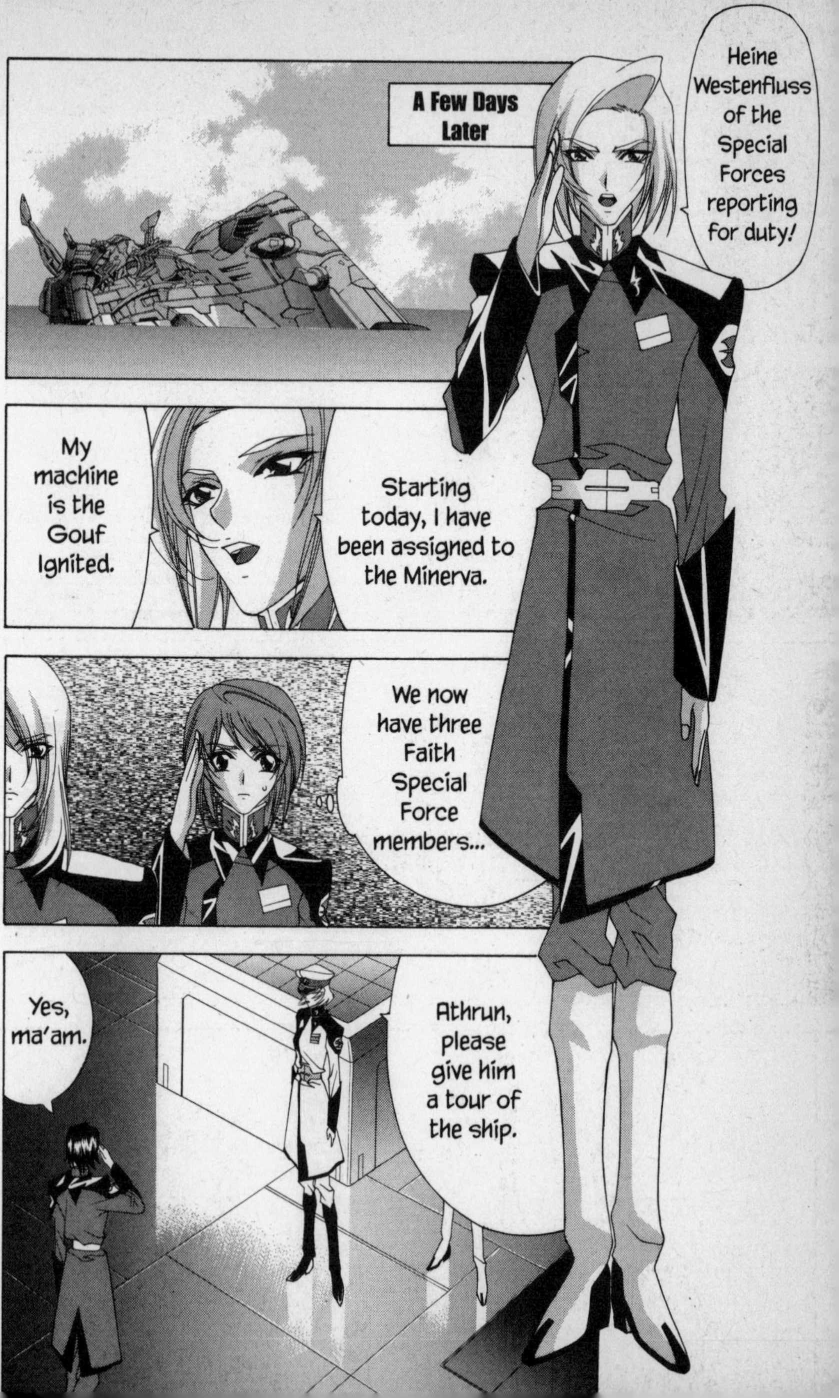
A Few Days Later
Heine Westenfluss of the Special Forces reporting for duty!
Starting today, I have been assigned to the Minerva.
My machine is the Gouf Ignited.
We now have three Faith Special Force members...
Athrun, please give him a tour of the ship.
Yes, ma'am.

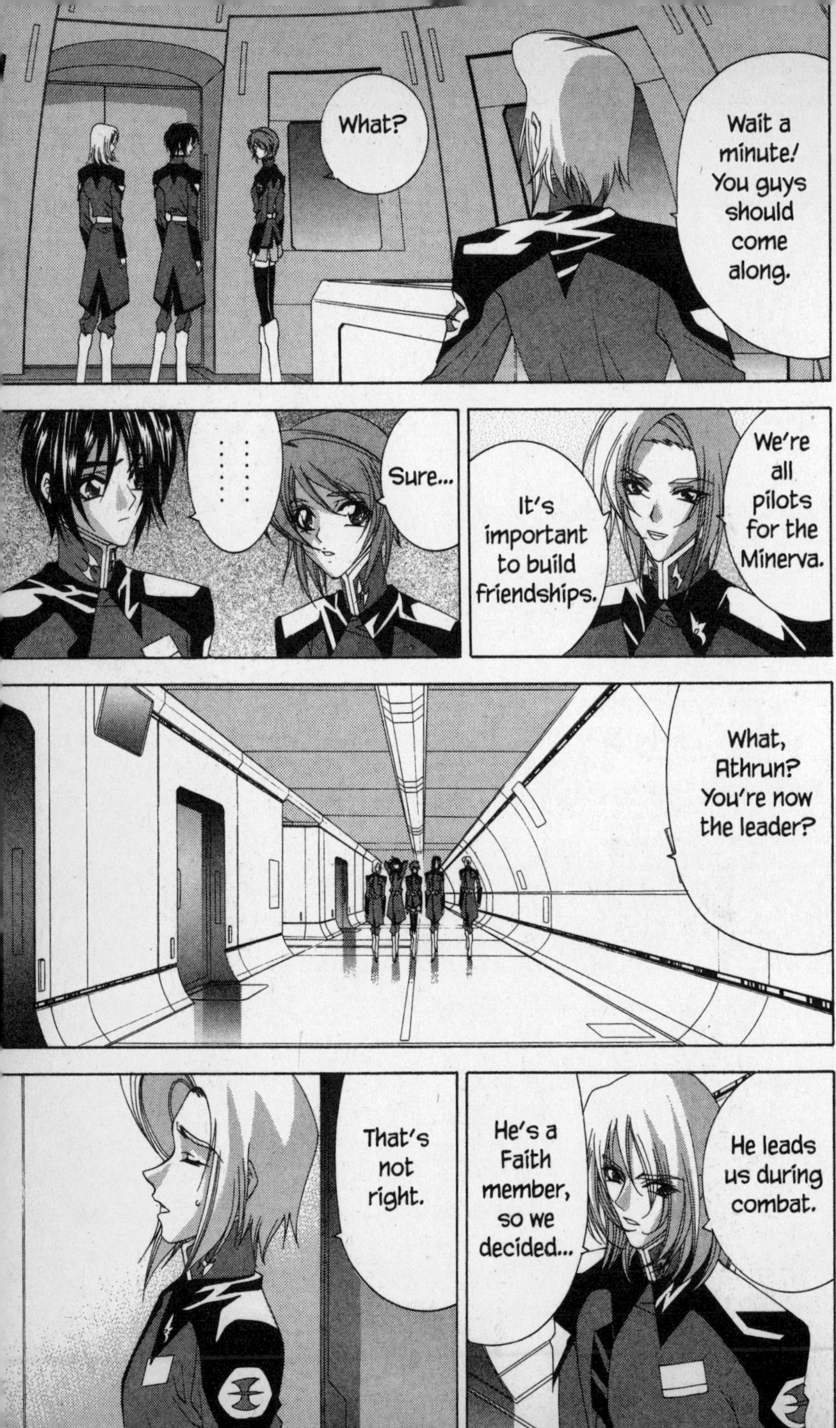
Wait a minute! You guys should come along.
What?
We're all pilots for the Minerva.
It's important to build friendships.
Sure...
......
What, Athrun? You're now the leader?
He leads us during combat.
He's a Faith member, so we decided...
That's not right.

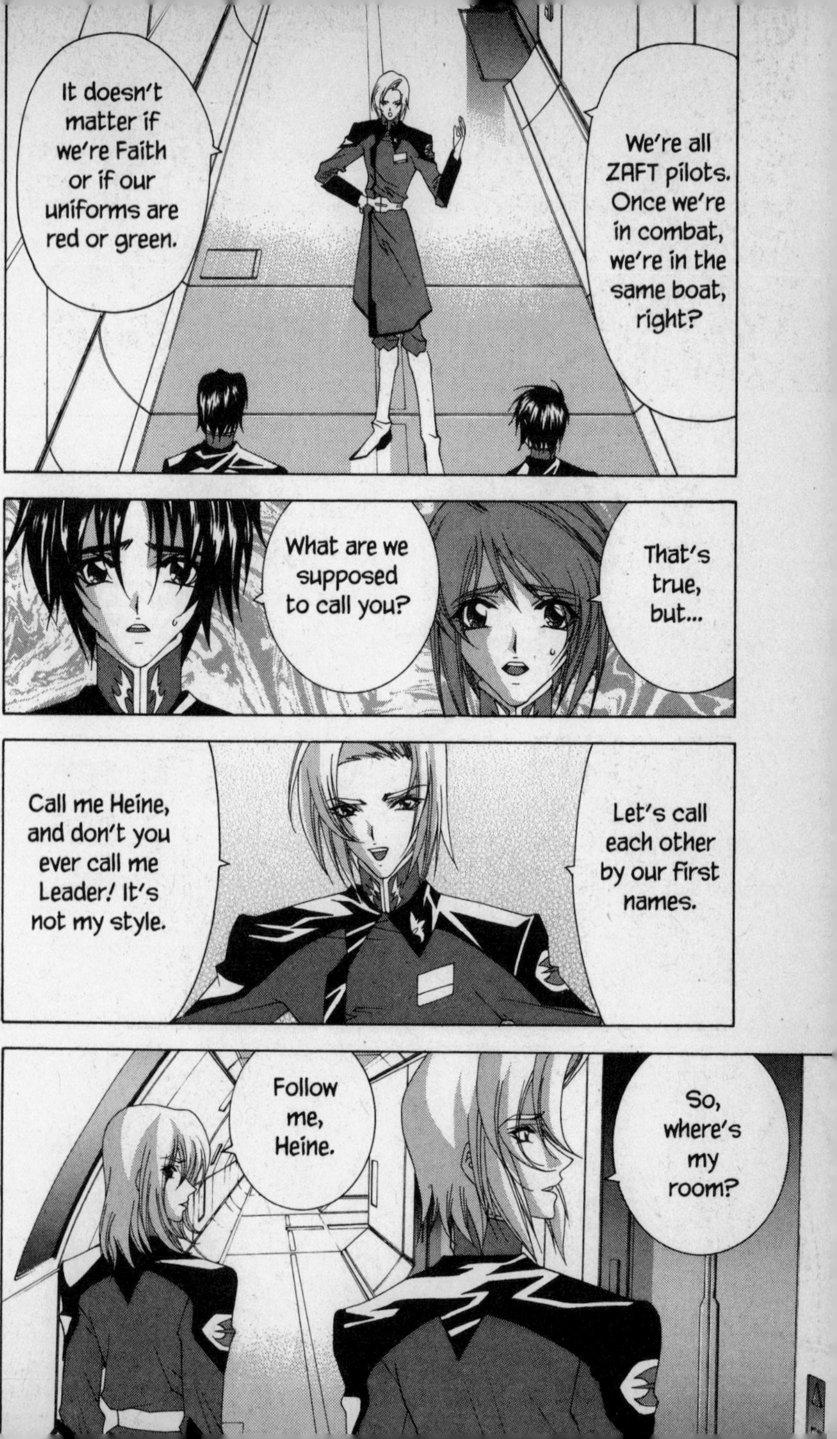
We're all ZAFT pilots. Once we're in combat, we're in the same boat, right?
It doesn't matter if we're Faith or if our uniforms are red or green.
That's true, but...
What are we supposed to call you?
Let's call each other by our first names.
Call me Heine, and don't you ever call me Leader! It's not my style.
So, where's my room?
Follow me, Heine.

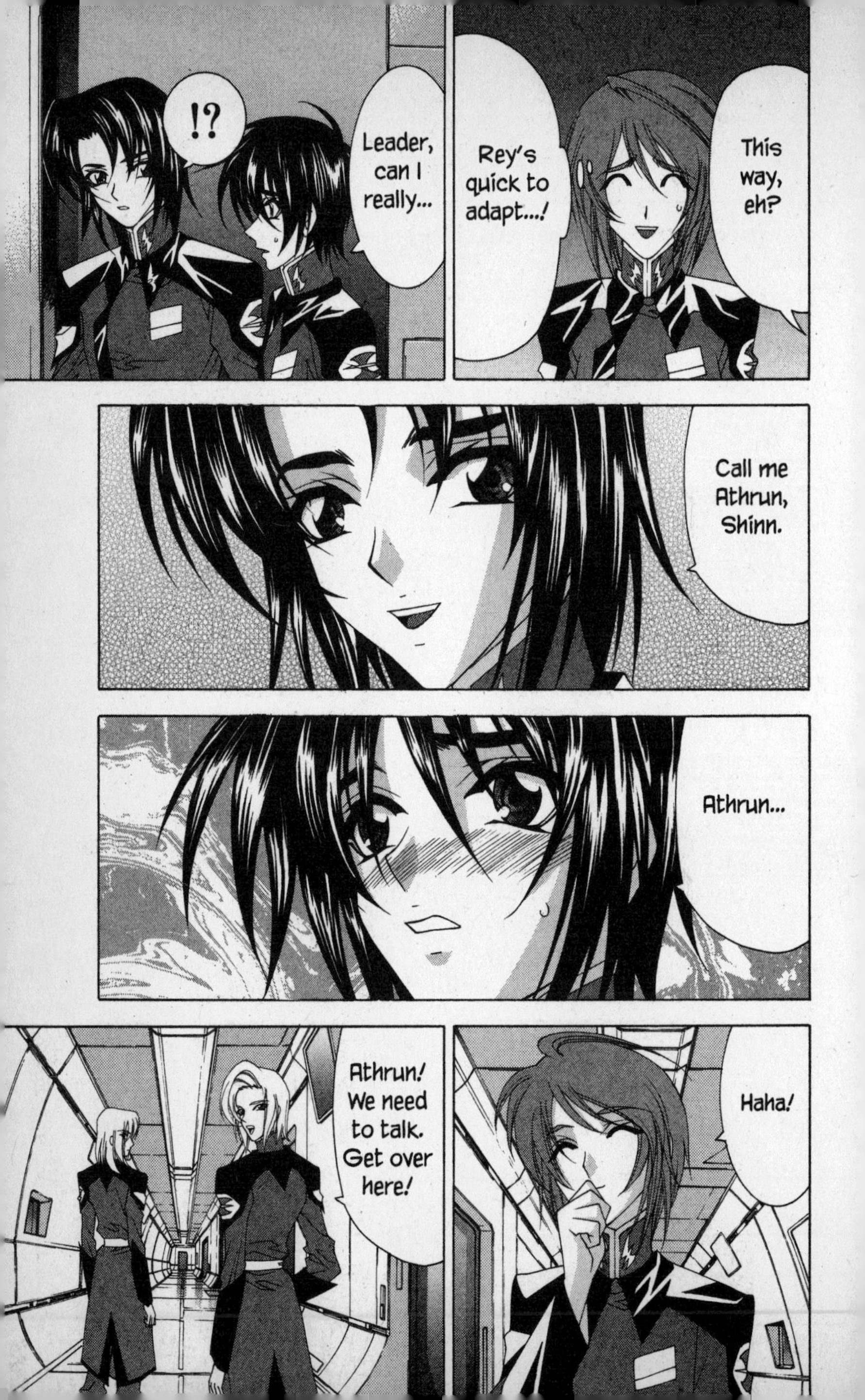
This way, eh?
Rey's quick to adapt...!
Leader, can I really...
!?
Call me Athrun, Shinn.
Athrun...
Haha!
Athrun! We need to talk. Get over here!

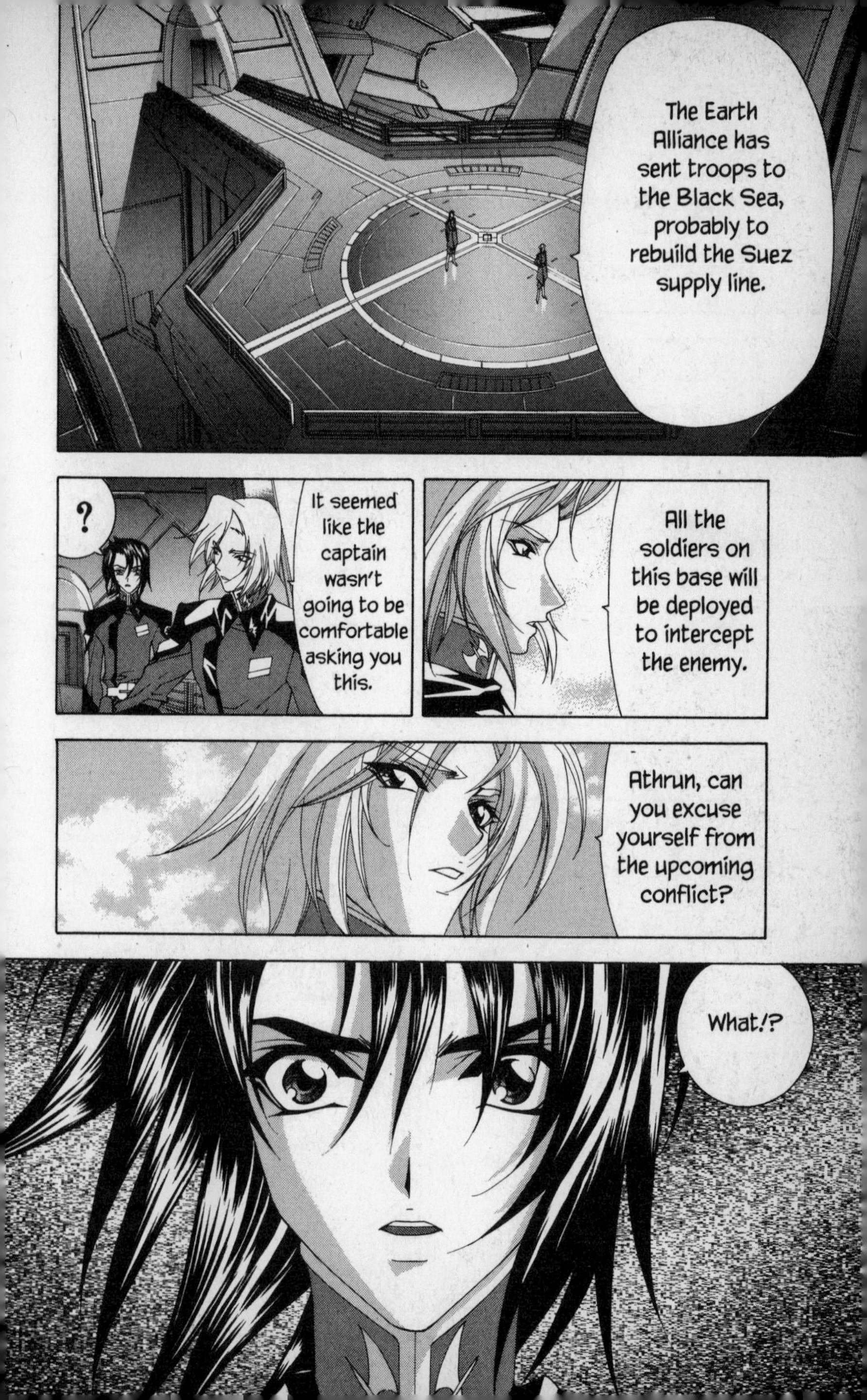
The Earth Alliance has sent troops to the Black Sea, probably to rebuild the Suez supply line.
All the soldiers on this base will be deployed to intercept the enemy.
It seemed like the captain wasn't going to be comfortable asking you this.
?
Athrun, can you excuse yourself from the upcoming conflict?
What!?

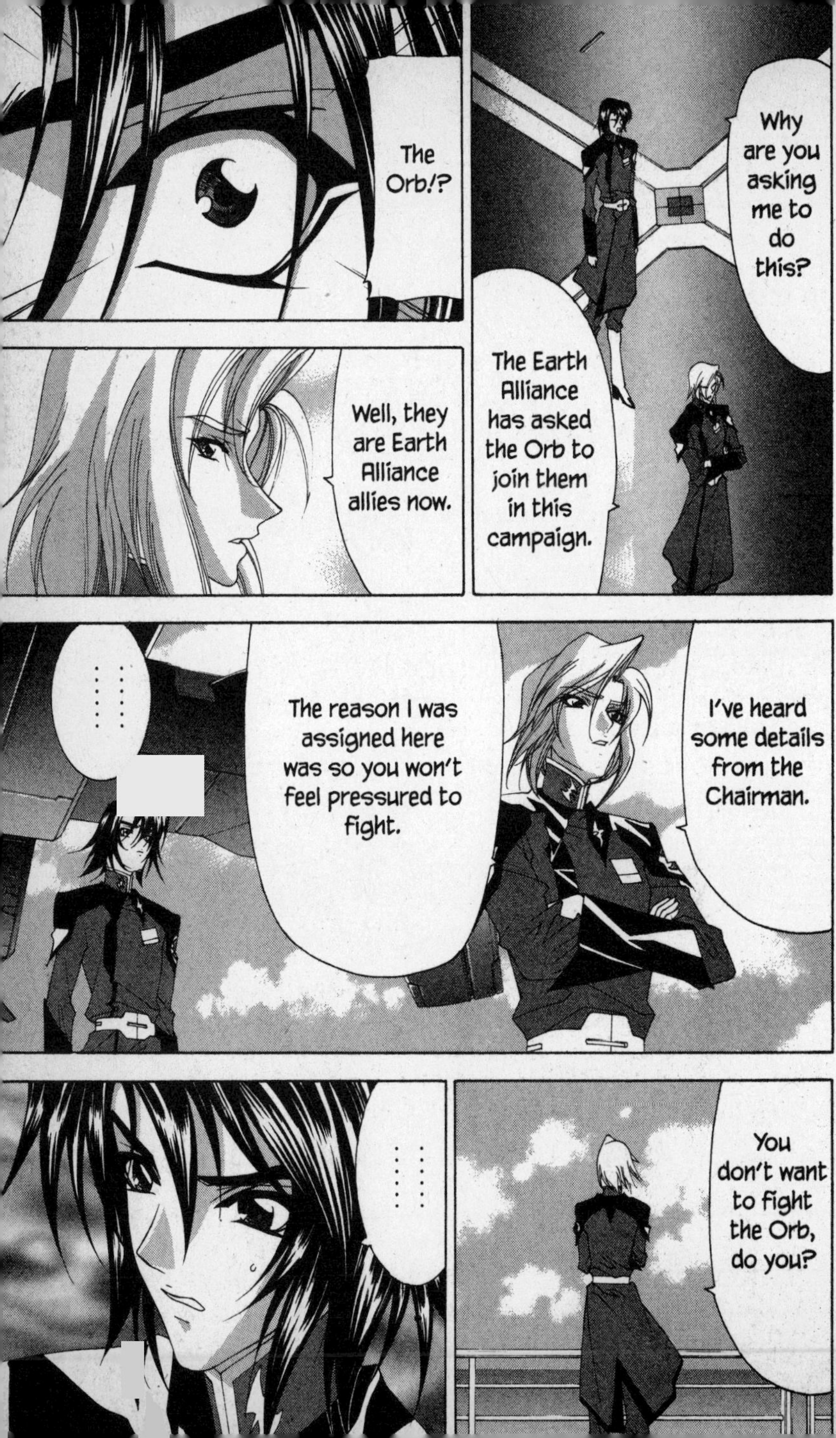
Why are you asking me to do this?
The Earth Alliance has asked the Orb to join them in this campaign.
The Orb!?
Well, they are Earth Alliance allies now.
I've heard some details from the Chairman.
The reason I was assigned here was so you won't feel pressured to fight.
......
You don't want to fight the Orb, do you?
......

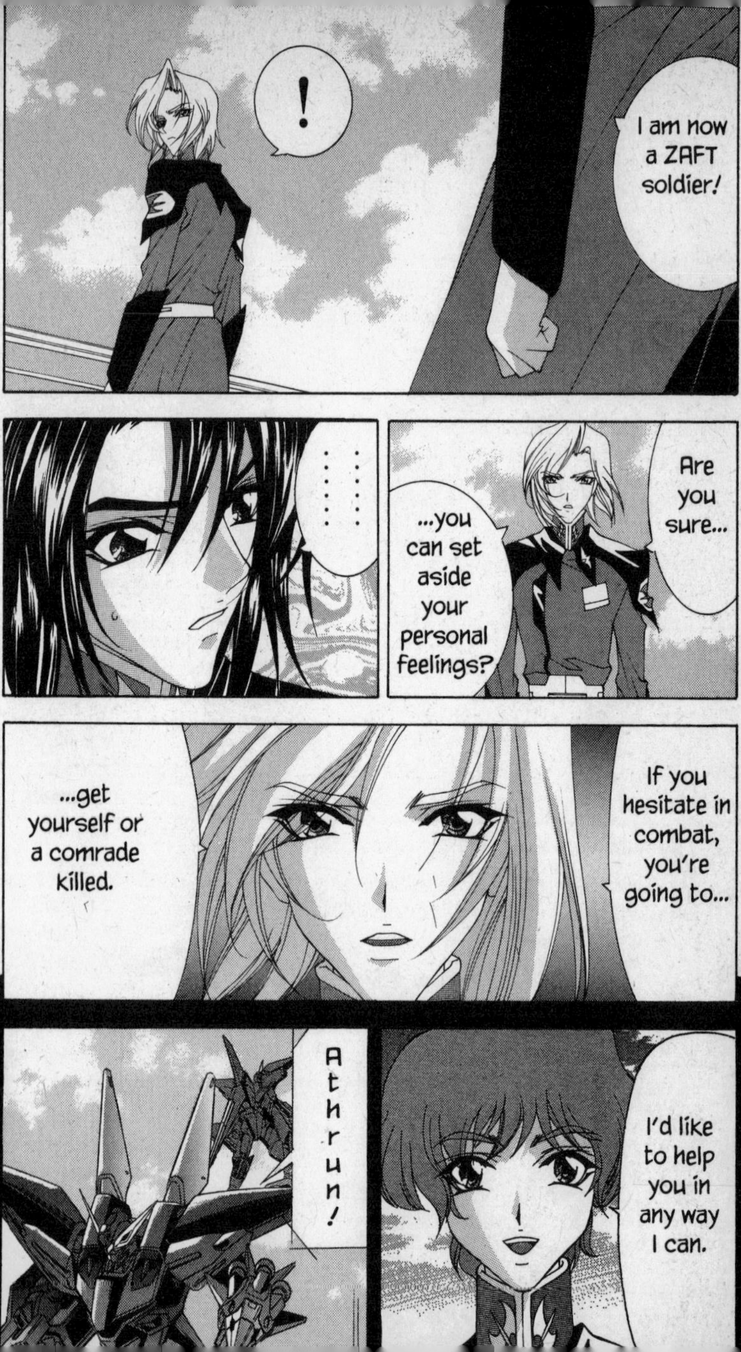
I am now a ZAFT soldier!
!
Are you sure...
...you can set aside your personal feelings?
......
If you hesitate in combat, you're going to...
...get yourself or a comrade killed.
I'd like to help you in any way I can.
Athrun!

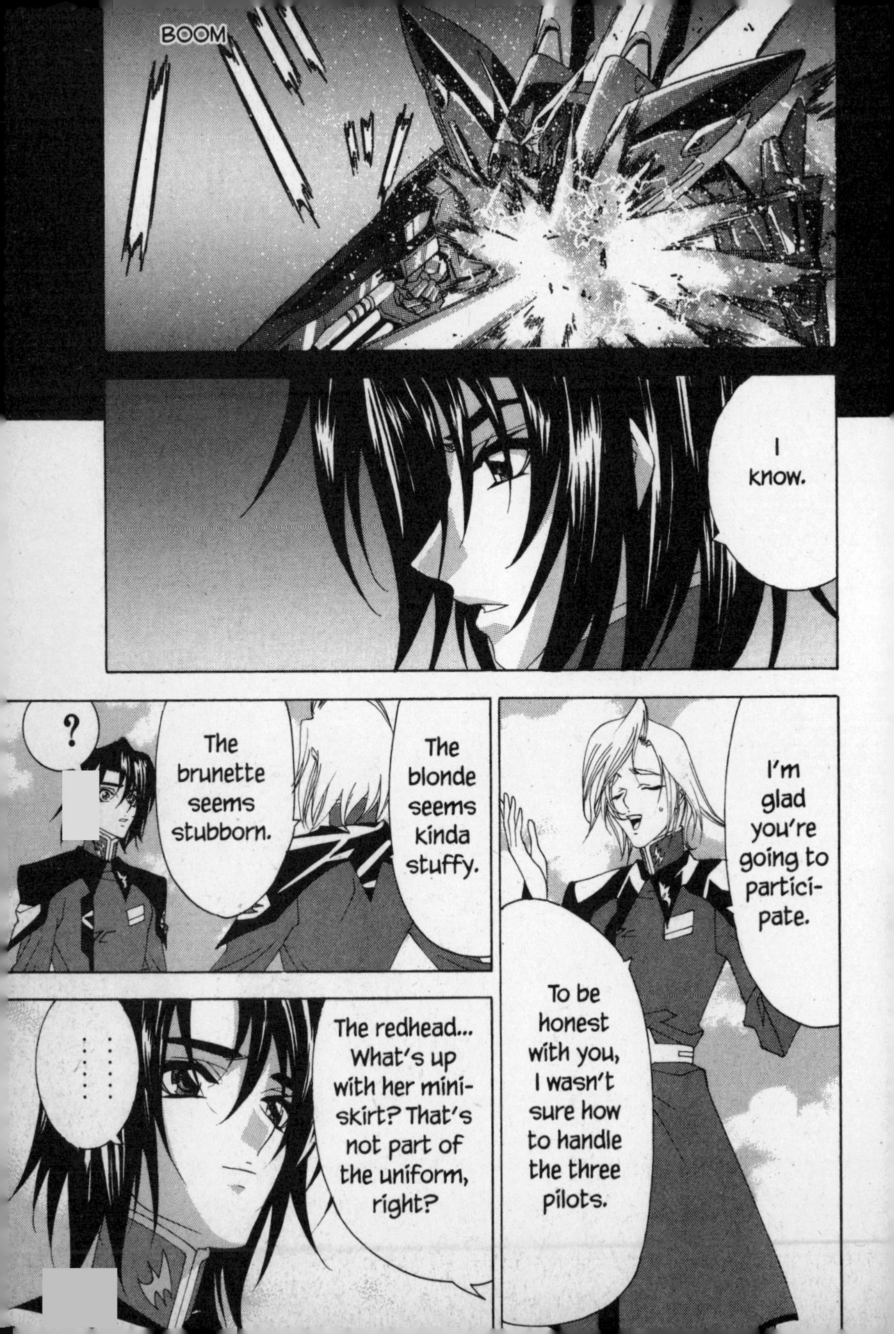
BOOM
I know.
I'm glad you're going to partici-pate.
To be honest with you, I wasn't sure how to handle the three pilots.
The blonde seems kinda stuffy.
The brunette seems stubborn.
?
The redhead... What's up with her mini-skirt? That's not part of the uniform, right?
......

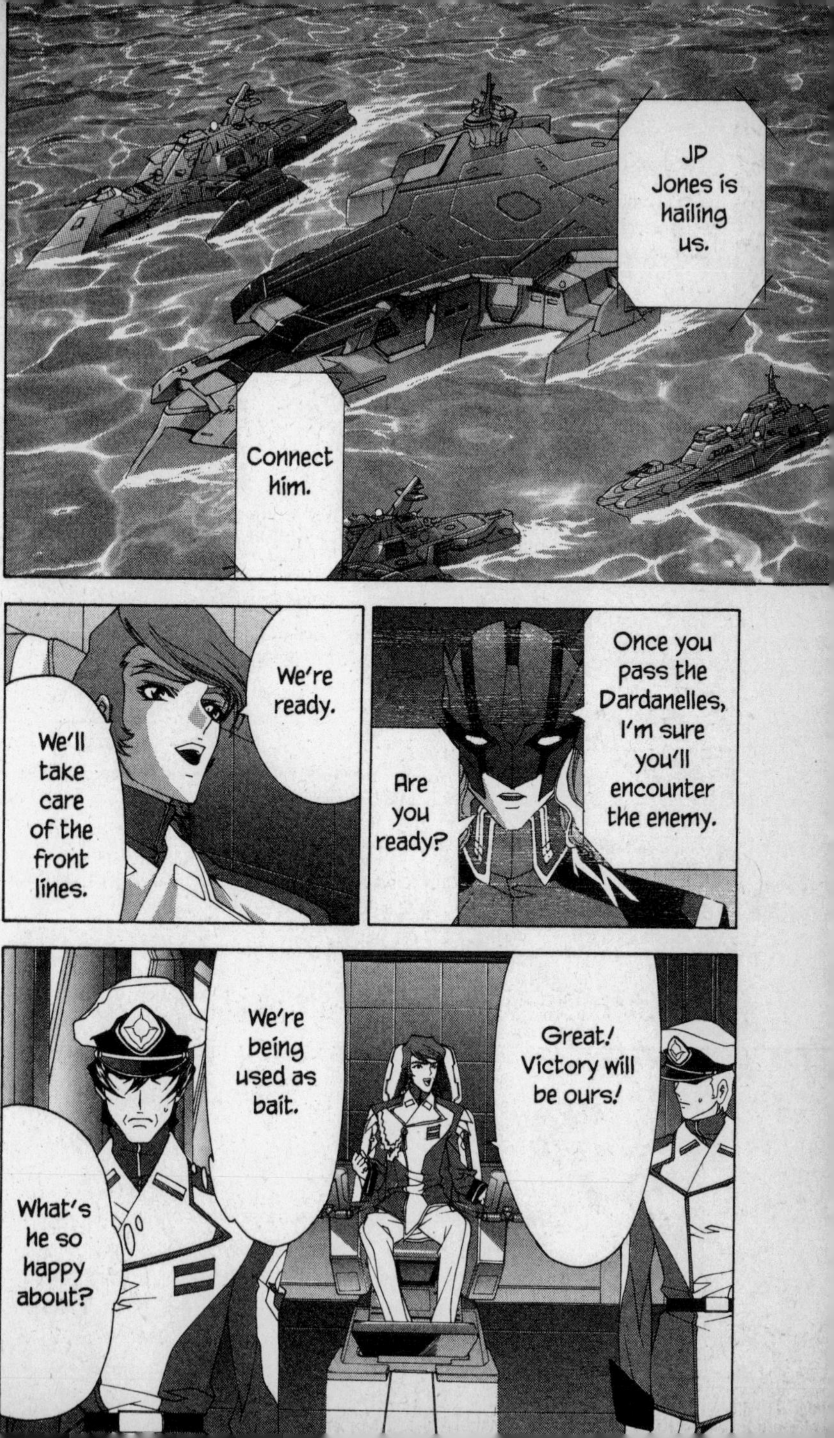
JP Jones is hailing us.
Connect him.
Once you pass the Dardanelles, I'm sure you'll encounter the enemy.
Are you ready?
We're ready.
We'll take care of the front lines.
Great! Victory will be ours!
We're being used as bait.
What's he so happy about?

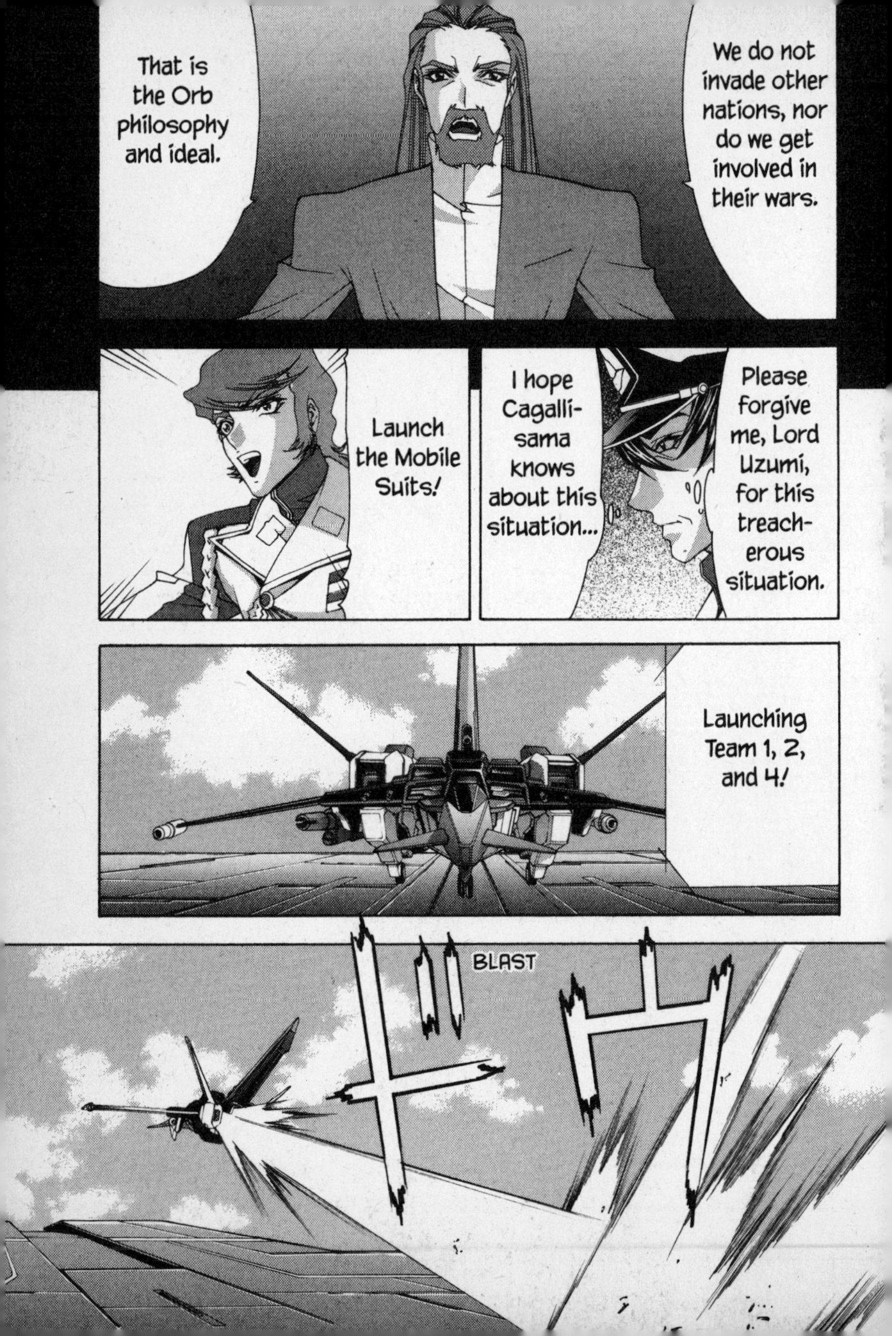
We do not invade other nations, nor do we get involved in their wars.
That is the Orb philosophy and ideal.
Please forgive me, Lord Uzumi, for this treacherous situation.
I hope Cagalli-sama knows about this situation...
Launch the Mobile Suits!
Launching Team 1, 2, and 4!
BLAST

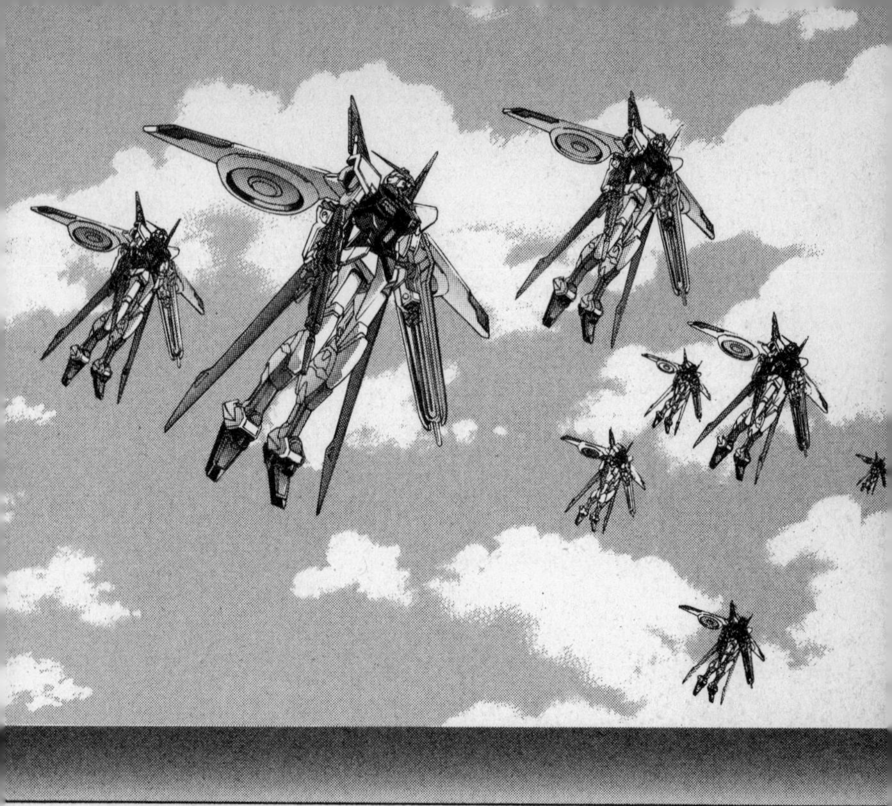

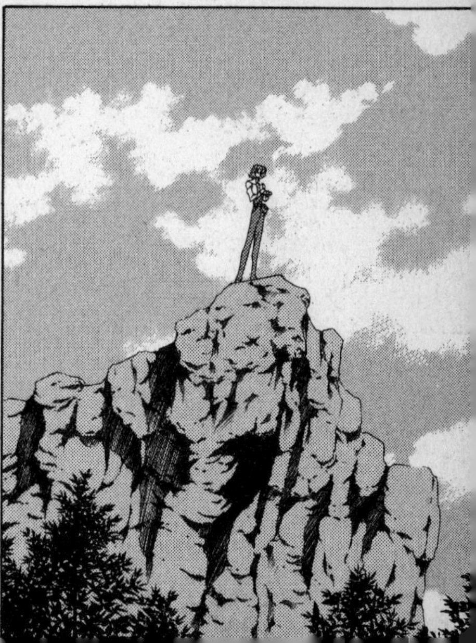

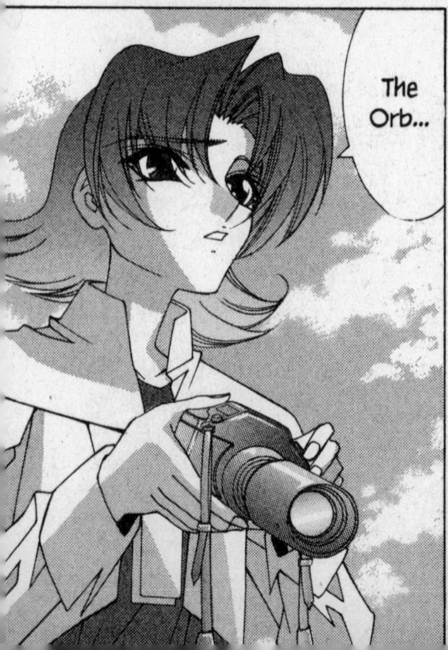
The Orb...

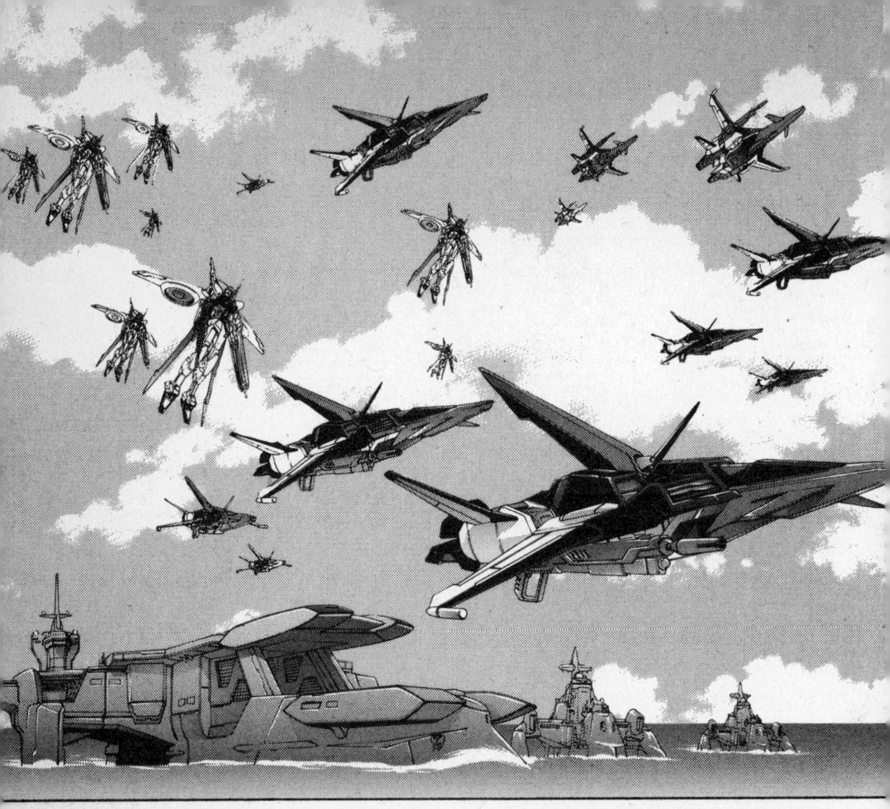

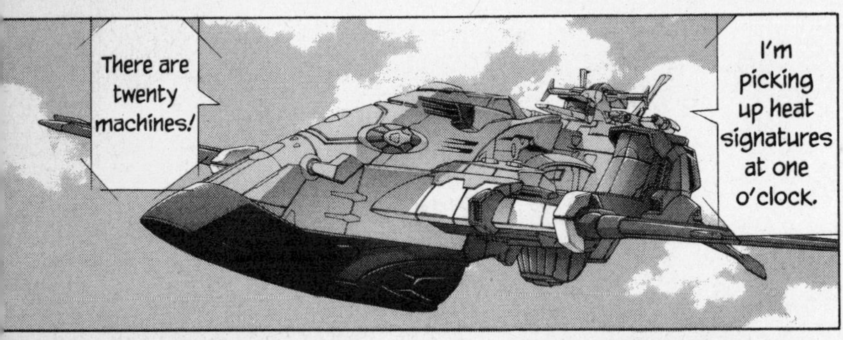
I'm picking up heat signatures at one o'clock.
There are twenty machines!

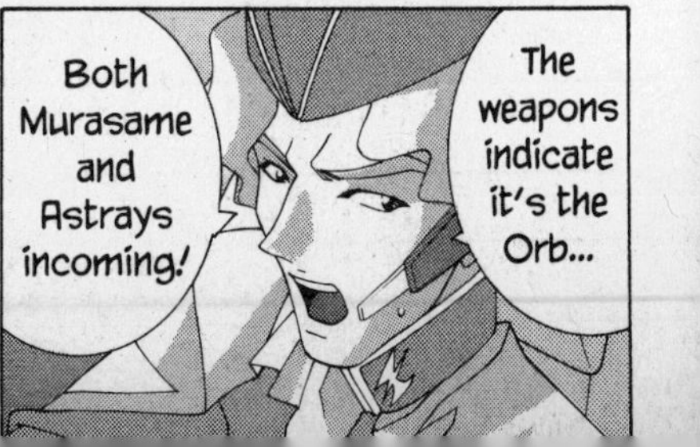
The weapons indicate it's the Orb...
Both Murasame and Astrays incoming!

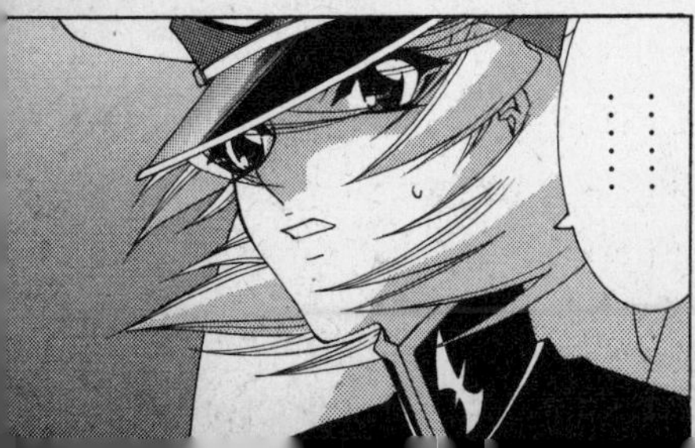
......

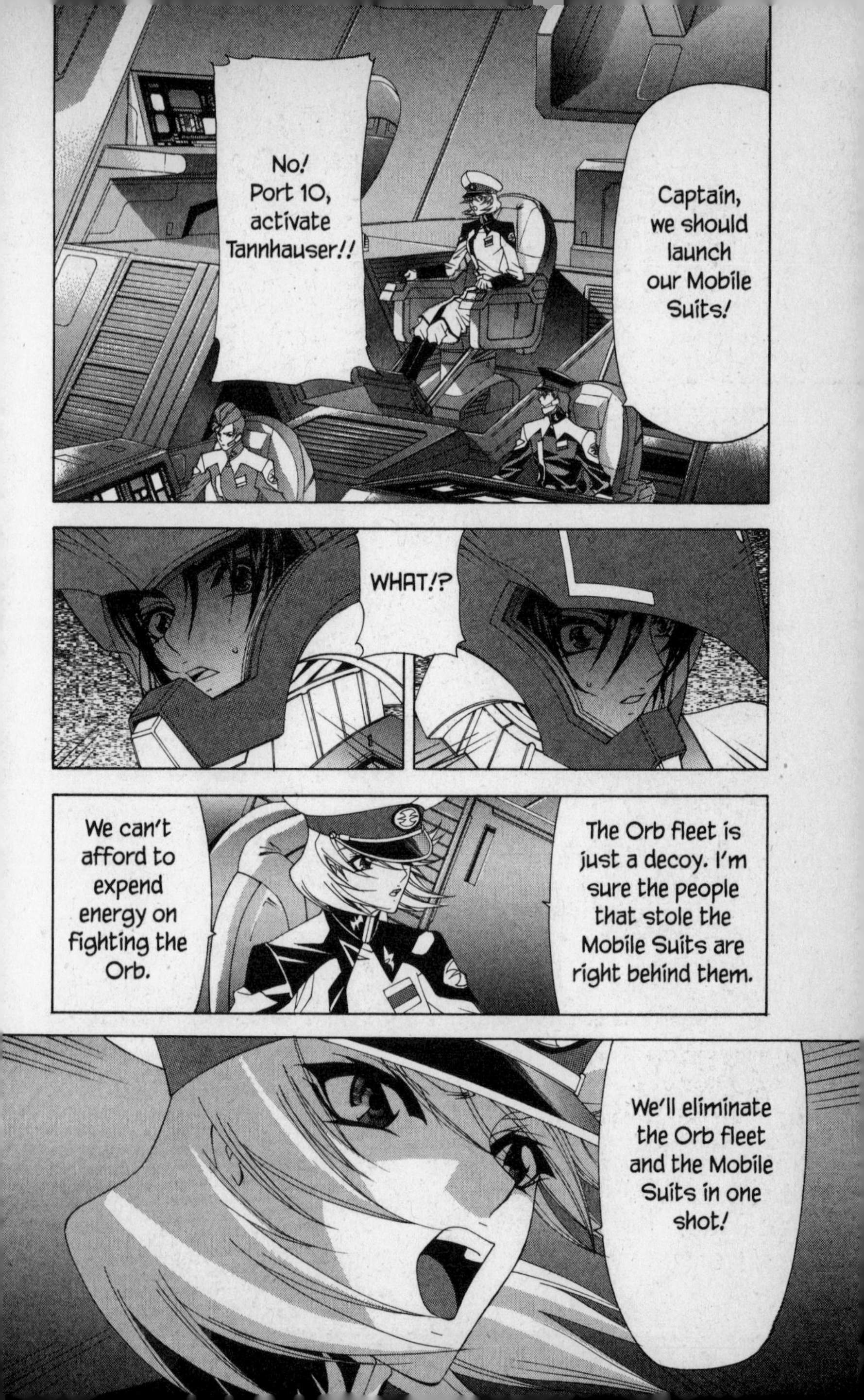
Captain, we should launch our Mobile Suits!
No! Port 10, activate Tannhauser!!
WHAT!?
The Orb fleet is just a decoy. I'm sure the people that stole the Mobile Suits are right behind them.
We can't afford to expend energy on fighting the Orb.
We'll eliminate the Orb fleet and the Mobile Suits in one shot!

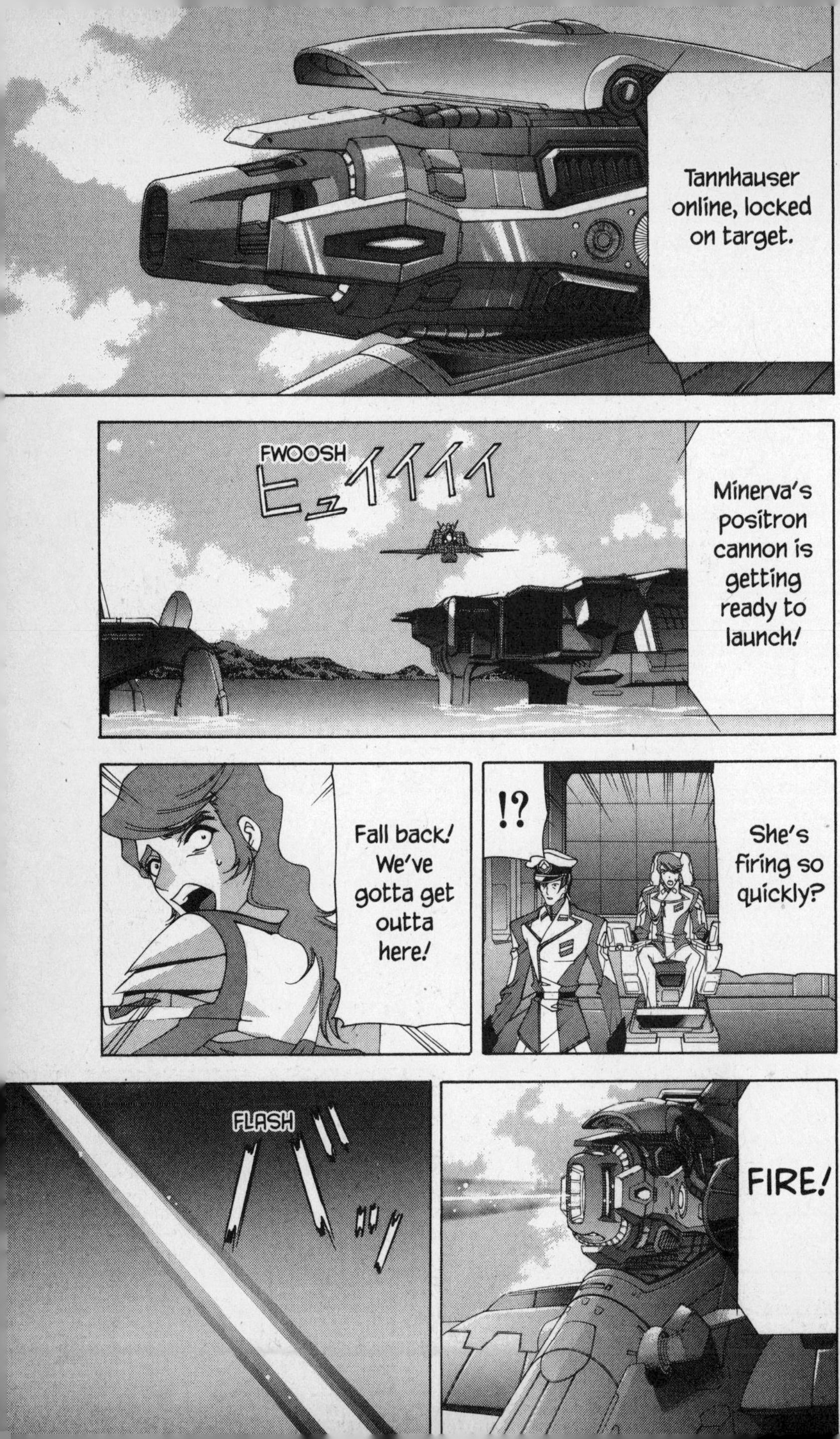
Tannhauser online, locked on target.
Minerva's positron cannon is getting ready to launch!
FWOOSH
ヒュイイイイ
!?
She's firing so quickly?
Fall back! We've gotta get outta here!
FIRE!
FLASH

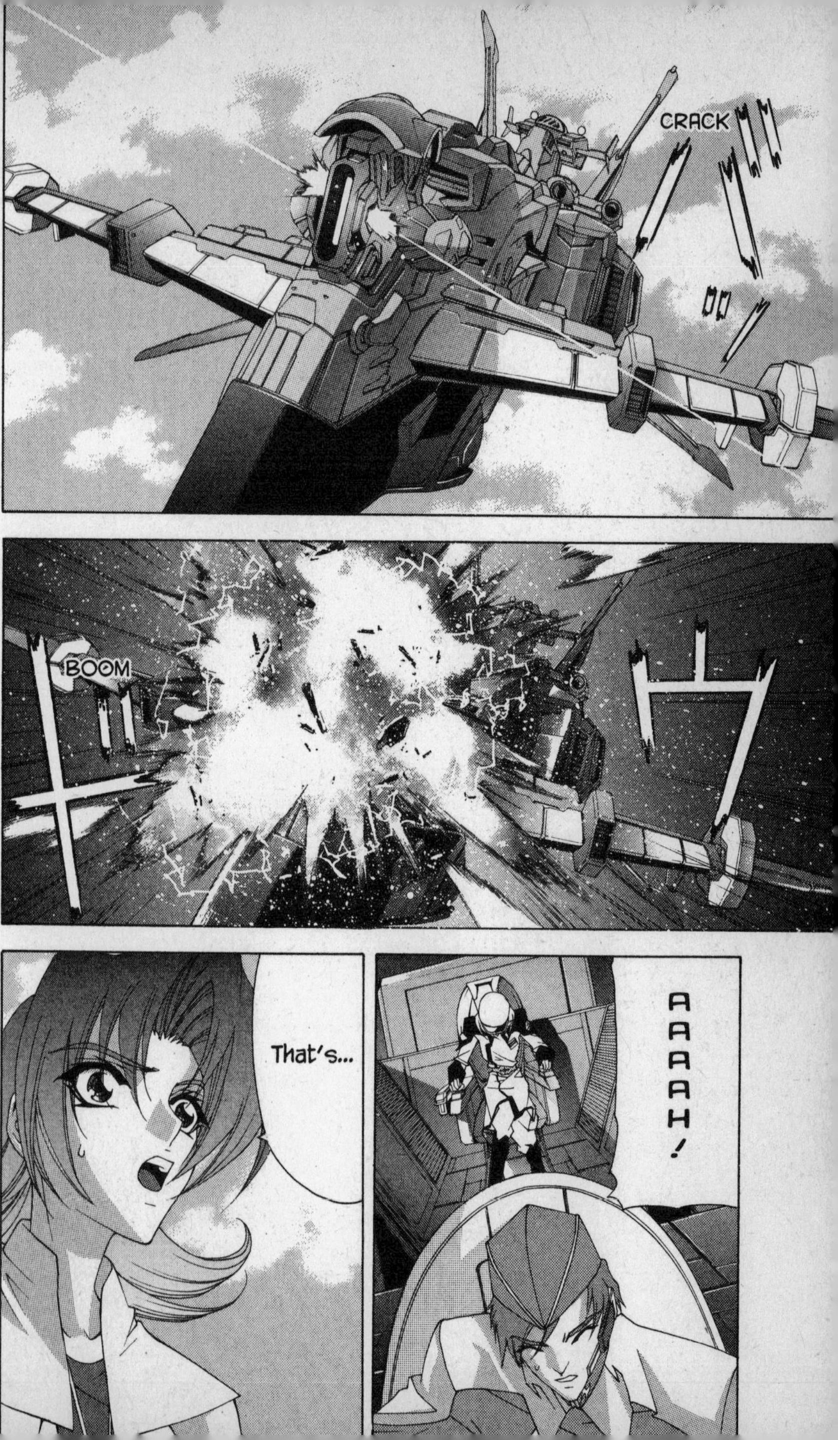
CRACK
BOOM
AAAAH!
That's...

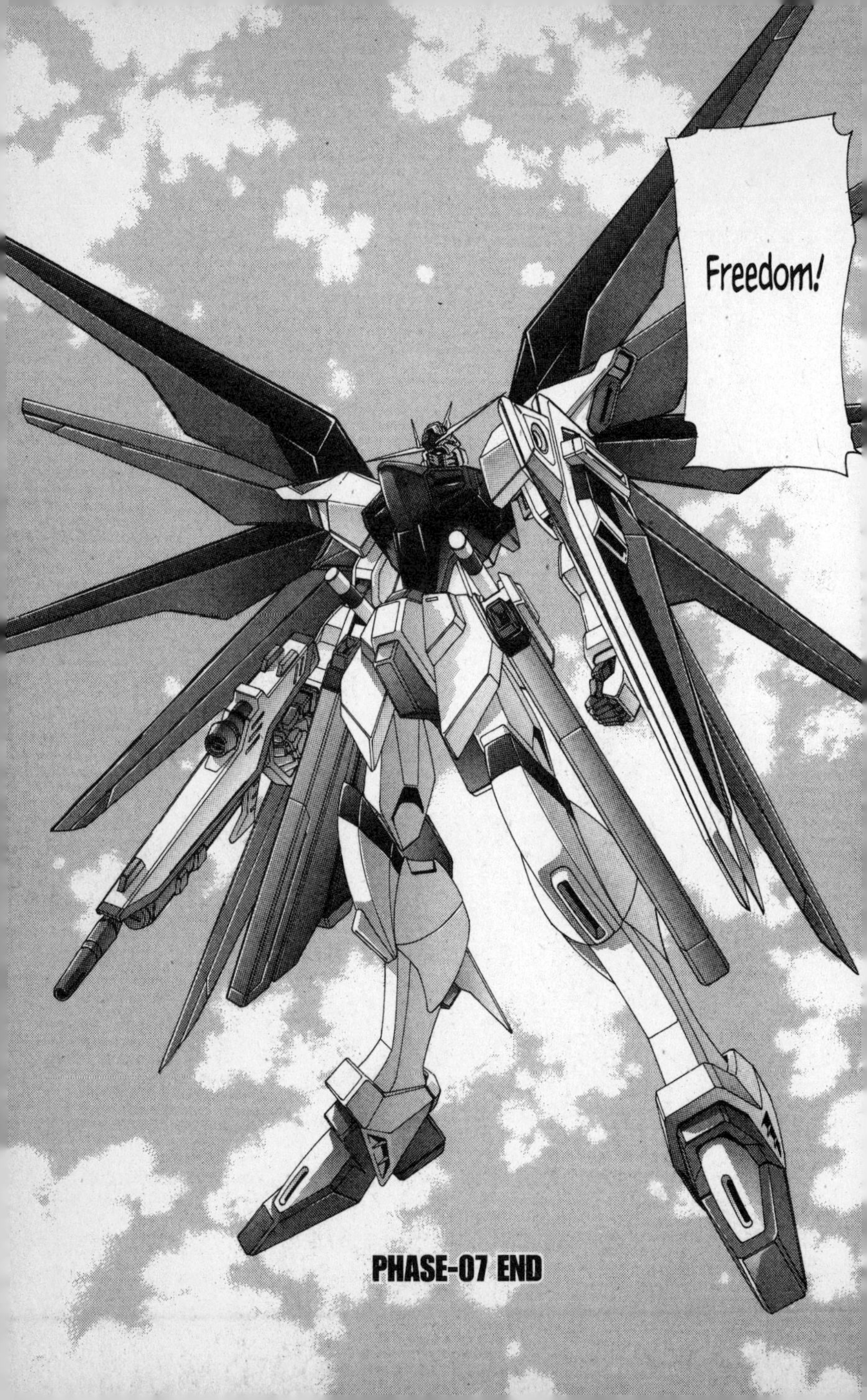
Freedom!
PHASE-07 END

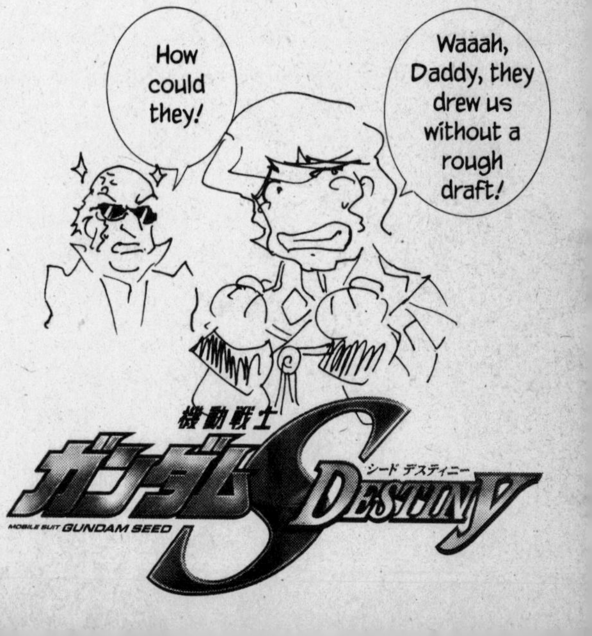
Waaah, Daddy, they drew us without a rough draft!
How could they!

機動戦士 ガンダム SEED DESTINY
シード デスティニー
MOBILE SUIT GUNDAM SEED

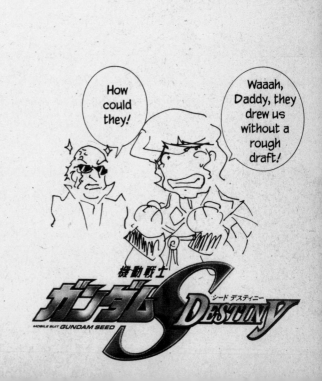

PHASE-08 The Shadows of War

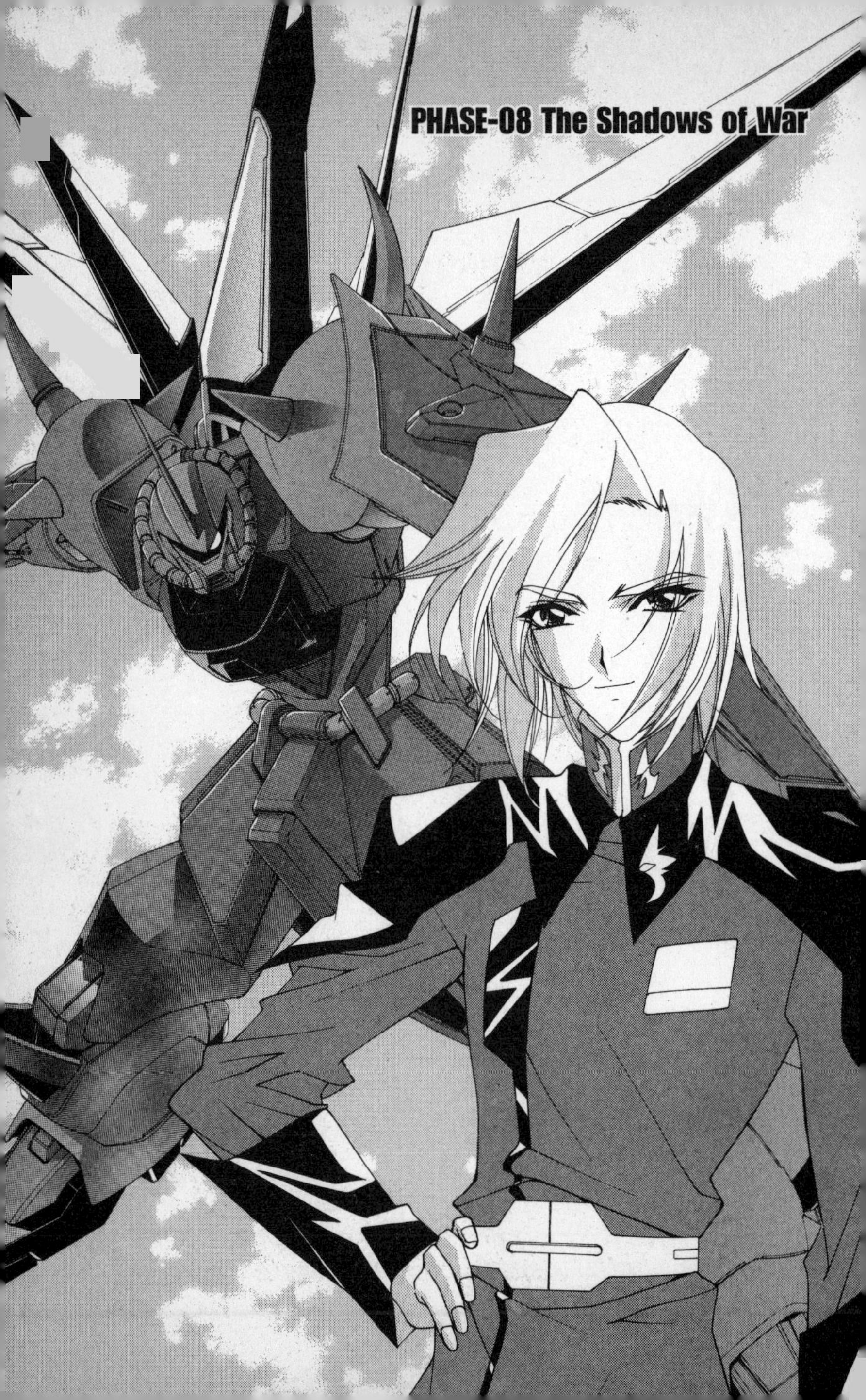

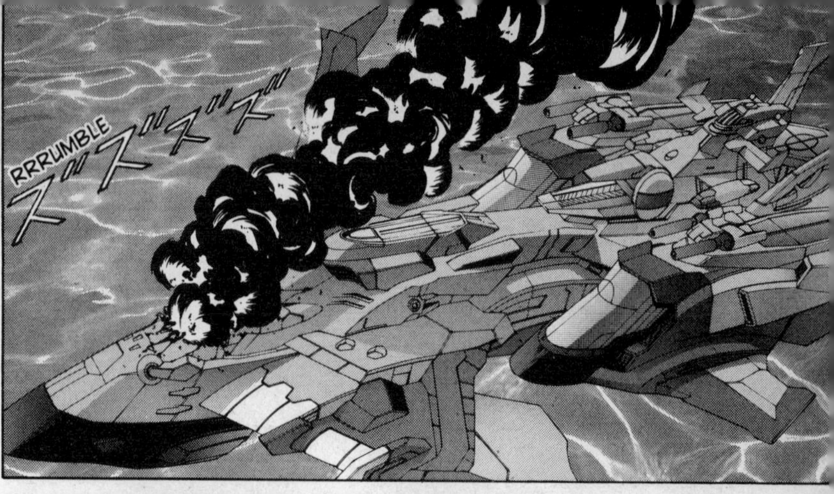
RRRUMBLE
ズズズズ
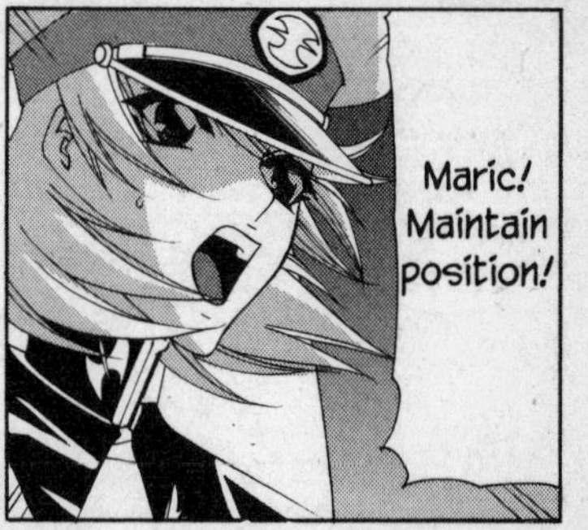
Maric! Maintain position!
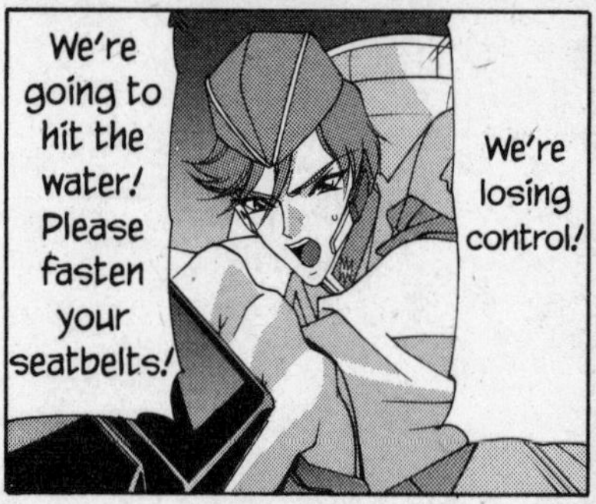
We're losing control!
We're going to hit the water! Please fasten your seatbelts!
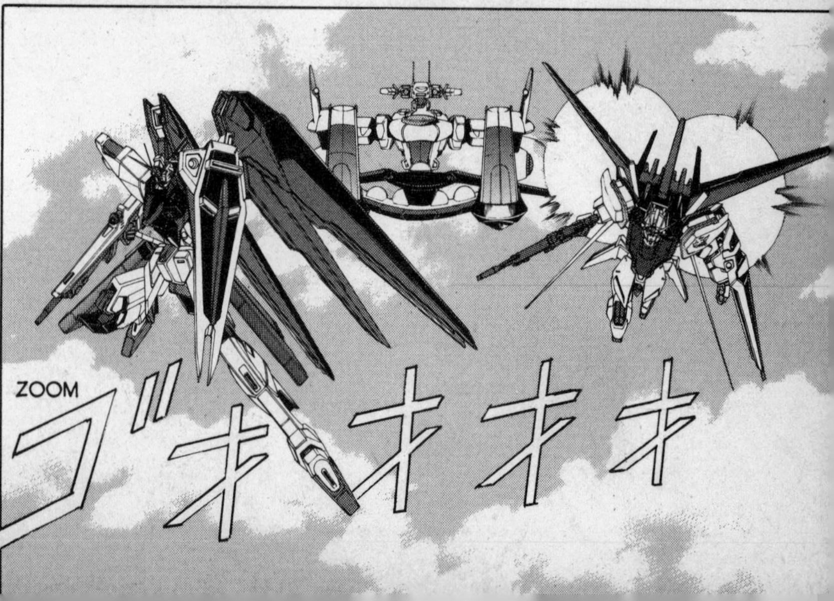
ZOOM
ゴオオオオ

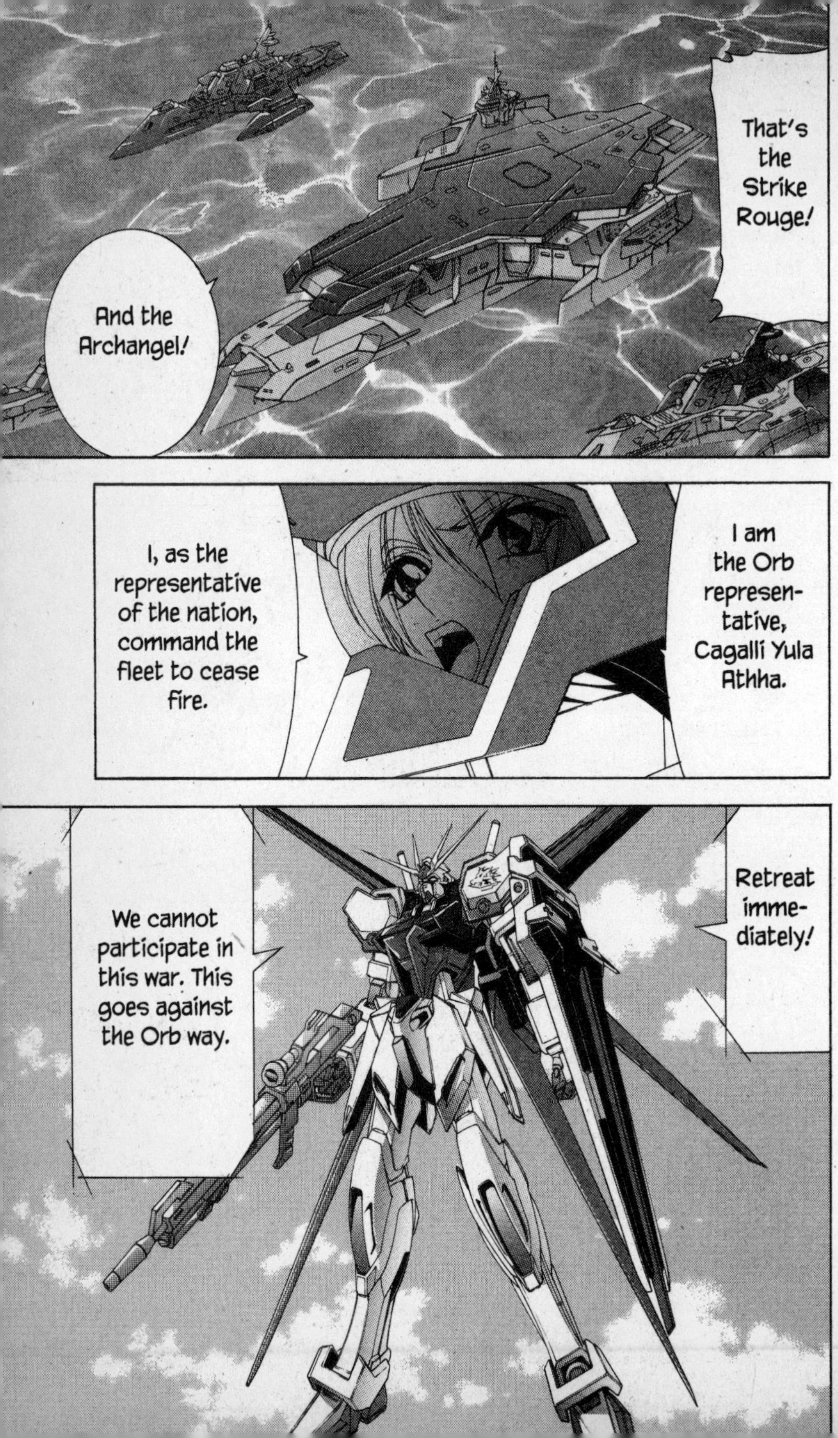
That's the Strike Rouge!
And the Archangel!
I am the Orb representative, Cagalli Yula Athha.
I, as the representative of the nation, command the fleet to cease fire.
Retreat immediately!
We cannot participate in this war. This goes against the Orb way.

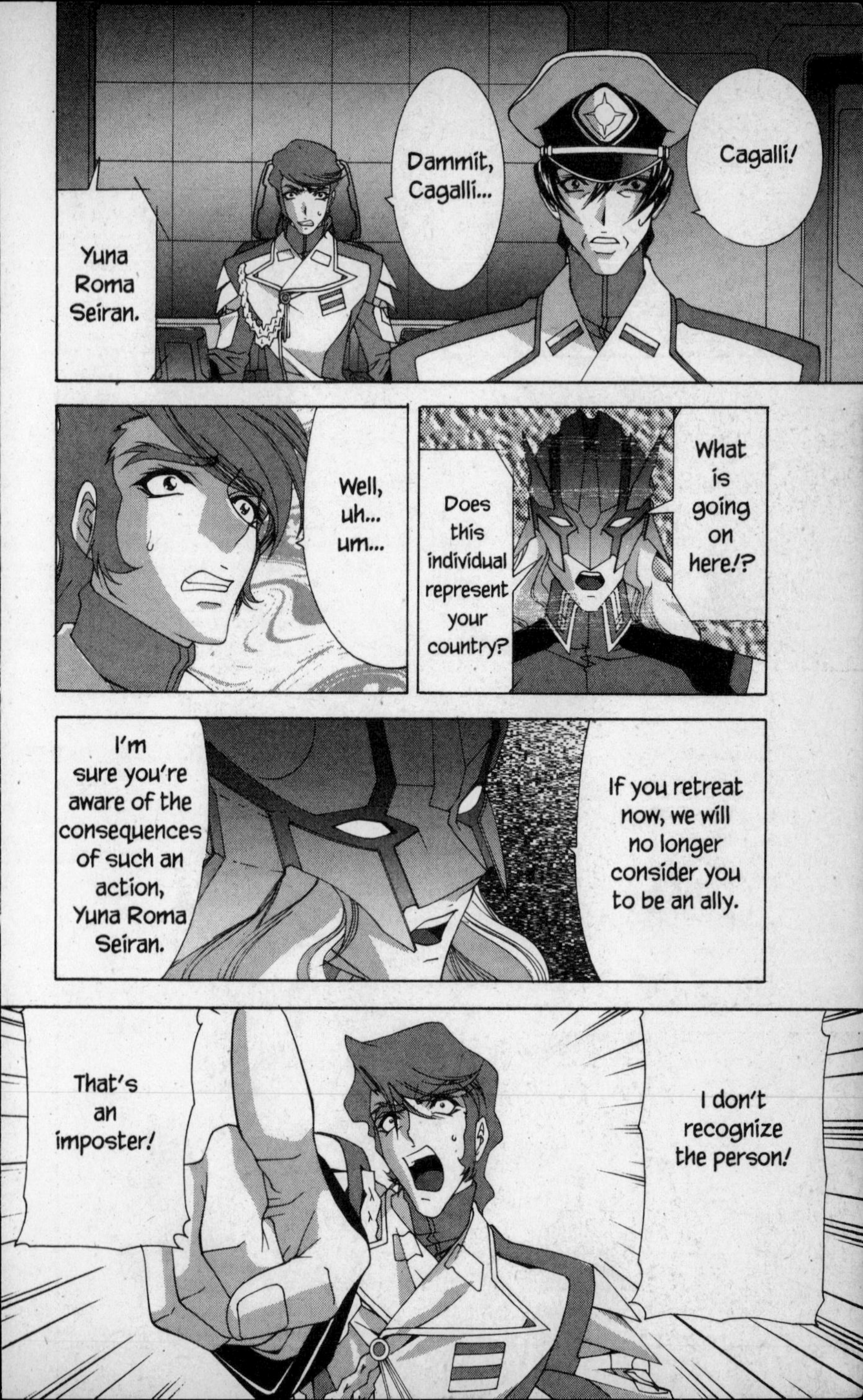
Cagalli!
Dammit, Cagalli...
Yuna Roma Seiran.
What is going on here!?
Does this individual represent your country?
Well, uh... um...
If you retreat now, we will no longer consider you to be an ally.
I'm sure you're aware of the consequences of such an action, Yuna Roma Seiran.
I don't recognize the person!
That's an imposter!

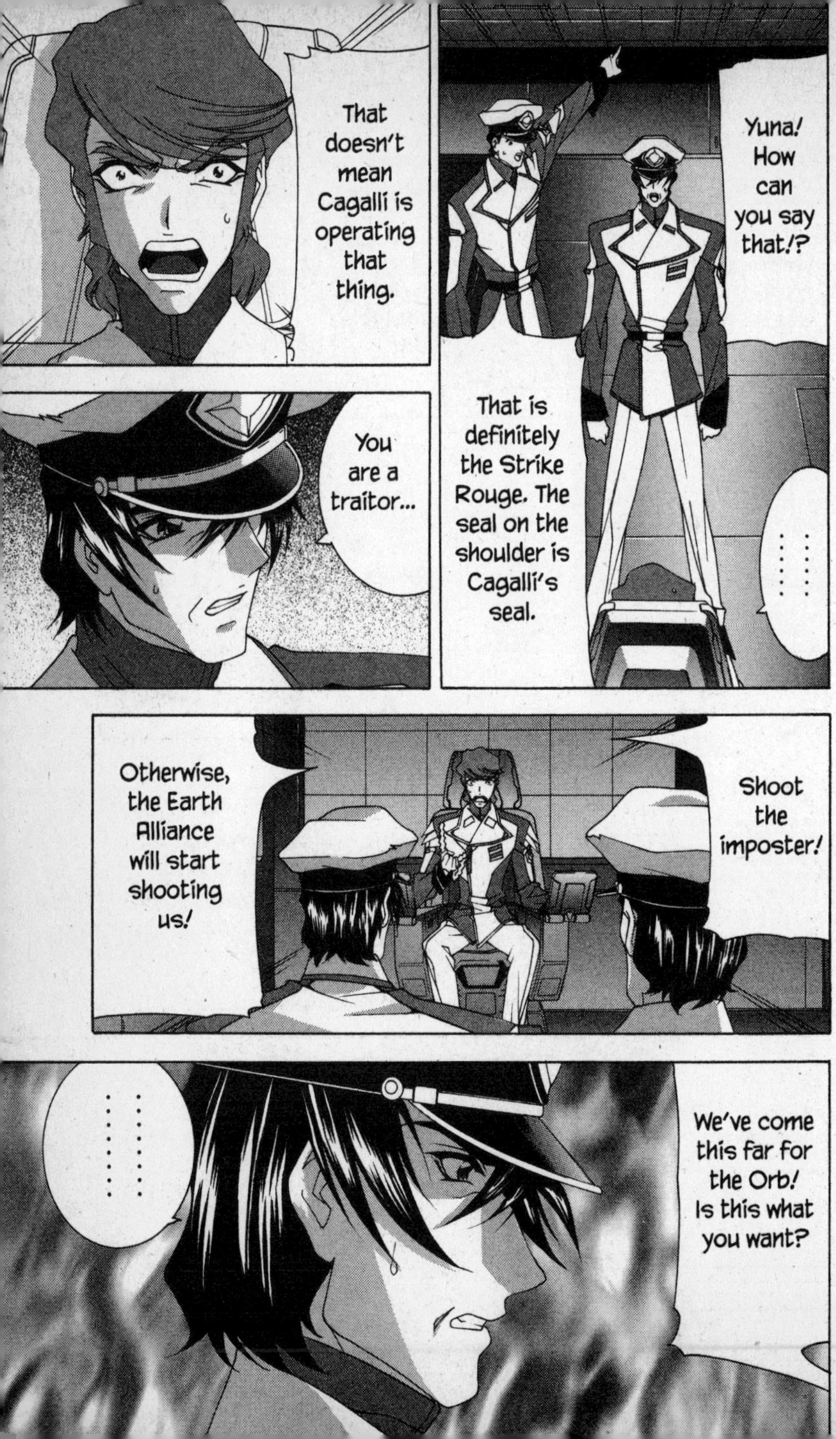
Yuna! How can you say that!?
That doesn't mean Cagalli is operating that thing.
That is definitely the Strike Rouge. The seal on the shoulder is Cagalli's seal.
......
You are a traitor...
Shoot the imposter!
Otherwise, the Earth Alliance will start shooting us!
We've come this far for the Orb! Is this what you want?
......

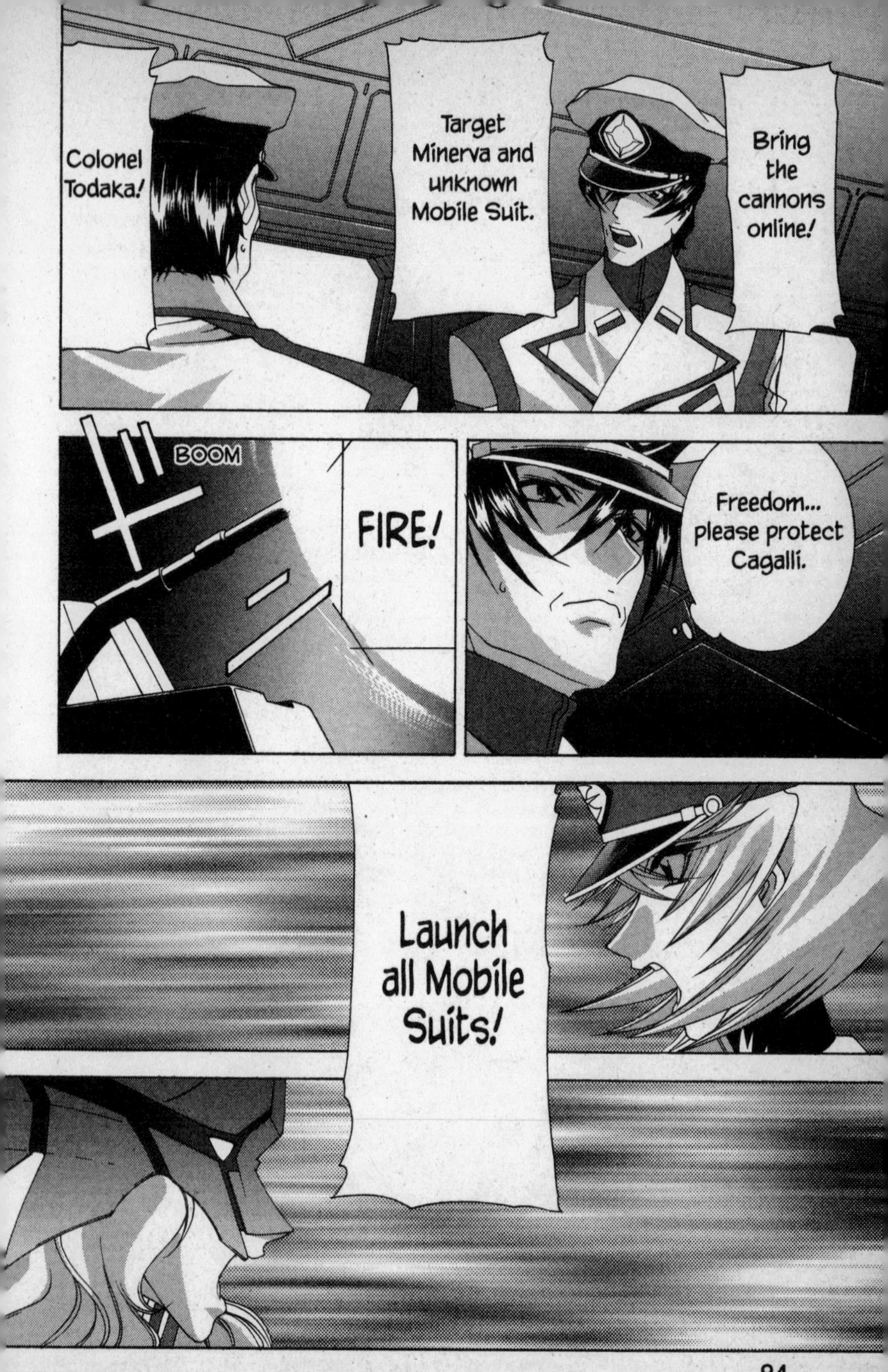
Bring the cannons online!
Target Minerva and unknown Mobile Suit.
Colonel Todaka!
Freedom... please protect Cagalli.
FIRE!
BOOM
Launch all Mobile Suits!

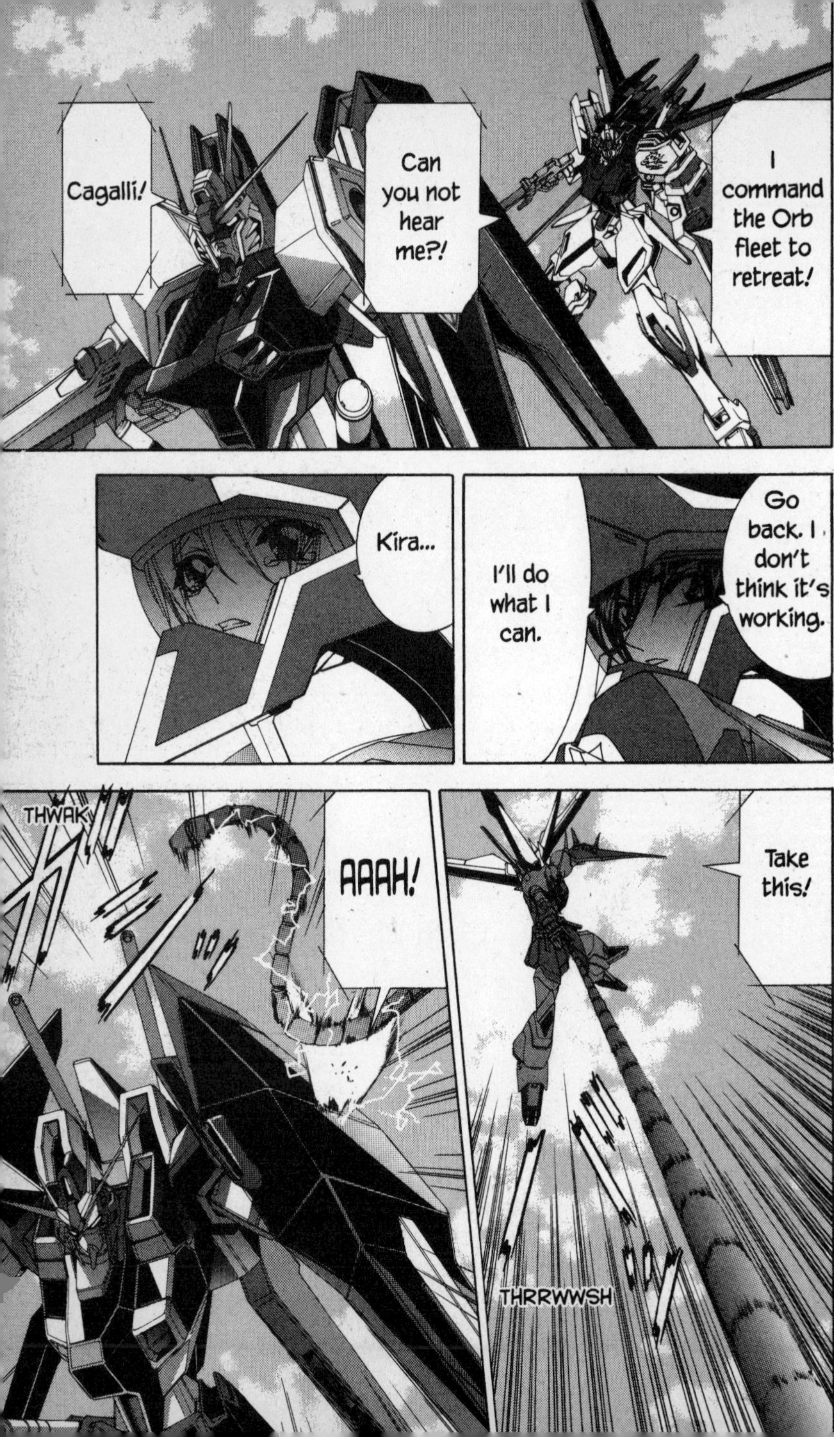
I command the Orb fleet to retreat!
Can you not hear me?!
Cagalli!
Go back. I don't think it's working.
I'll do what I can.
Kira...
Take this!
THRRWWSH
AAAH!
THWAK

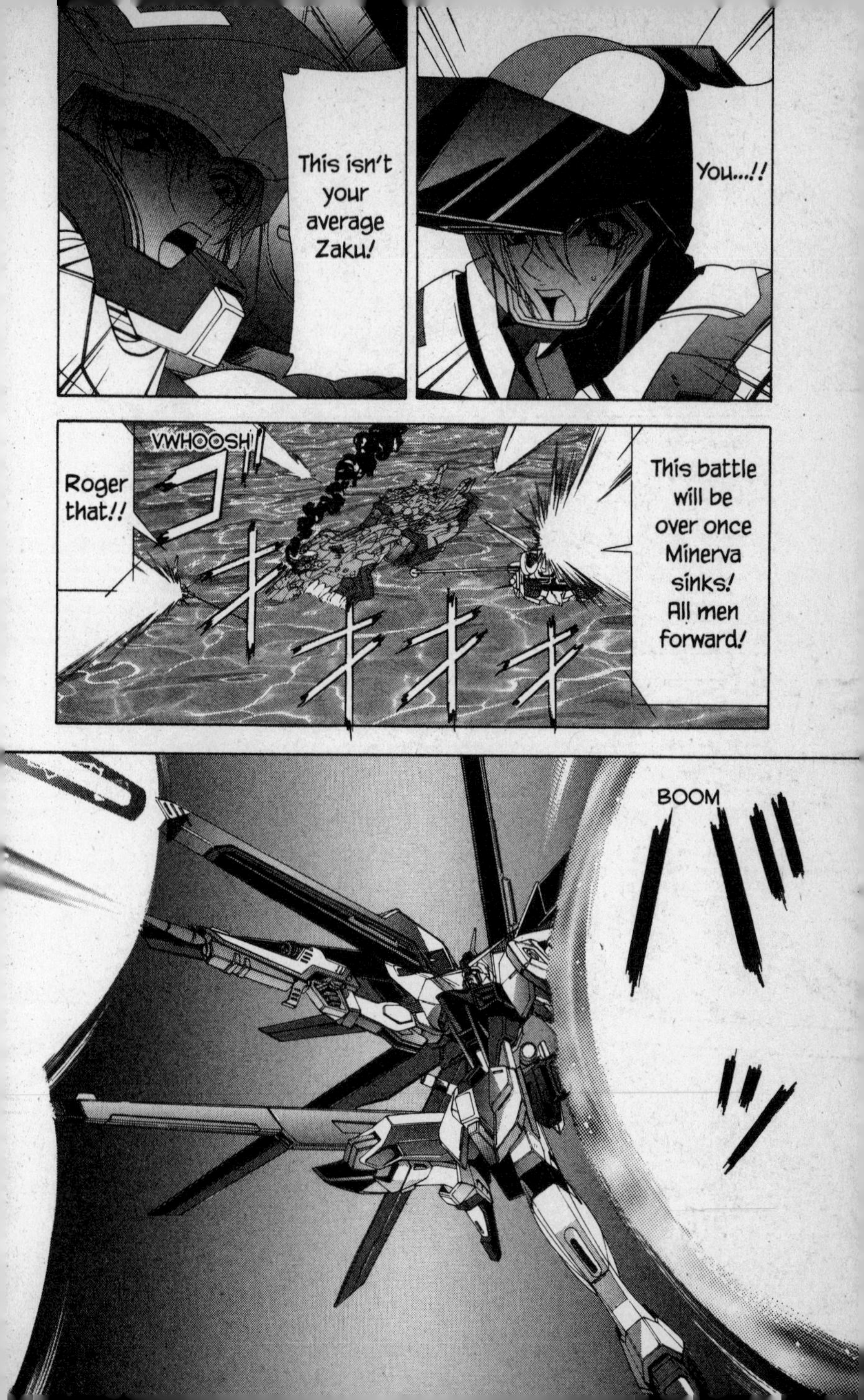
You...!!
This isn't your average Zaku!
This battle will be over once Minerva sinks! All men forward!
VWHOOSH
Roger that!!
BOOM

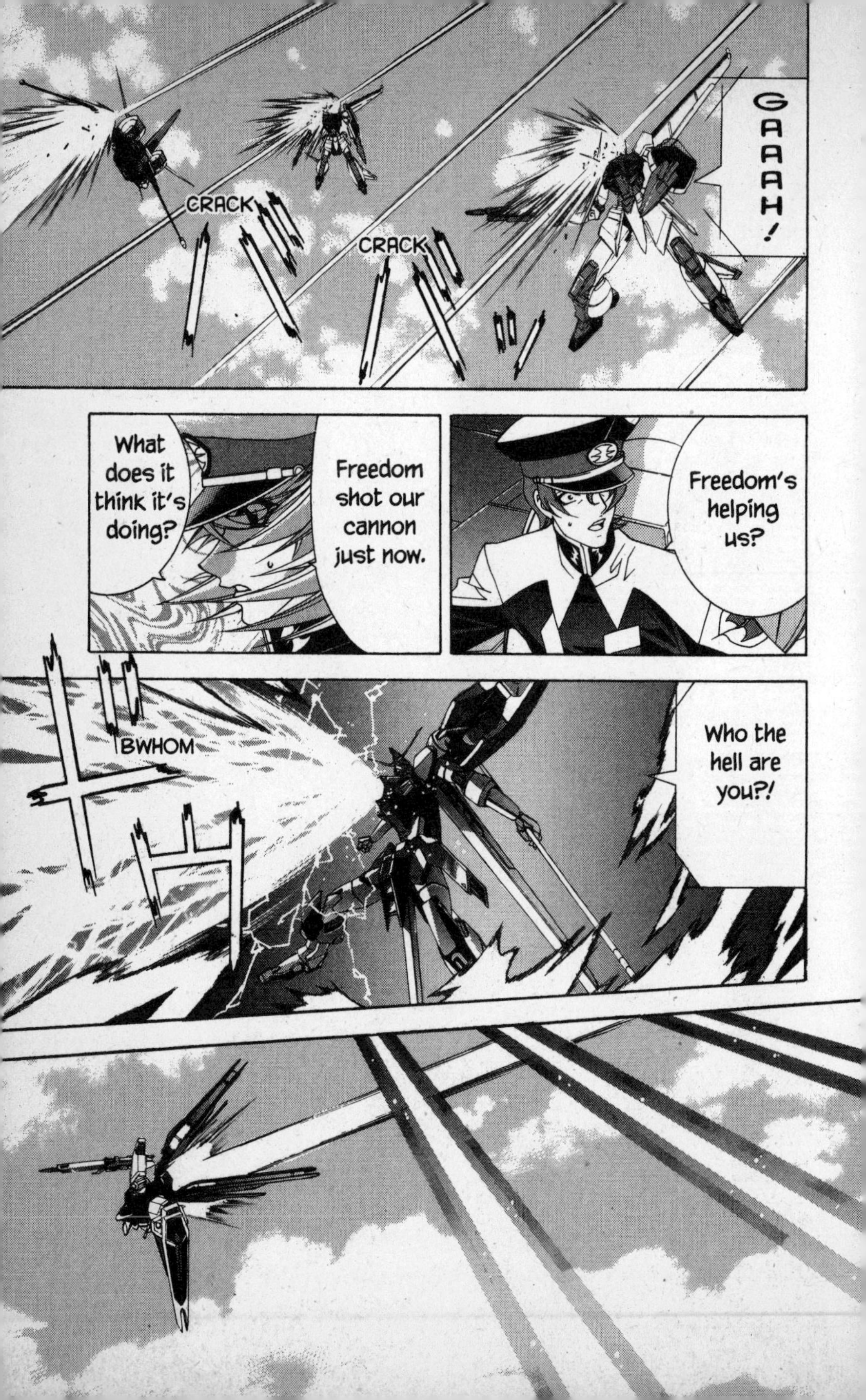
GAAAH!
CRACK
CRACK
Freedom's helping us?
Freedom shot our cannon just now.
What does it think it's doing?
Who the hell are you?!
BWHOM

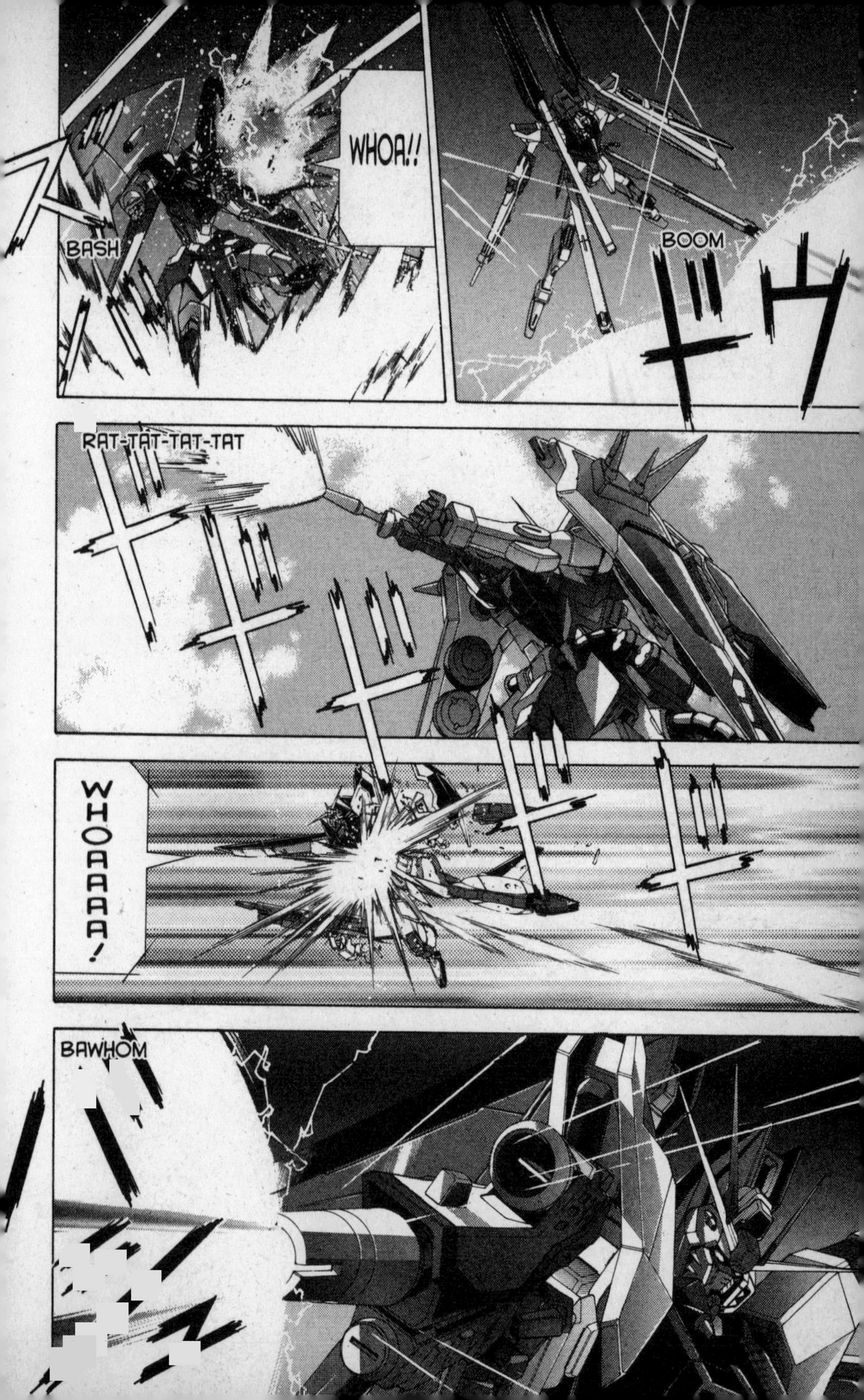
BOOM
WHOA!!
BASH
RAT-TAT-TAT-TAT
WHOAAAAA!
BAWHOM

!!

SHATTER

You dirt-bag!

Stop, Shinn!

Rey!

Which side are you on?!

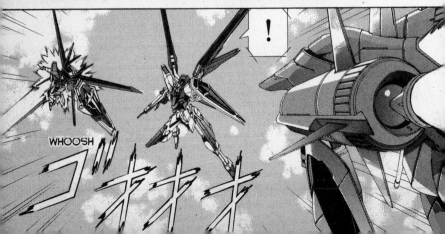

!

WHOOSH

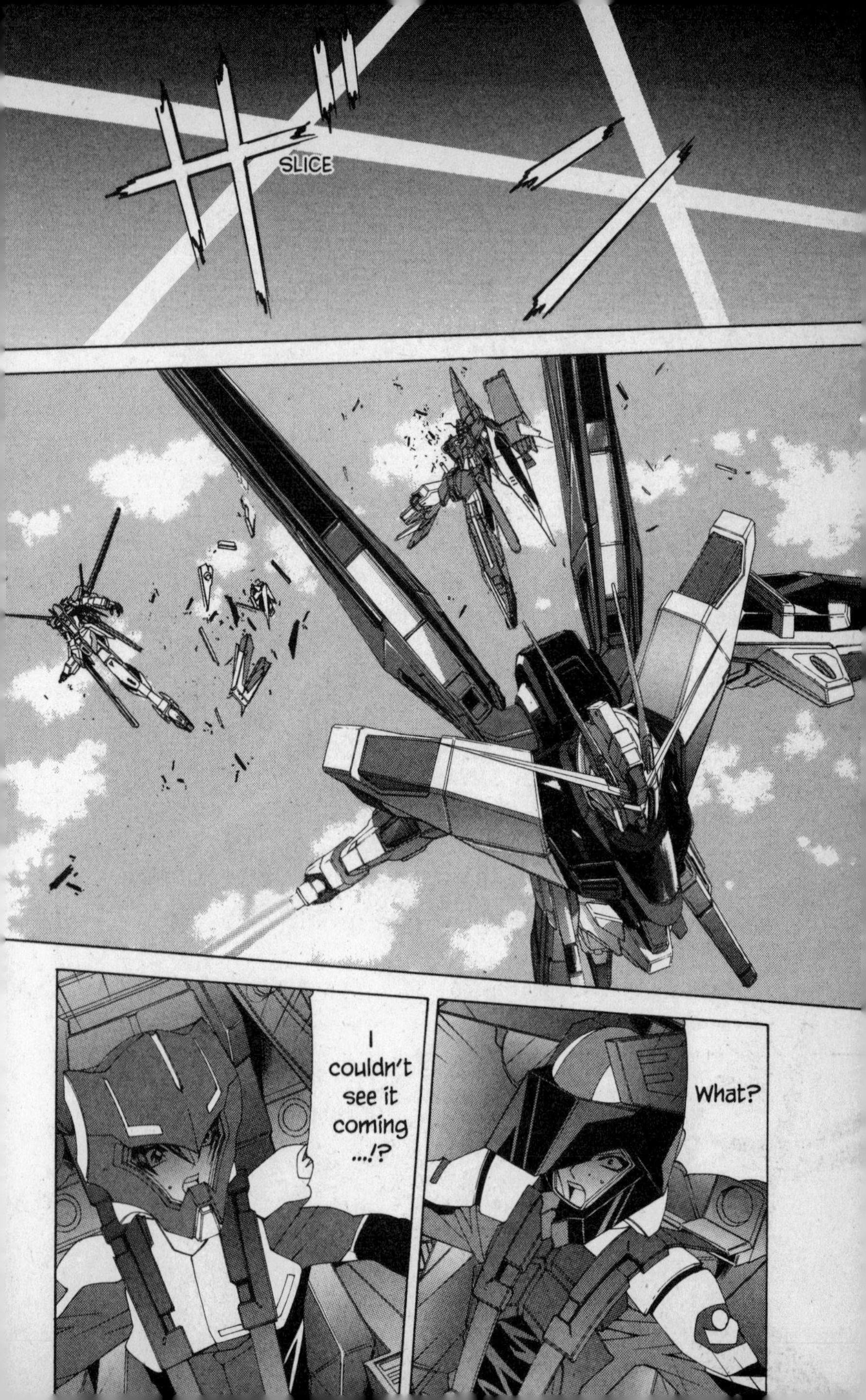
SLICE
What?
I couldn't see it coming ...!?

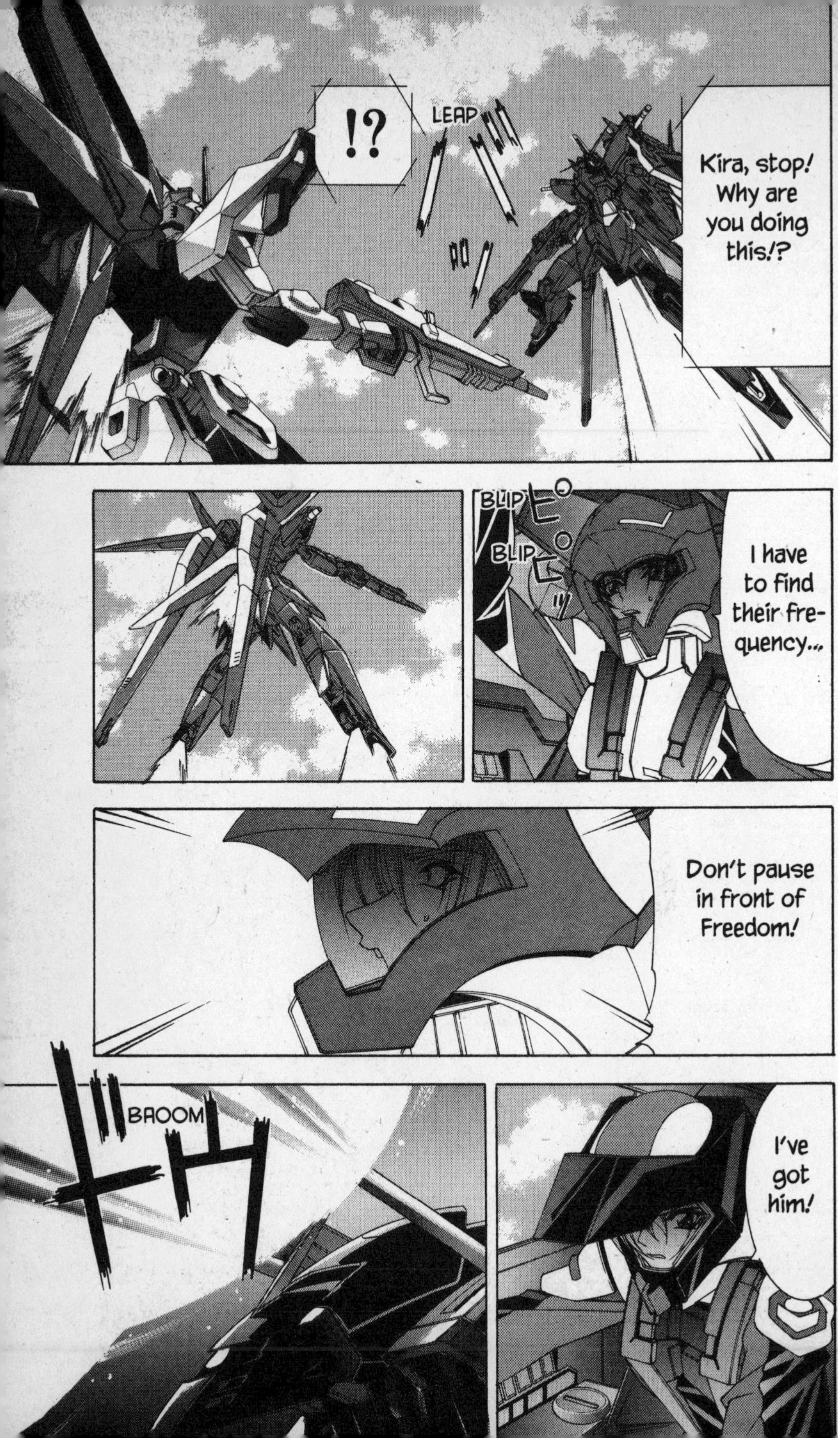
Kira, stop! Why are you doing this!?
LEAP
!?
I have to find their fre-quency...
BLIP
BLIP
Don't pause in front of Freedom!
I've got him!
BAOOM

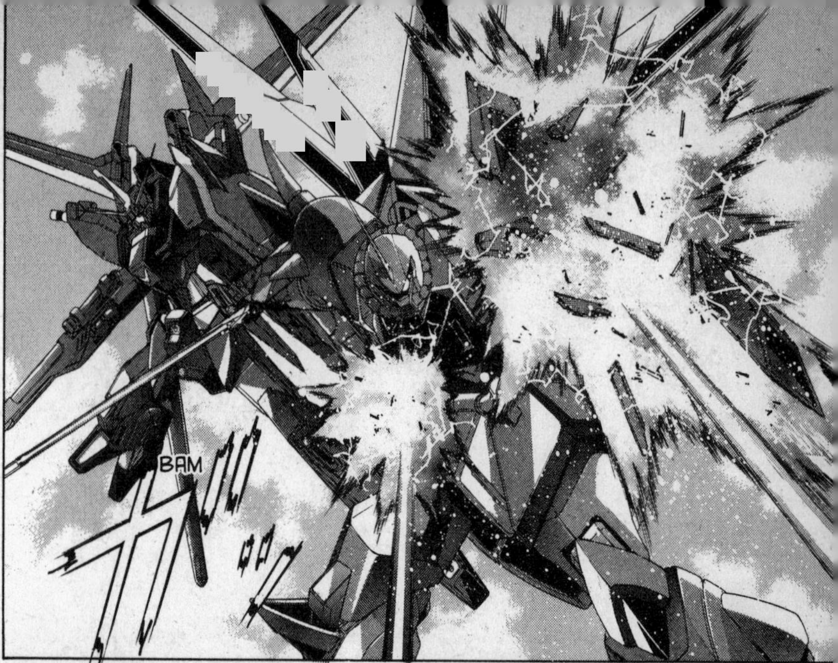
BAM
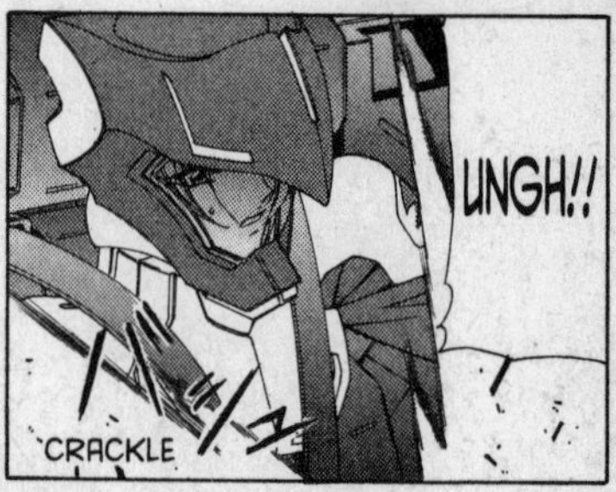
UNGH!!
CRACKLE
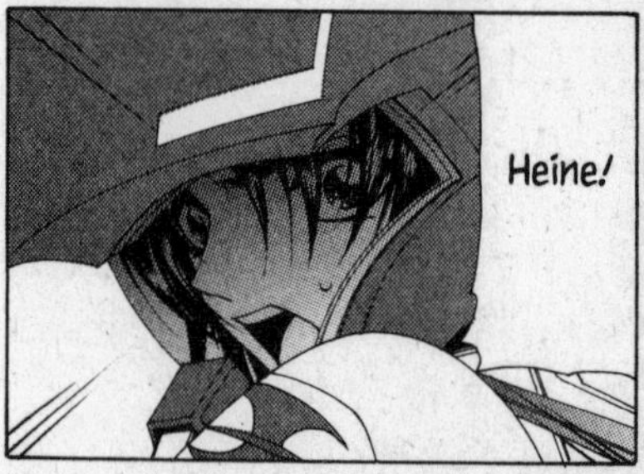
Heine!
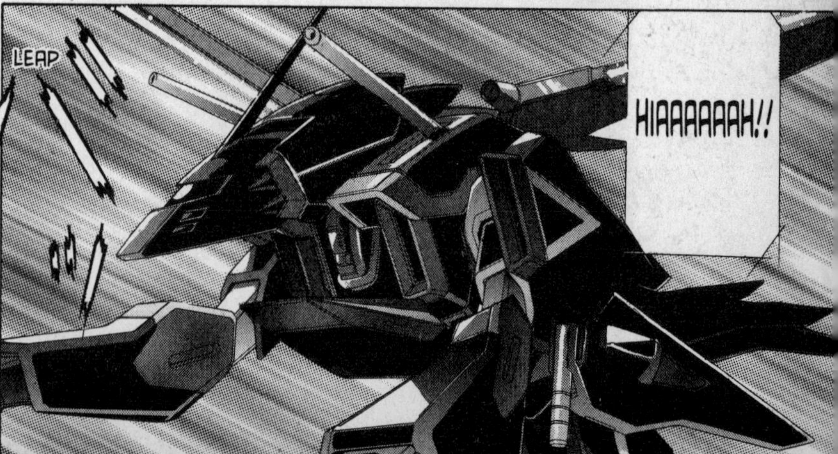
HIAAAAAAH!!
LEAP

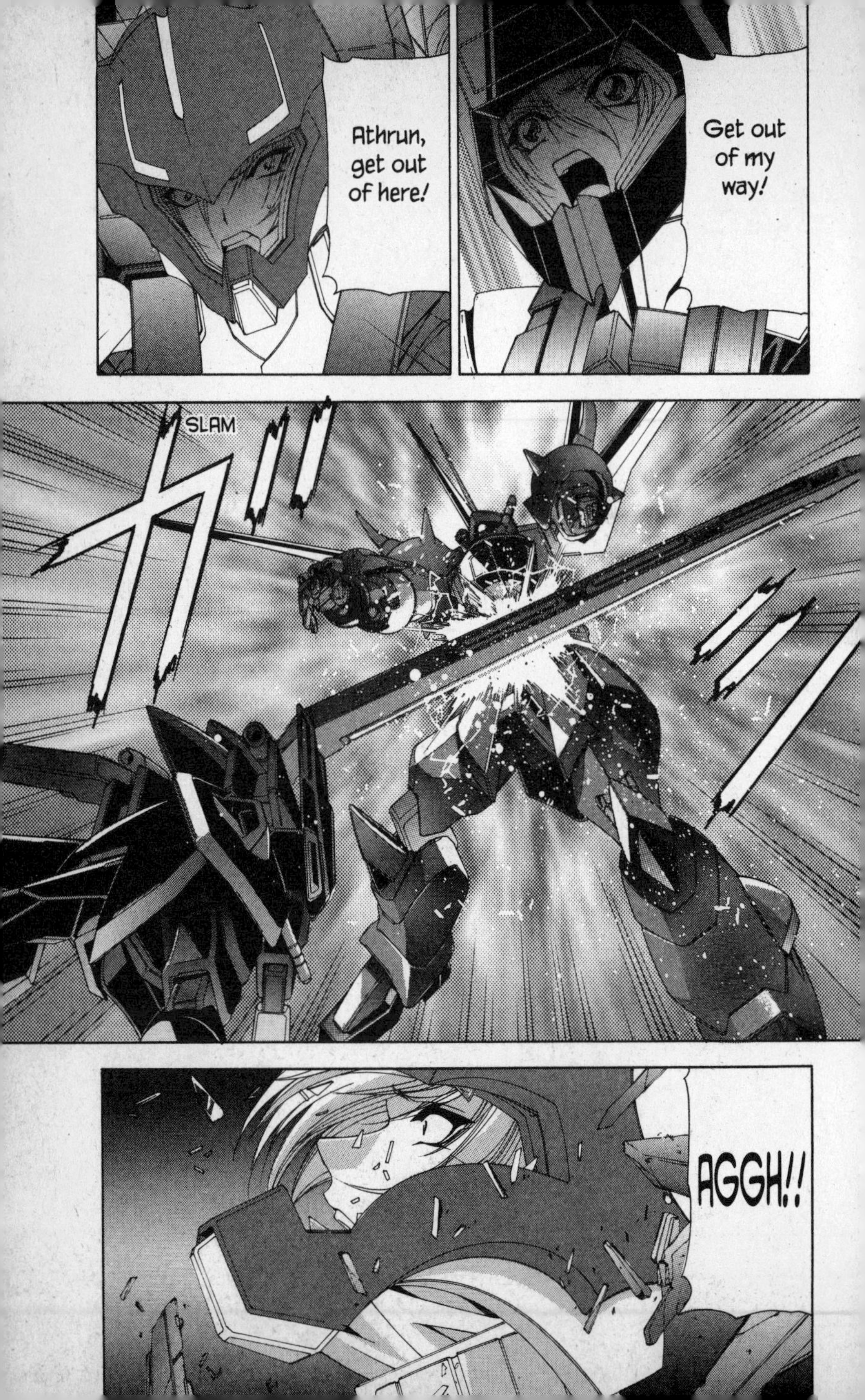
Get out of my way!
Athrun, get out of here!
SLAM
AGGH!!

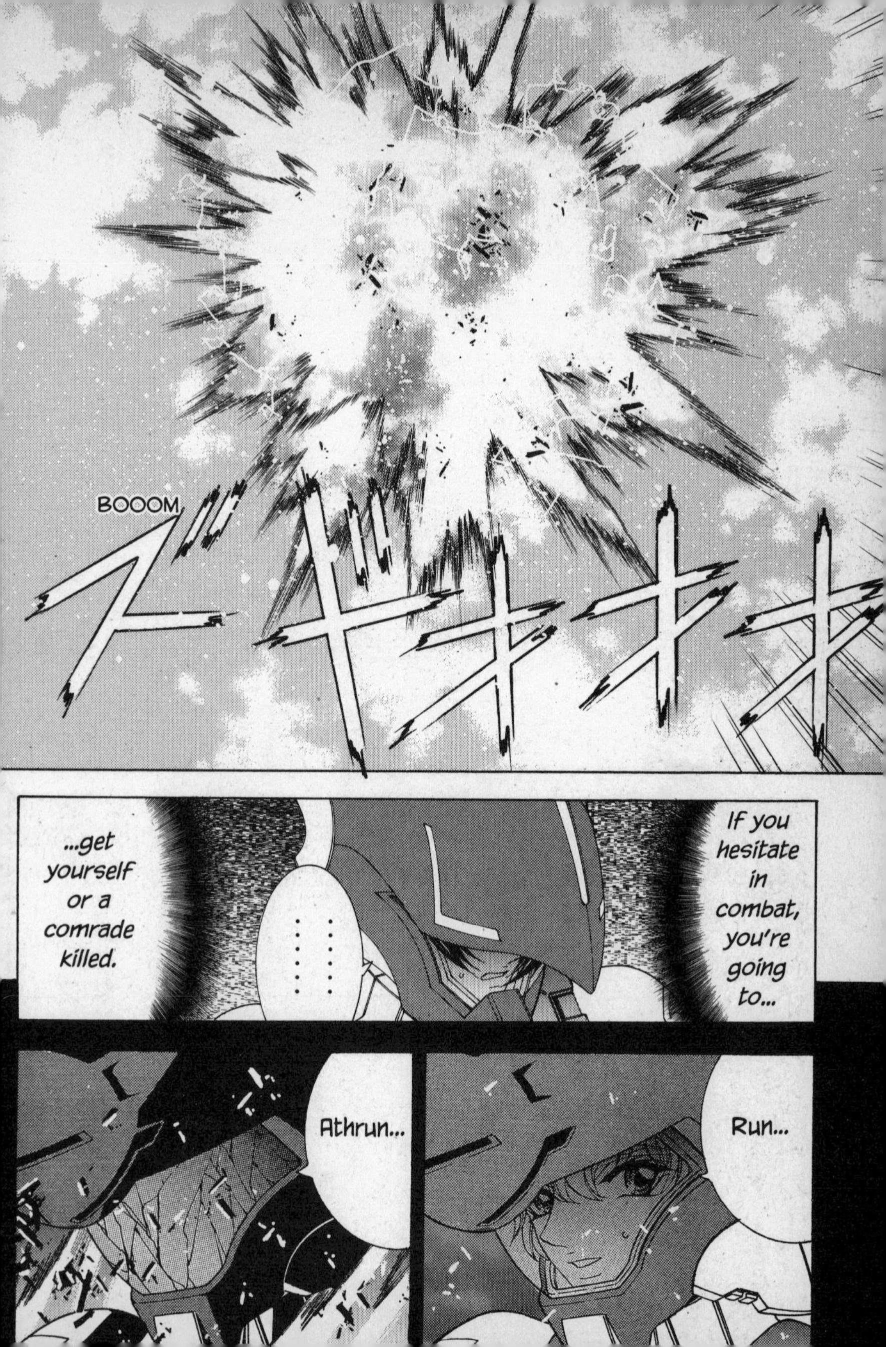
BOOOM
If you hesitate in combat, you're going to...
...get yourself or a comrade killed.
......
Run...
Athrun...

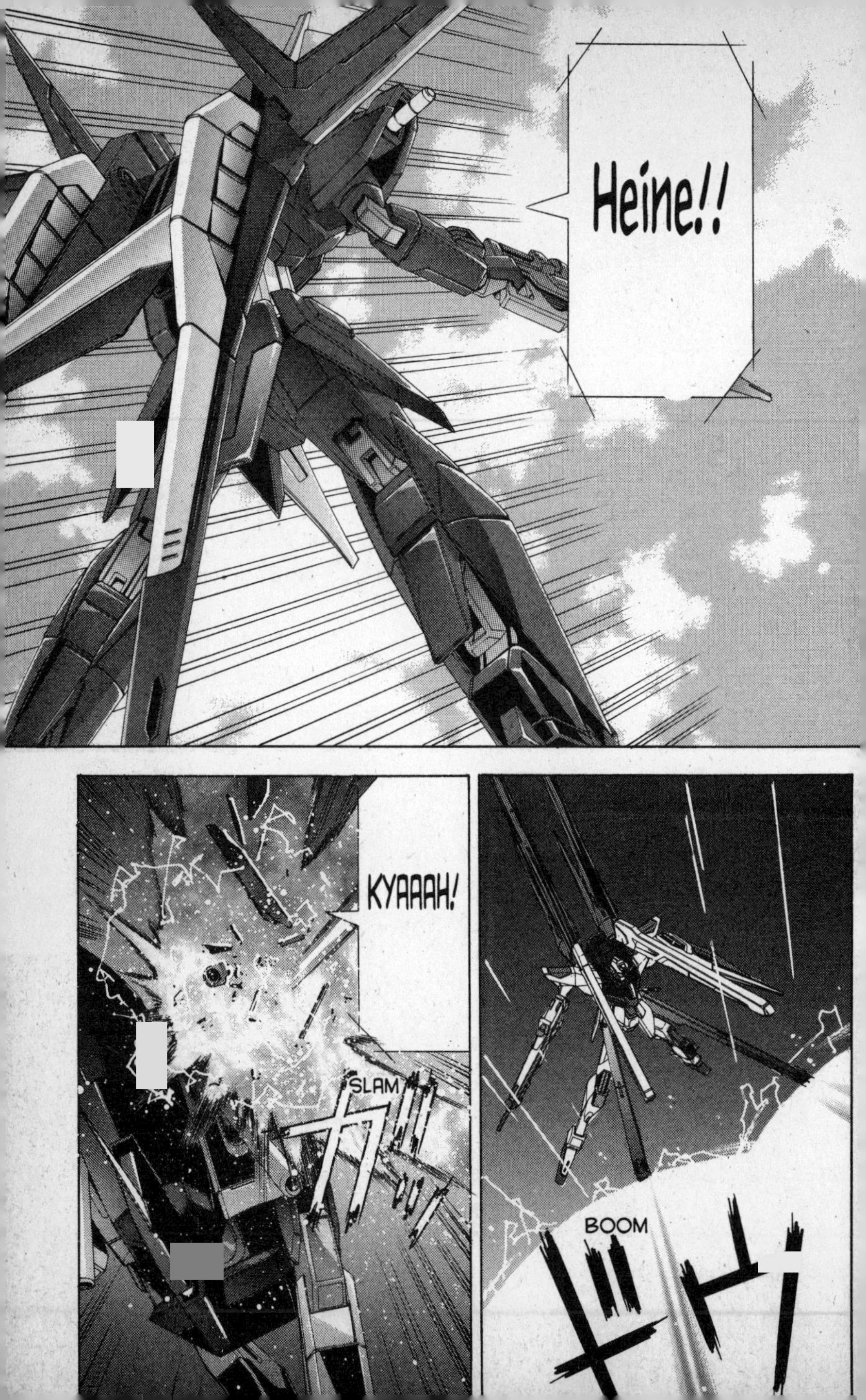
Heine!!
BOOM
KYAAAH!
SLAM

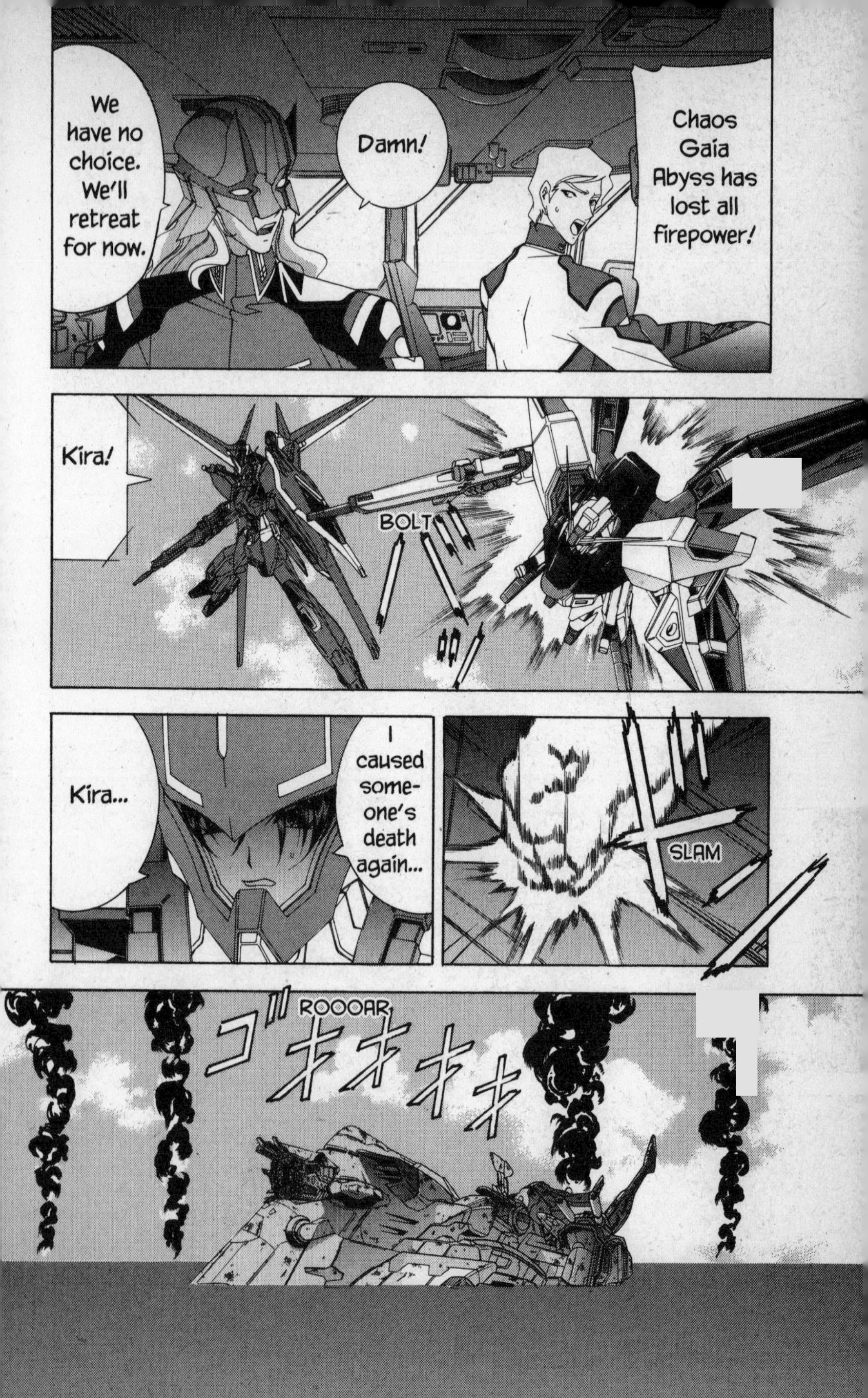
Chaos Gaia Abyss has lost all firepower!
Damn!
We have no choice. We'll retreat for now.
Kira!
BOLT
SLAM
I caused some-one's death again...
Kira...
ROOOAR
ゴオオオォ

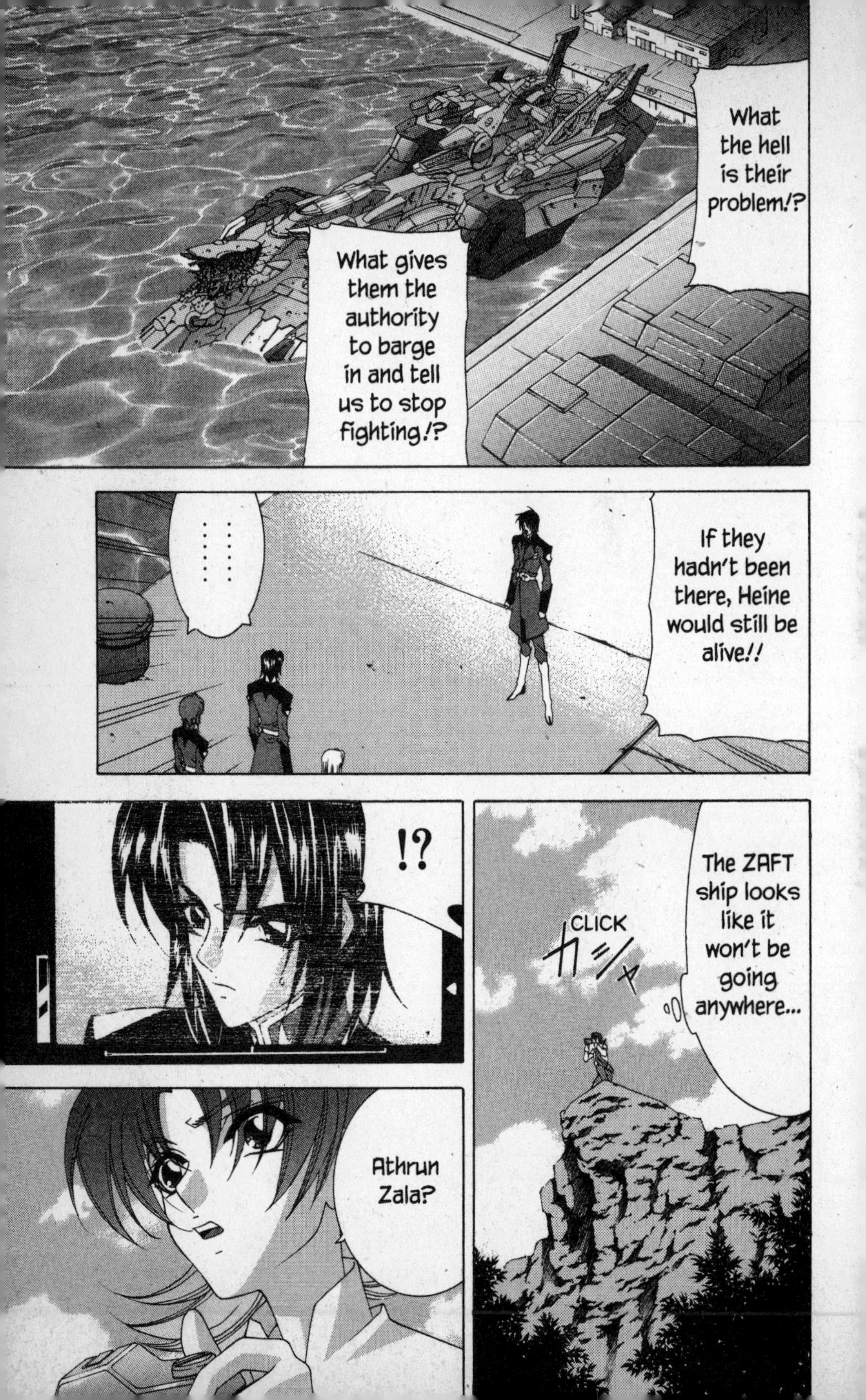
What the hell is their problem!?
What gives them the authority to barge in and tell us to stop fighting!?
If they hadn't been there, Heine would still be alive!!
......
The ZAFT ship looks like it won't be going anywhere...
CLICK
カシャ
!?
Athrun Zala?

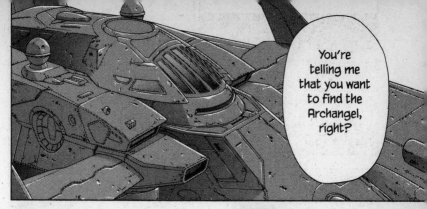

You're telling me that you want to find the Archangel, right?

Yes, they fought with us during Jachin Due.

I'm very familiar with the crew.

I don't think they understand what's going on.

That's the reason I'm confused about this situation.

I'd like permission to leave the ship and go talk to them in person.

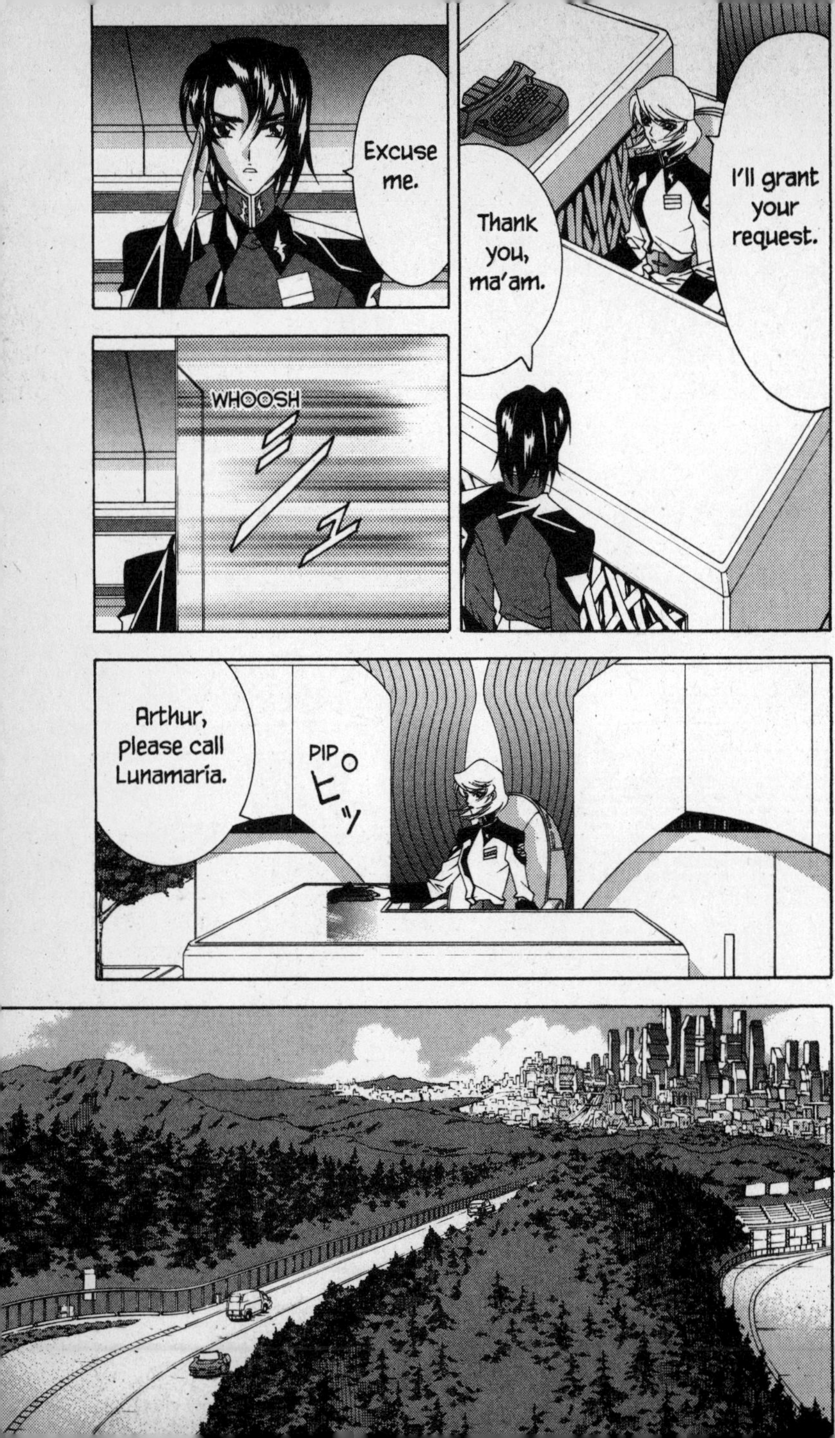
I'll grant your request.
Thank you, ma'am.
Excuse me.
WHOOSH
Arthur, please call Lunamaria.
PIP
ピッ

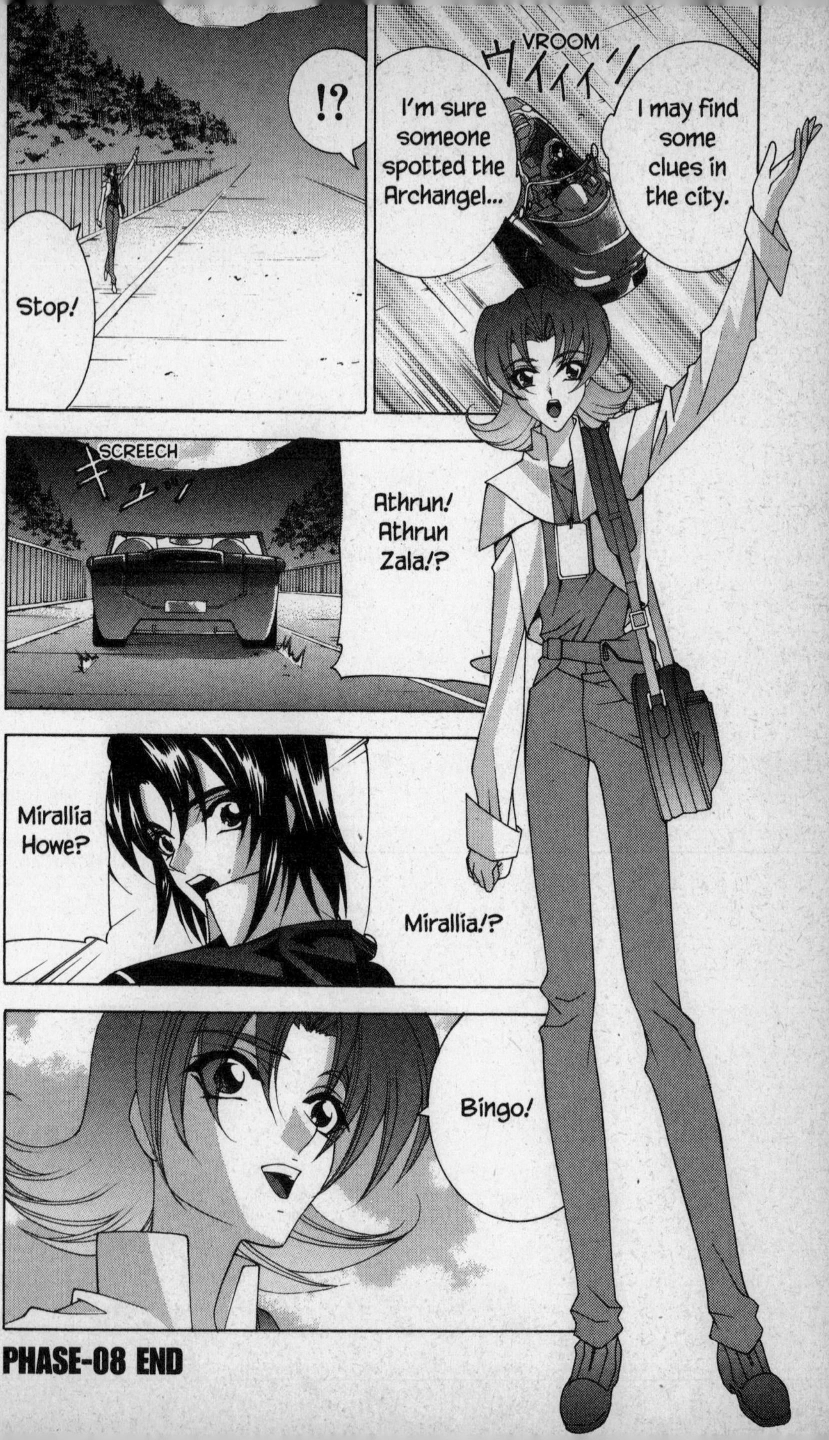
VROOM
I may find some clues in the city.
I'm sure someone spotted the Archangel...
!?
Stop!
SCREECH
Athrun! Athrun Zala!?
Miriallia Howe?
Miriallia!?
Bingo!

PHASE-08 END

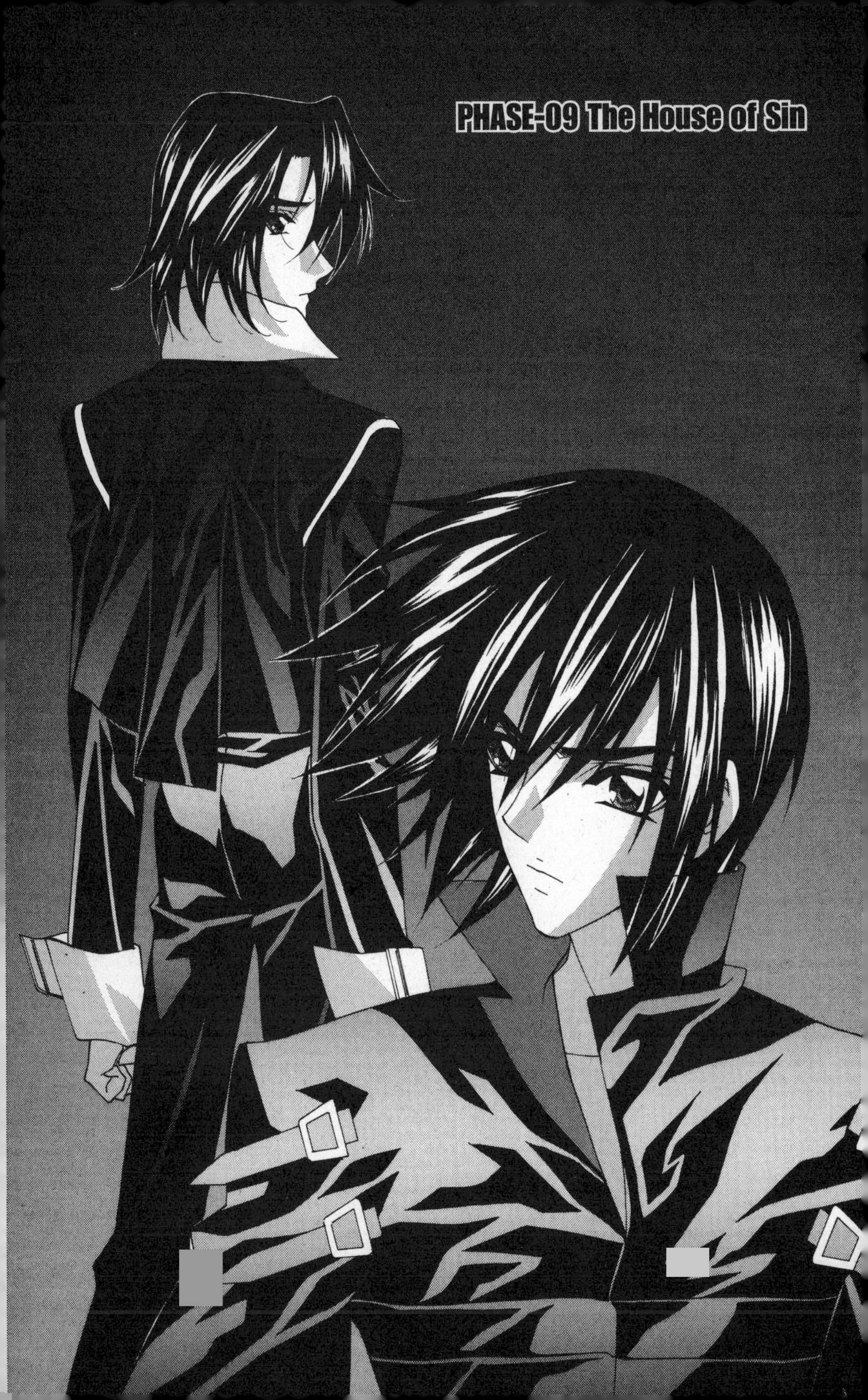
PHASE-09 The House of Sin

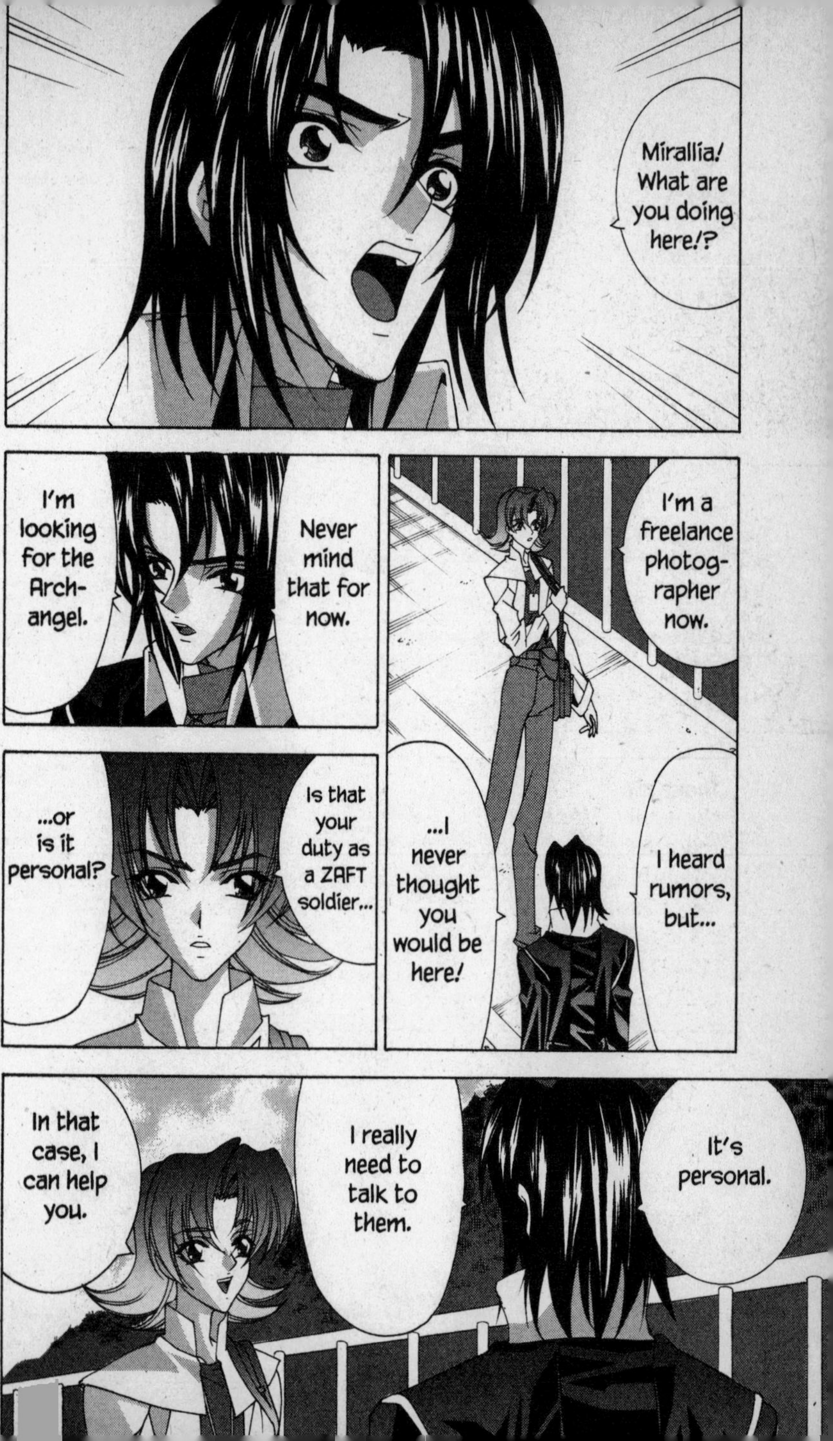
Mirallia! What are you doing here!?
I'm a freelance photog-rapher now.
I heard rumors, but...
...I never thought you would be here!
Never mind that for now.
I'm looking for the Arch-angel.
Is that your duty as a ZAFT soldier...
...or is it personal?
It's personal.
I really need to talk to them.
In that case, I can help you.

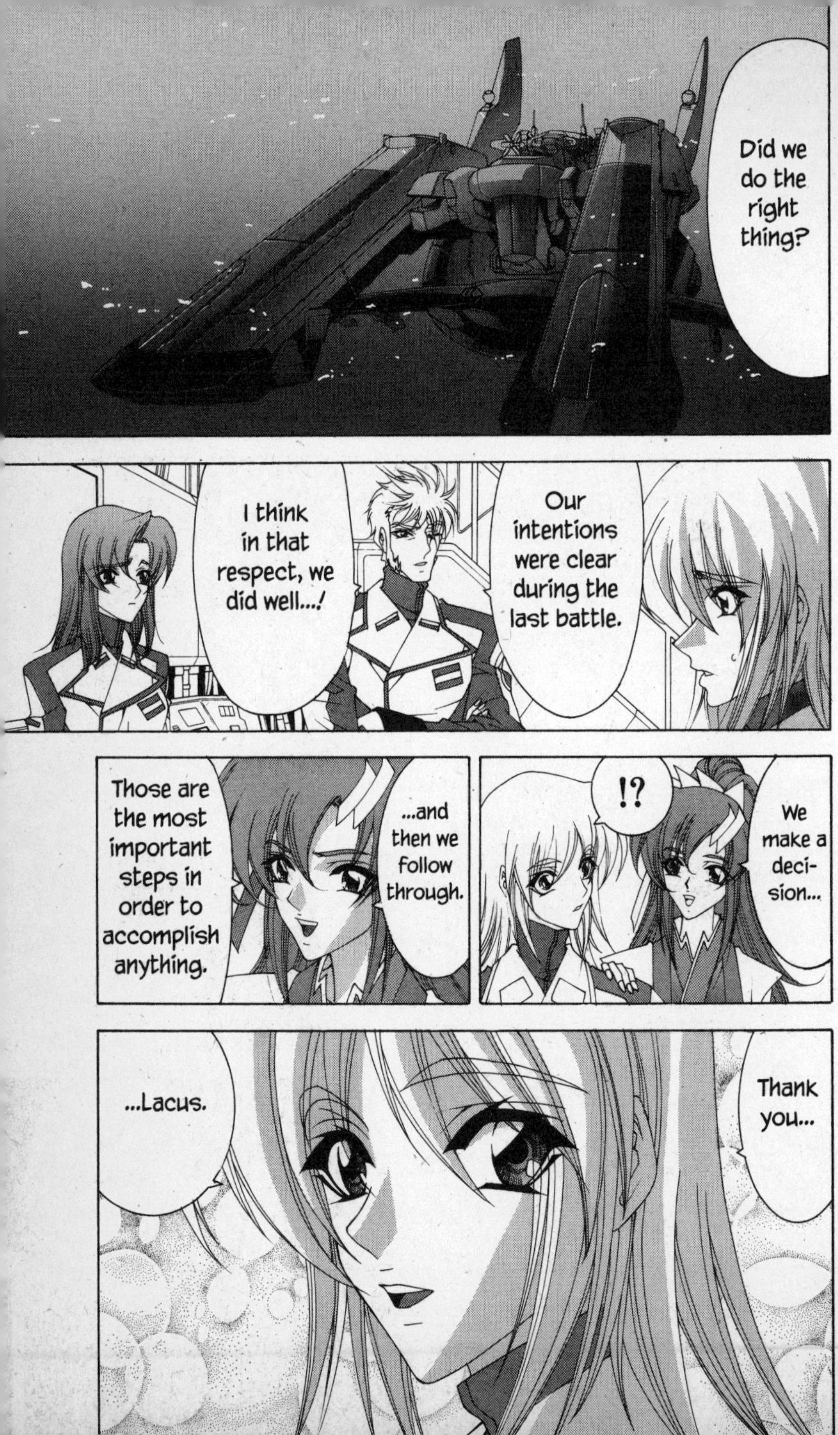
Did we do the right thing?
Our intentions were clear during the last battle.
I think in that respect, we did well...!
!?
We make a deci-sion...
...and then we follow through.
Those are the most important steps in order to accomplish anything.
Thank you...
...Lacus.

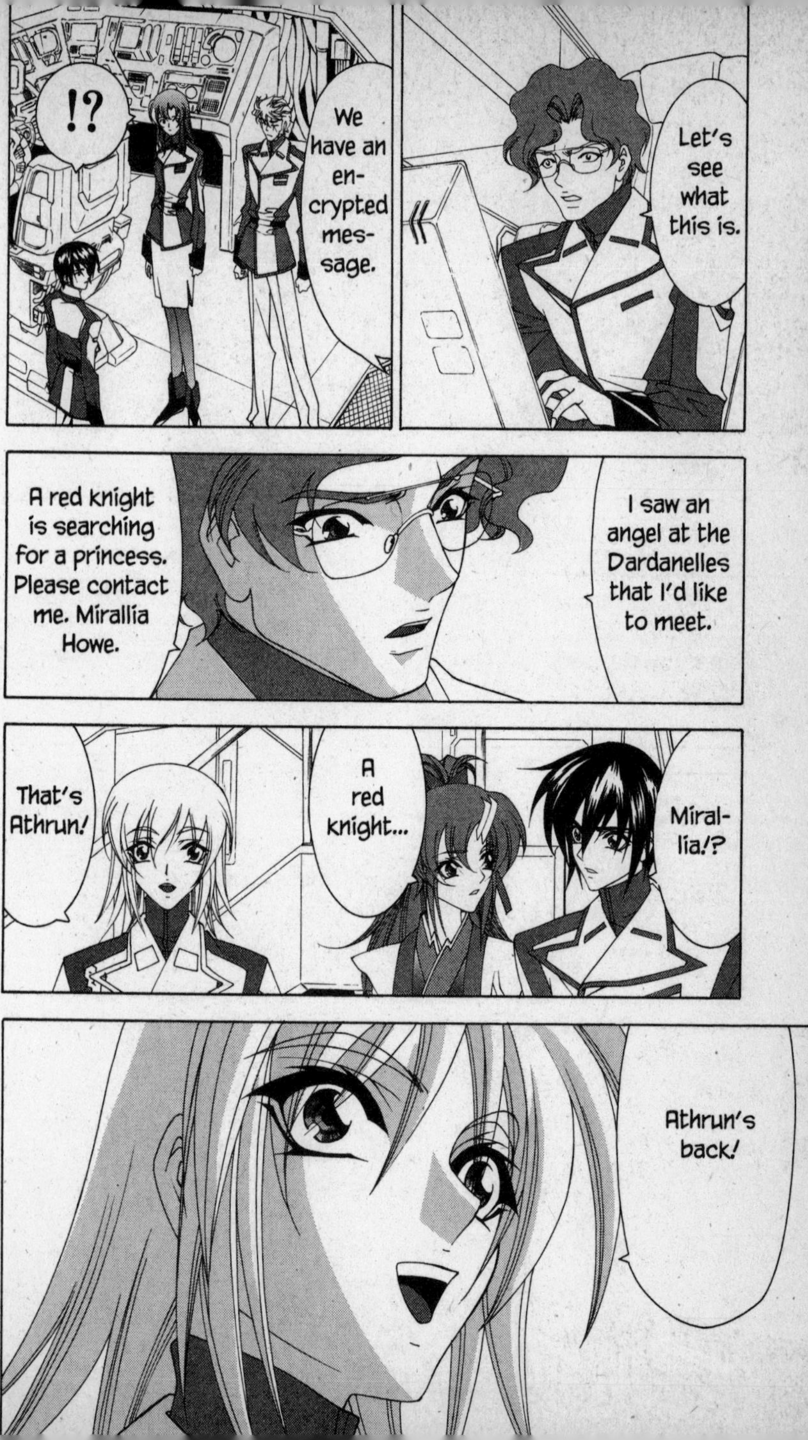
Let's see what this is.
We have an encrypted message.
!?
I saw an angel at the Dardanelles that I'd like to meet.
A red knight is searching for a princess. Please contact me. Mirallia Howe.
Mirallia!?
A red knight...
That's Athrun!
Athrun's back!

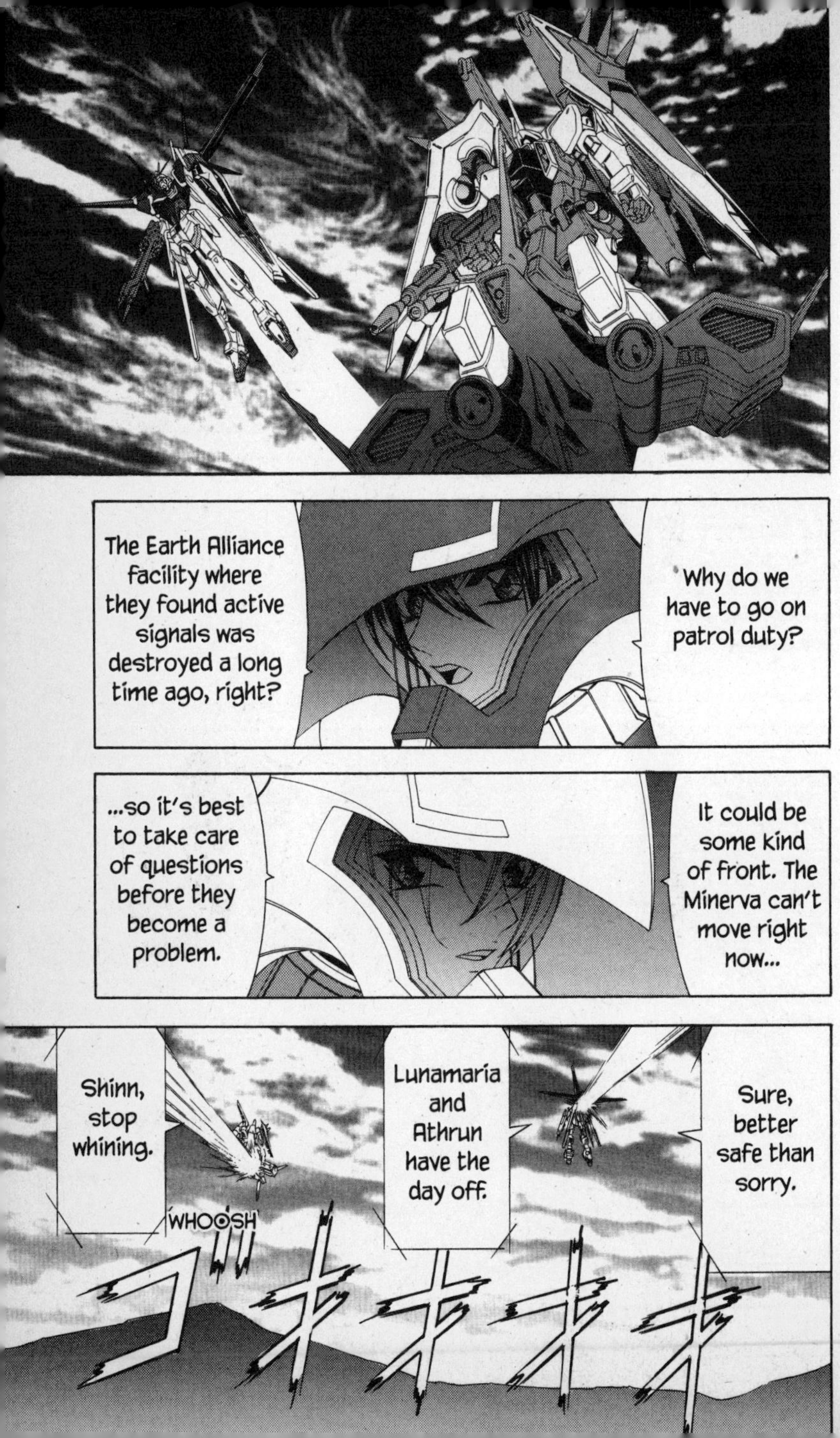
Why do we have to go on patrol duty?
The Earth Alliance facility where they found active signals was destroyed a long time ago, right?
It could be some kind of front. The Minerva can't move right now...
...so it's best to take care of questions before they become a problem.
Sure, better safe than sorry.
Lunamaria and Athrun have the day off.
Shinn, stop whining.
WHOOSH

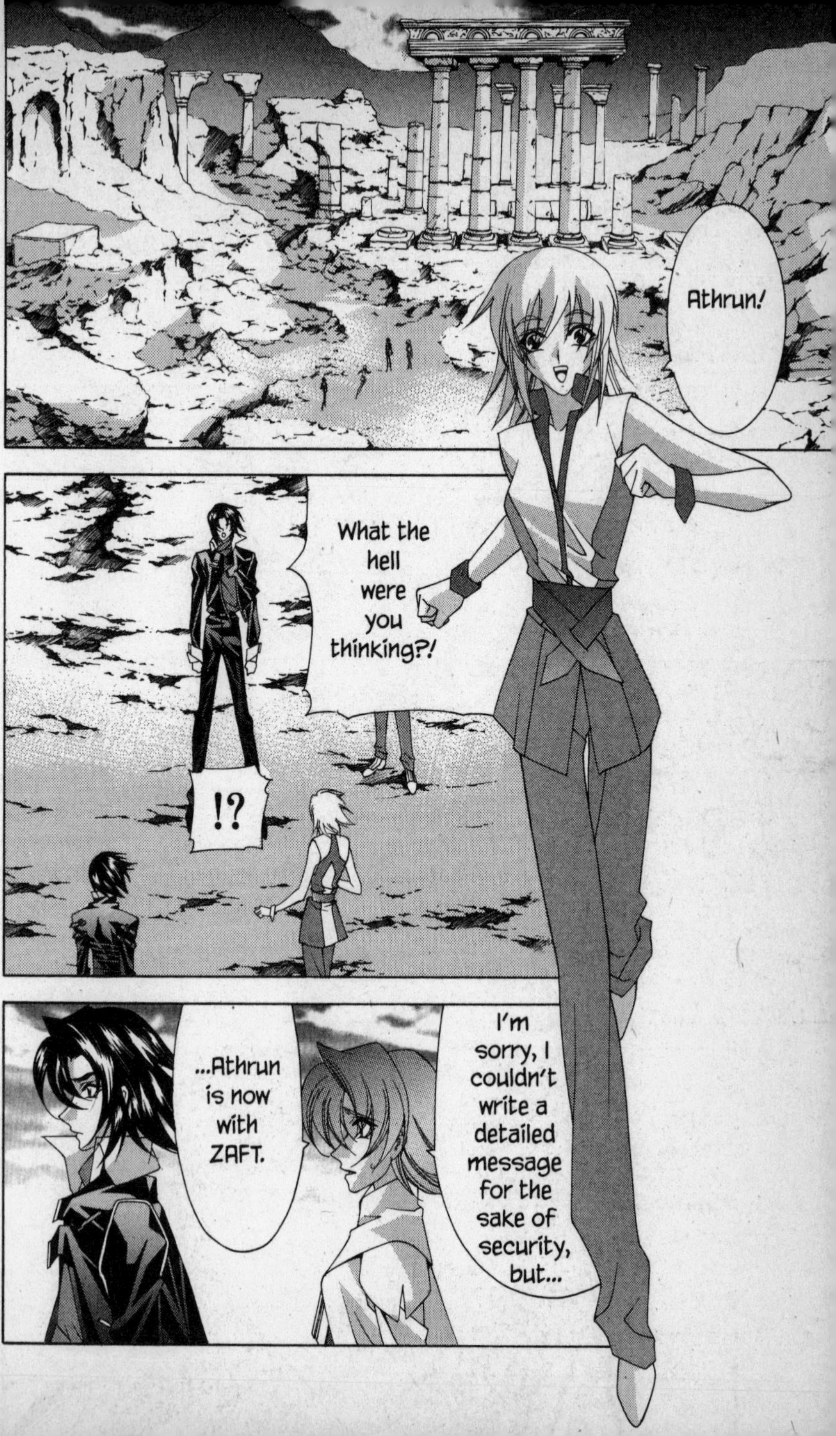
Athrun!
What the hell were you thinking?!
!?
I'm sorry, I couldn't write a detailed message for the sake of security, but...
...Athrun is now with ZAFT.

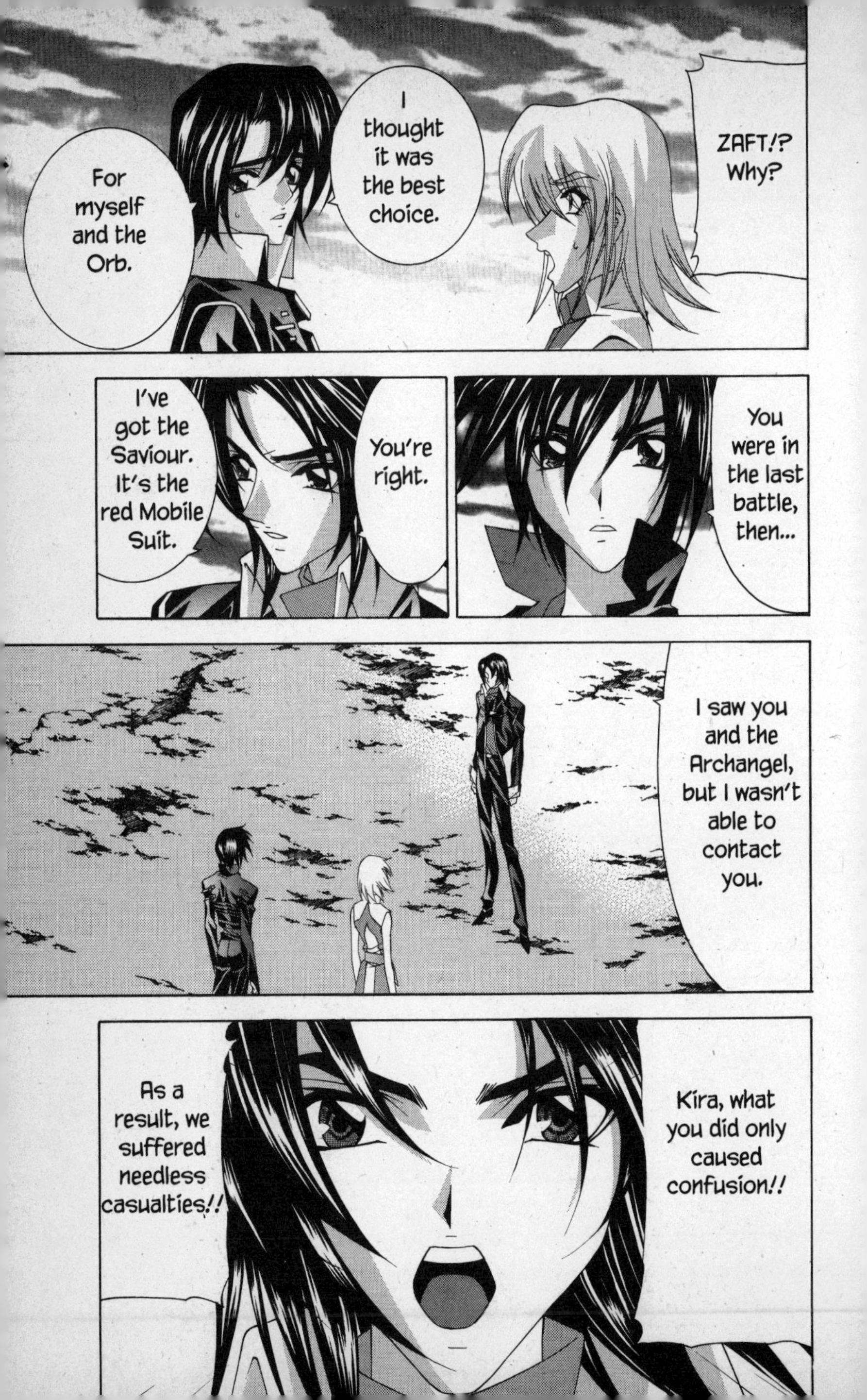
ZAFT!? Why?
I thought it was the best choice.
For myself and the Orb.
You were in the last battle, then...
You're right.
I've got the Saviour. It's the red Mobile Suit.
I saw you and the Archangel, but I wasn't able to contact you.
Kira, what you did only caused confusion!!
As a result, we suffered needless casualties!!

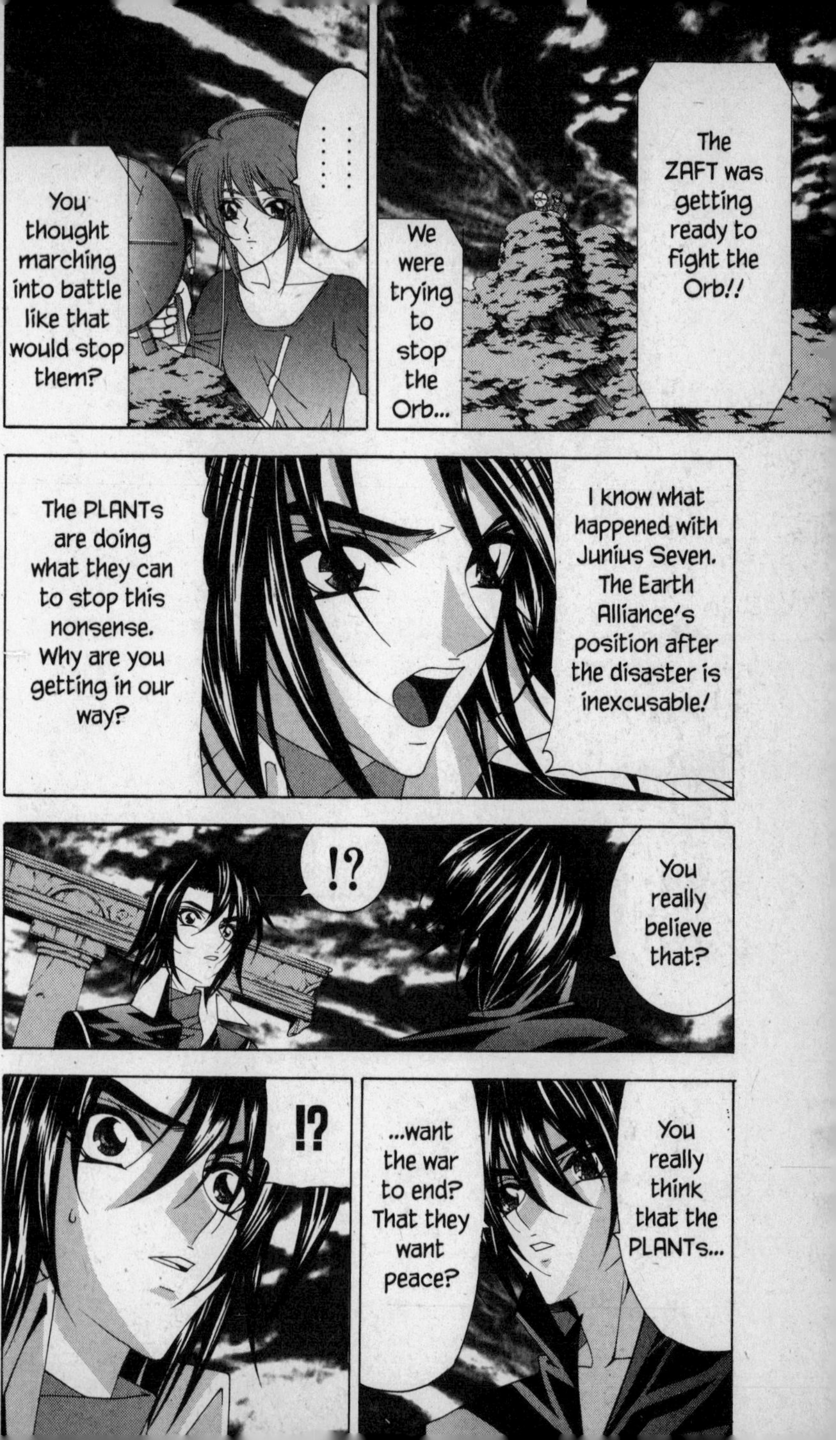
The ZAFT was getting ready to fight the Orb!!
We were trying to stop the Orb...
......
You thought marching into battle like that would stop them?
I know what happened with Junius Seven. The Earth Alliance's position after the disaster is inexcusable!
The PLANTs are doing what they can to stop this nonsense. Why are you getting in our way?
You really believe that?
!?
You really think that the PLANTs...
...want the war to end? That they want peace?
!?

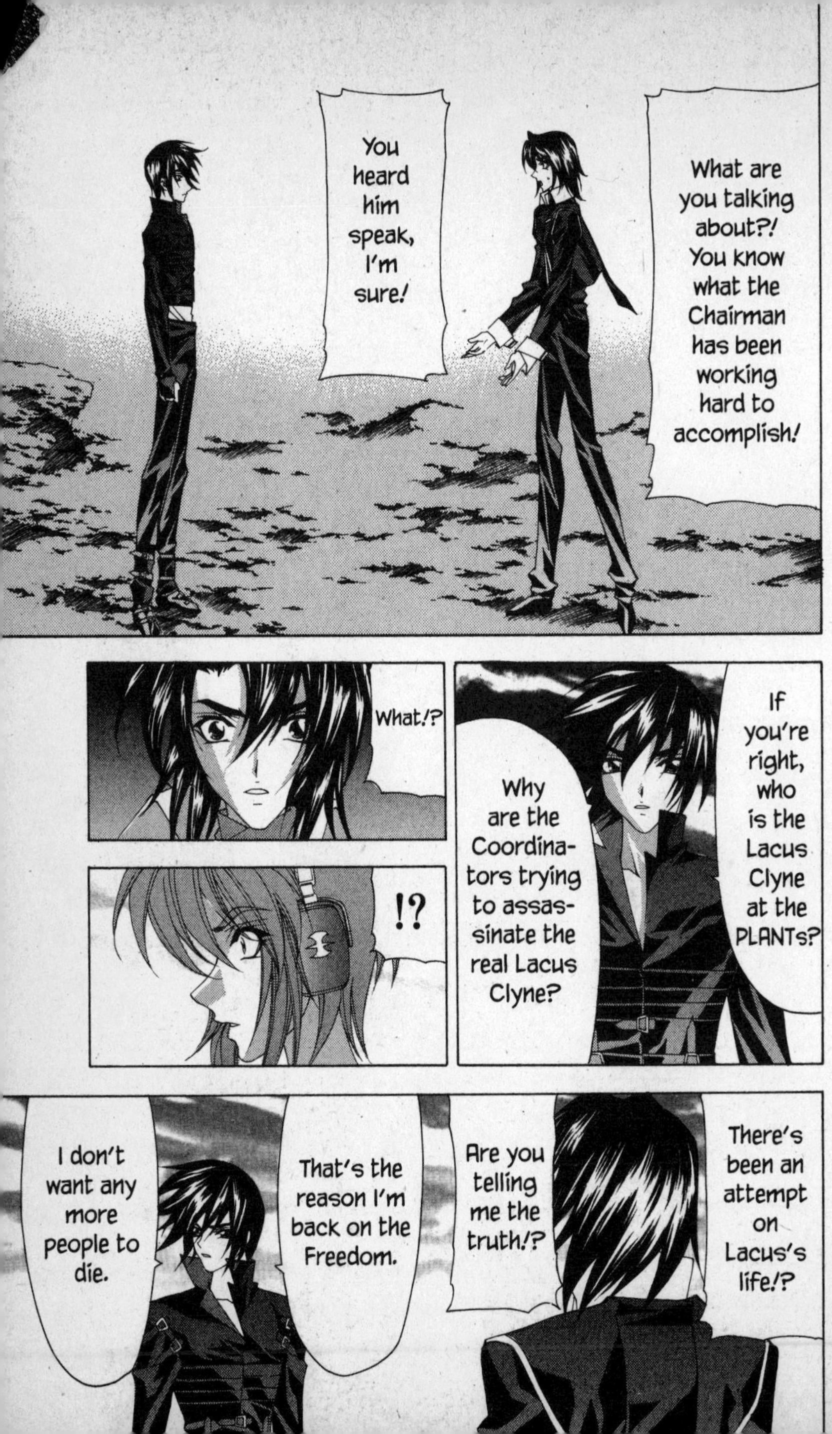
What are you talking about?! You know what the Chairman has been working hard to accomplish!
You heard him speak, I'm sure!
If you're right, who is the Lacus Clyne at the PLANTs?
Why are the Coordinators trying to assassinate the real Lacus Clyne?
What!?
!?
There's been an attempt on Lacus's life!?
Are you telling me the truth!?
That's the reason I'm back on the Freedom.
I don't want any more people to die.

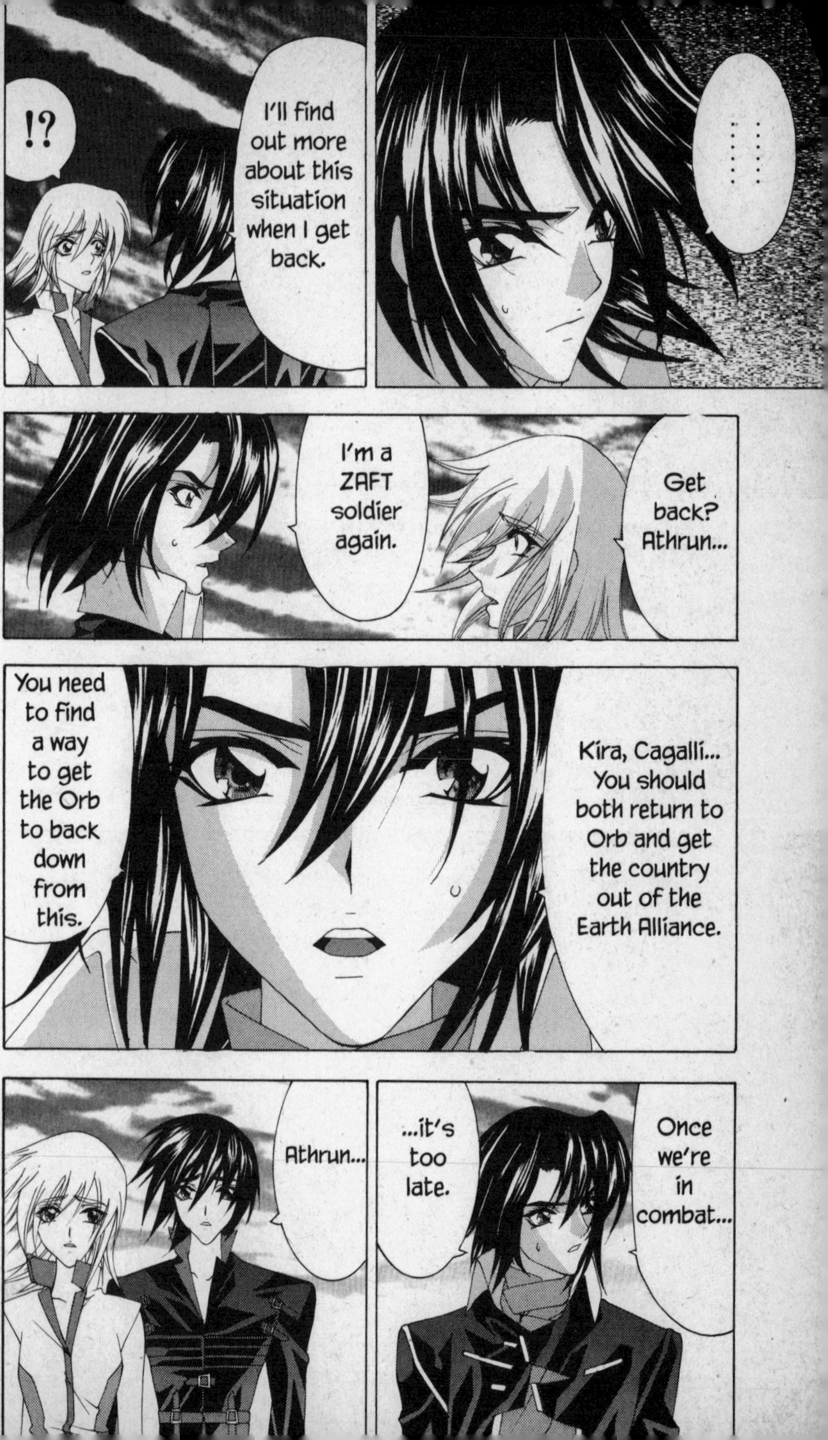
......
I'll find out more about this situation when I get back.
!?
Get back? Athrun...
I'm a ZAFT soldier again.
Kira, Cagalli... You should both return to Orb and get the country out of the Earth Alliance.
You need to find a way to get the Orb to back down from this.
Once we're in combat...
...it's too late.
Athrun...

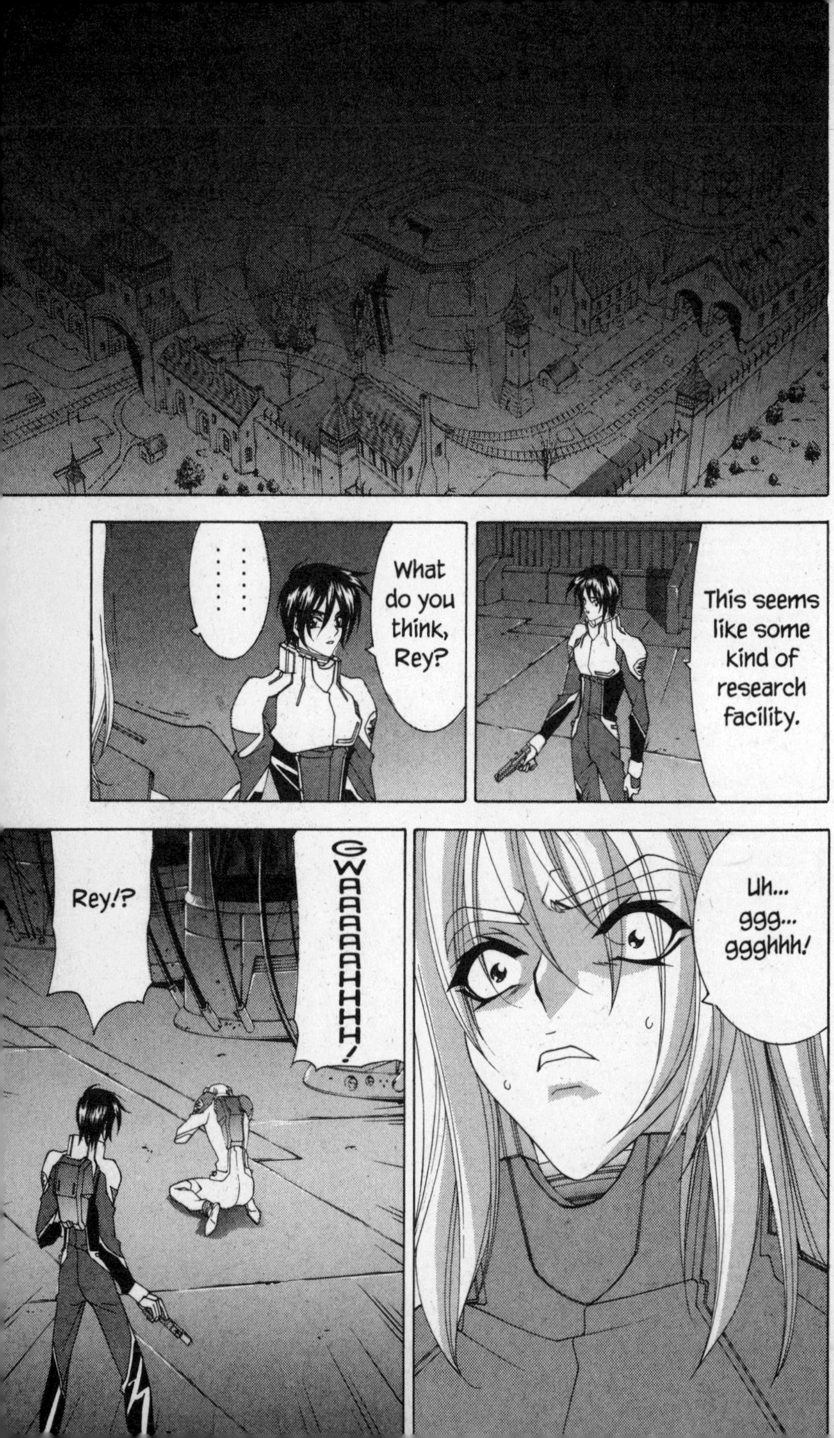
This seems like some kind of research facility.
What do you think, Rey?
......
Uh... ggg... ggghhh!
GWAAAAAHHHH!
Rey!?

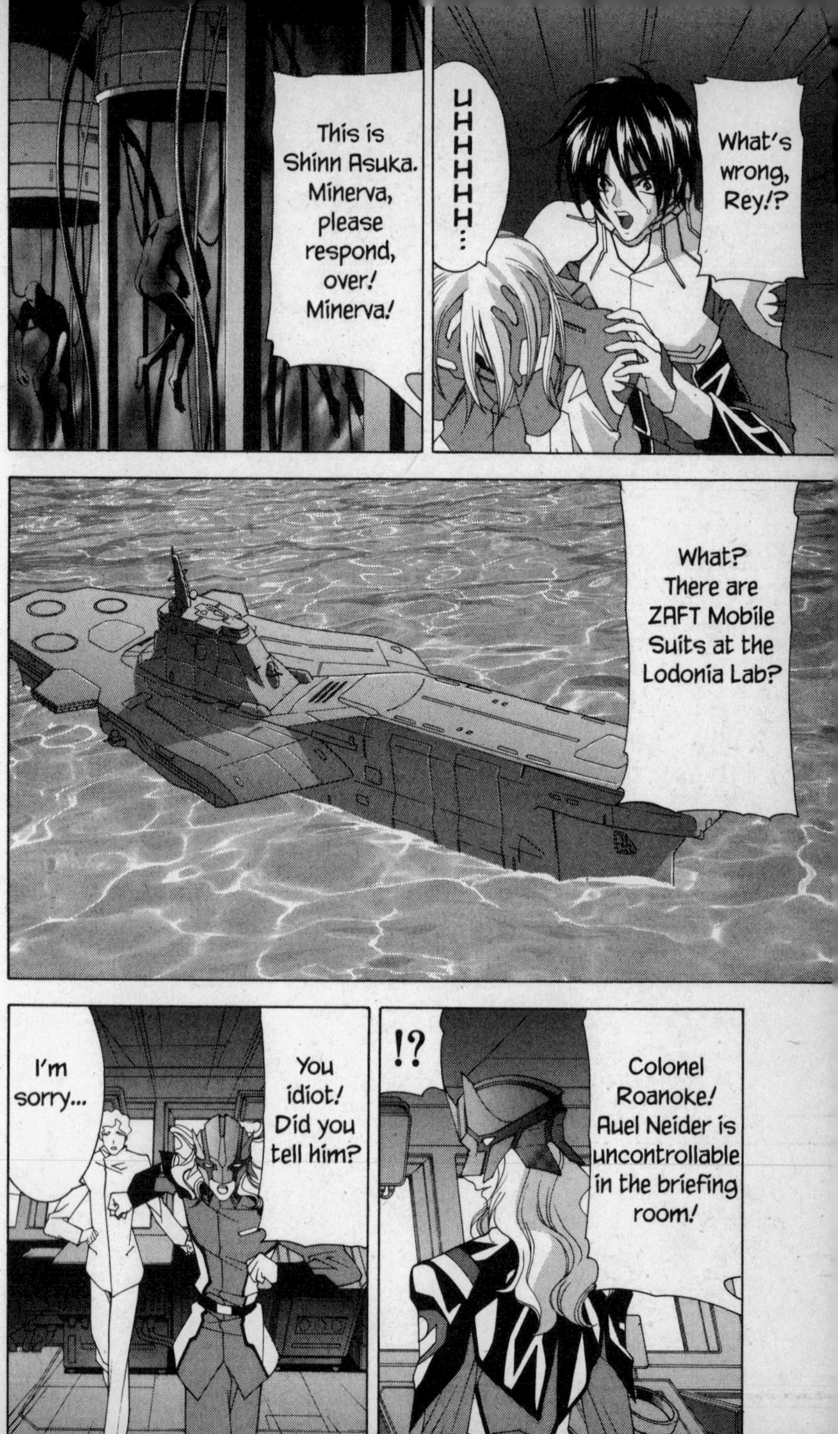
What's wrong, Rey!?
UHHHHH...
This is Shinn Asuka. Minerva, please respond, over! Minerva!
What? There are ZAFT Mobile Suits at the Lodonia Lab?
Colonel Roanoke! Auel Neider is uncontrollable in the briefing room!
!?
You idiot! Did you tell him?
I'm sorry...

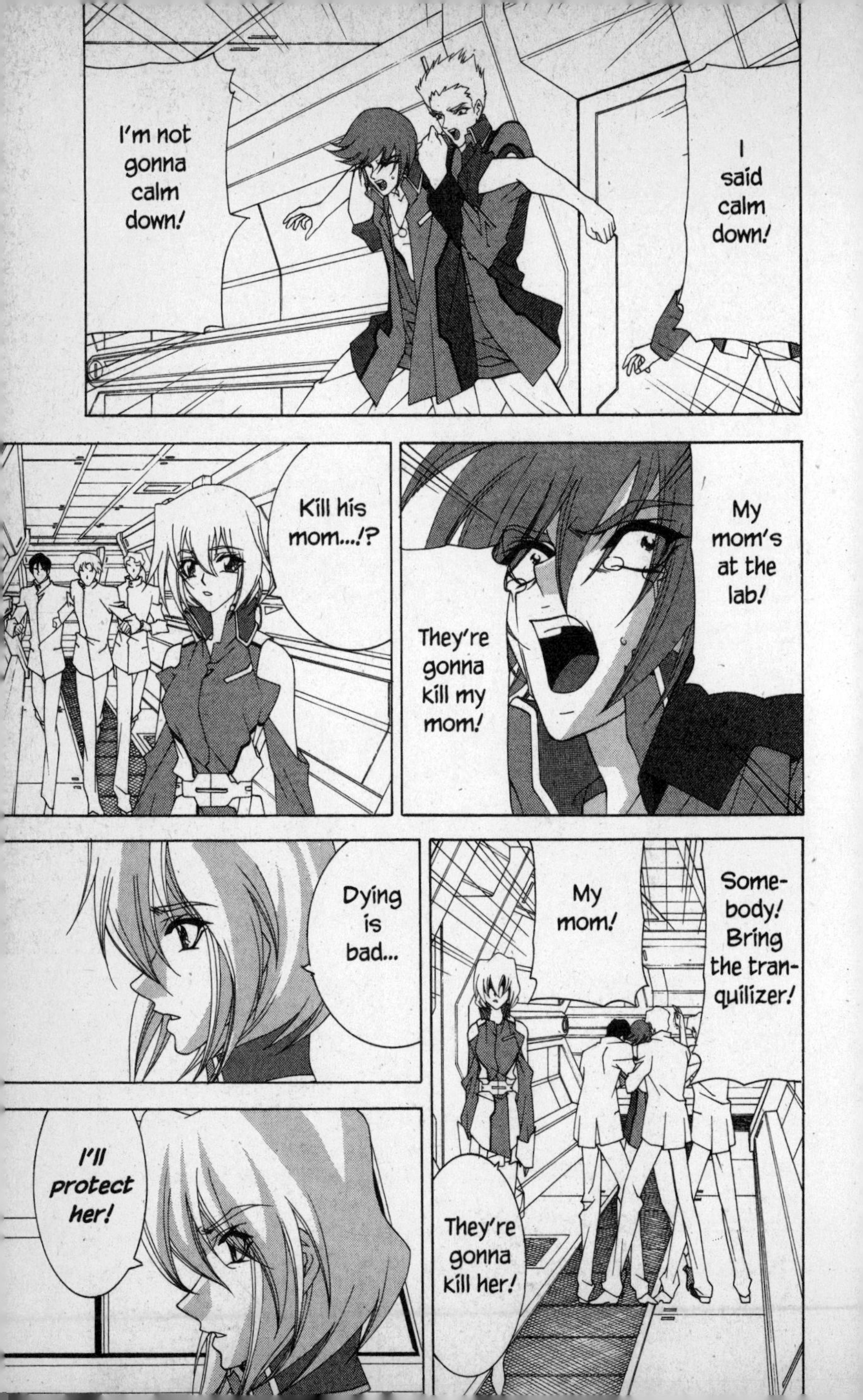
I said calm down!
I'm not gonna calm down!
My mom's at the lab!
They're gonna kill my mom!
Kill his mom...!?
Some-body! Bring the tran-quilizer!
My mom!
They're gonna kill her!
Dying is bad...
I'll protect her!

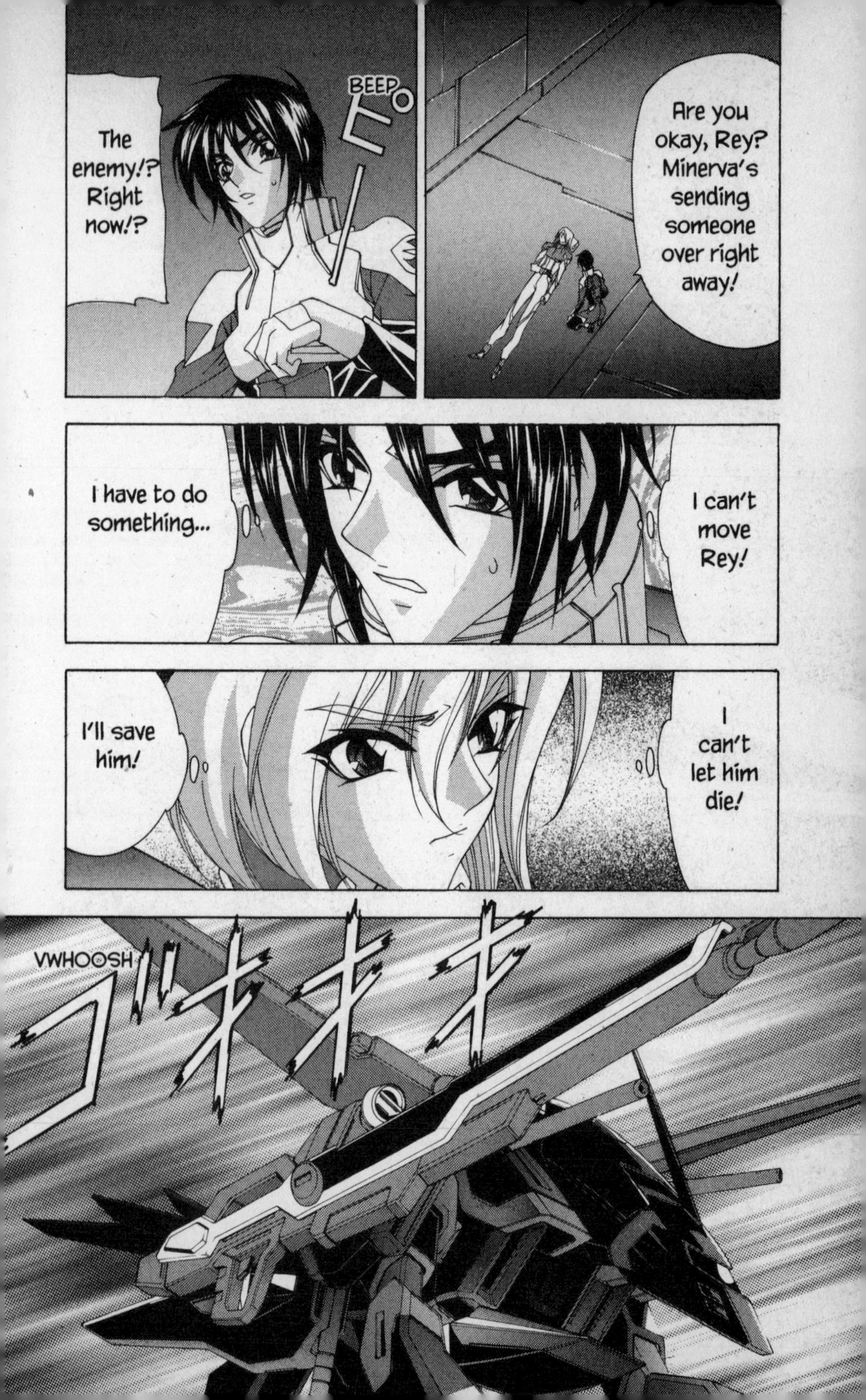
Are you okay, Rey? Minerva's sending someone over right away!
BEEP
The enemy!? Right now!?
I can't move Rey!
I have to do something...
I can't let him die!
I'll save him!
VWHOOSH

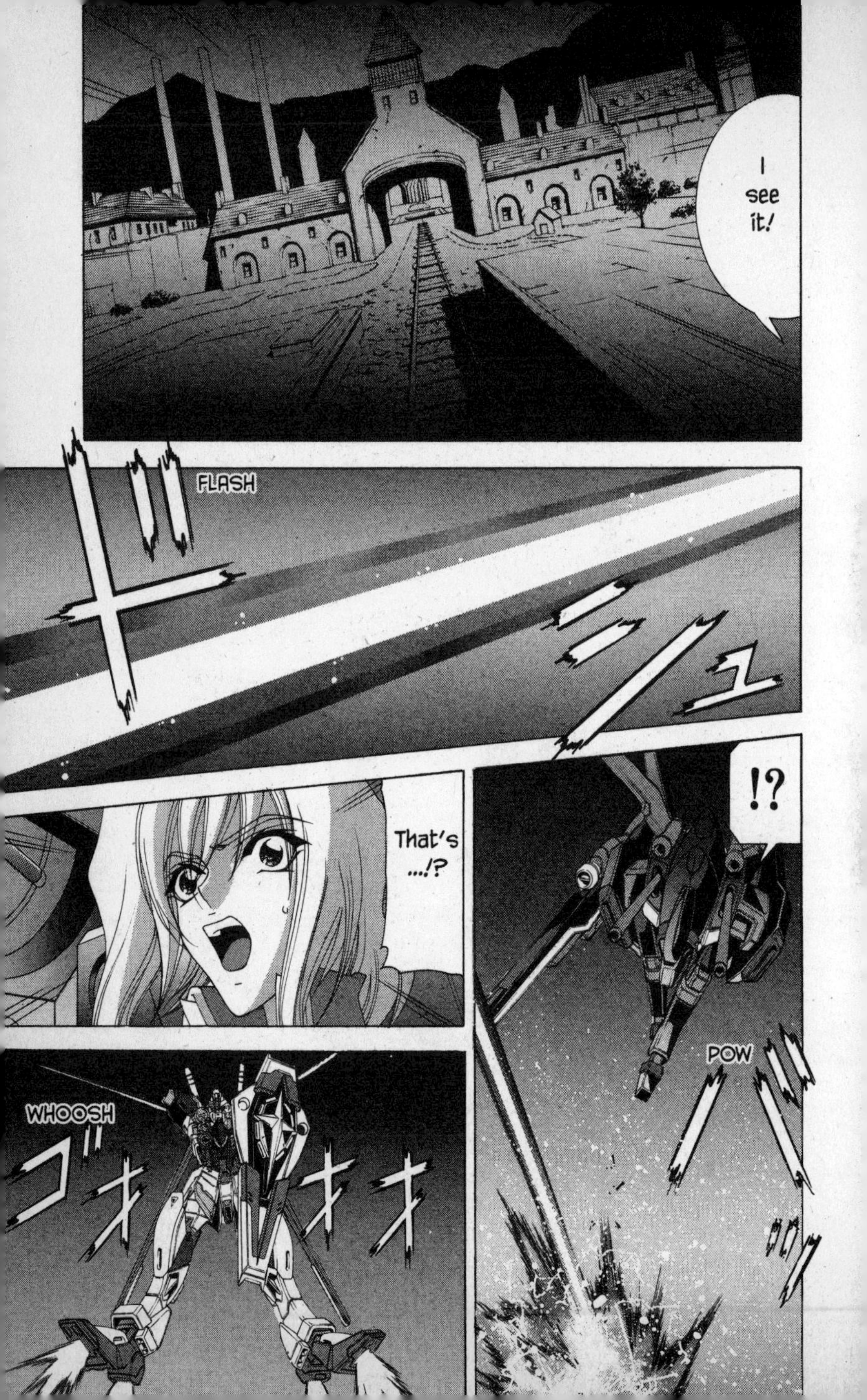
I see it!
FLASH
!?
POW
That's ...!?
WHOOSH

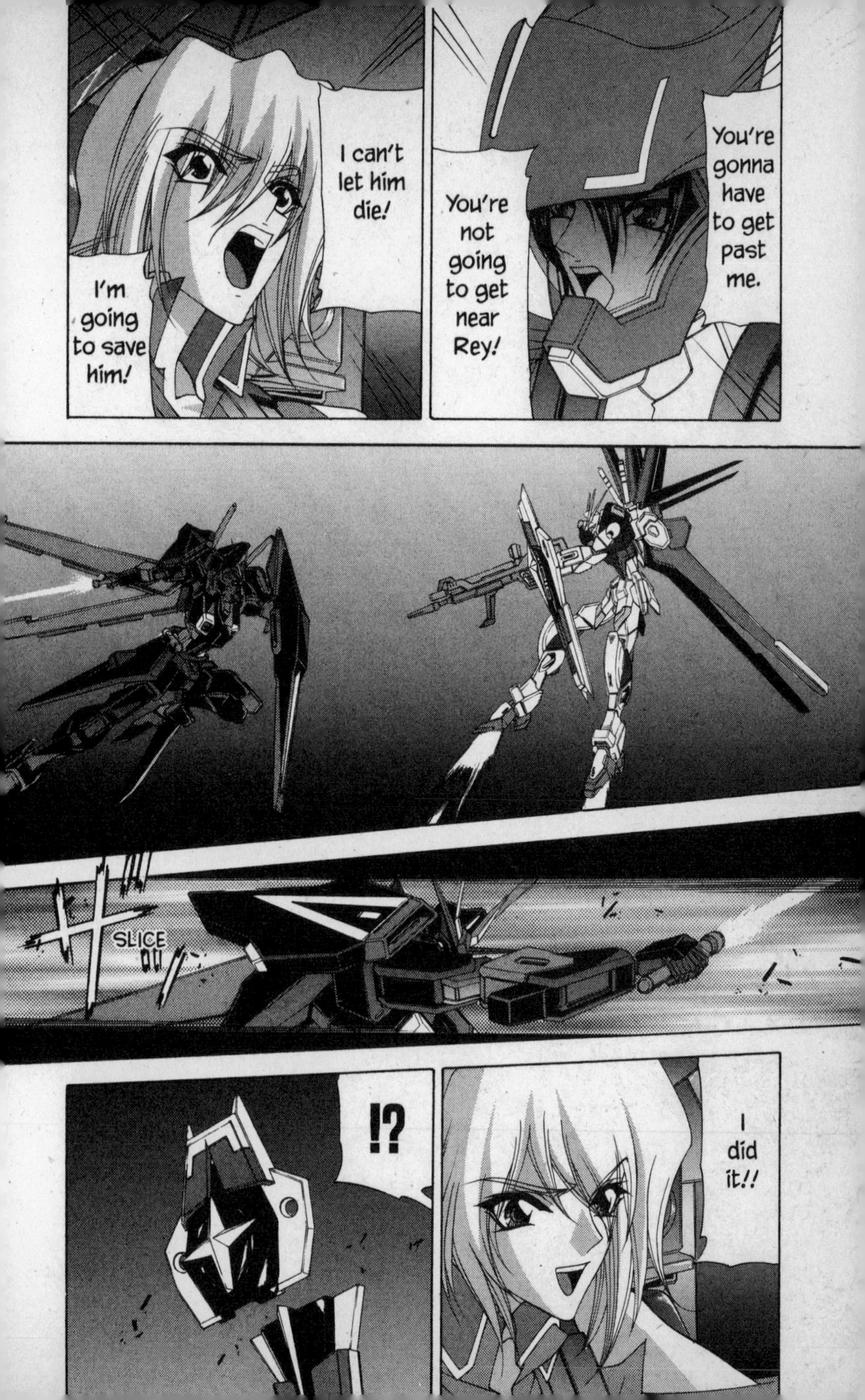
You're gonna have to get past me.
You're not going to get near Rey!
I can't let him die!
I'm going to save him!
SLICE
I did it!!
!?

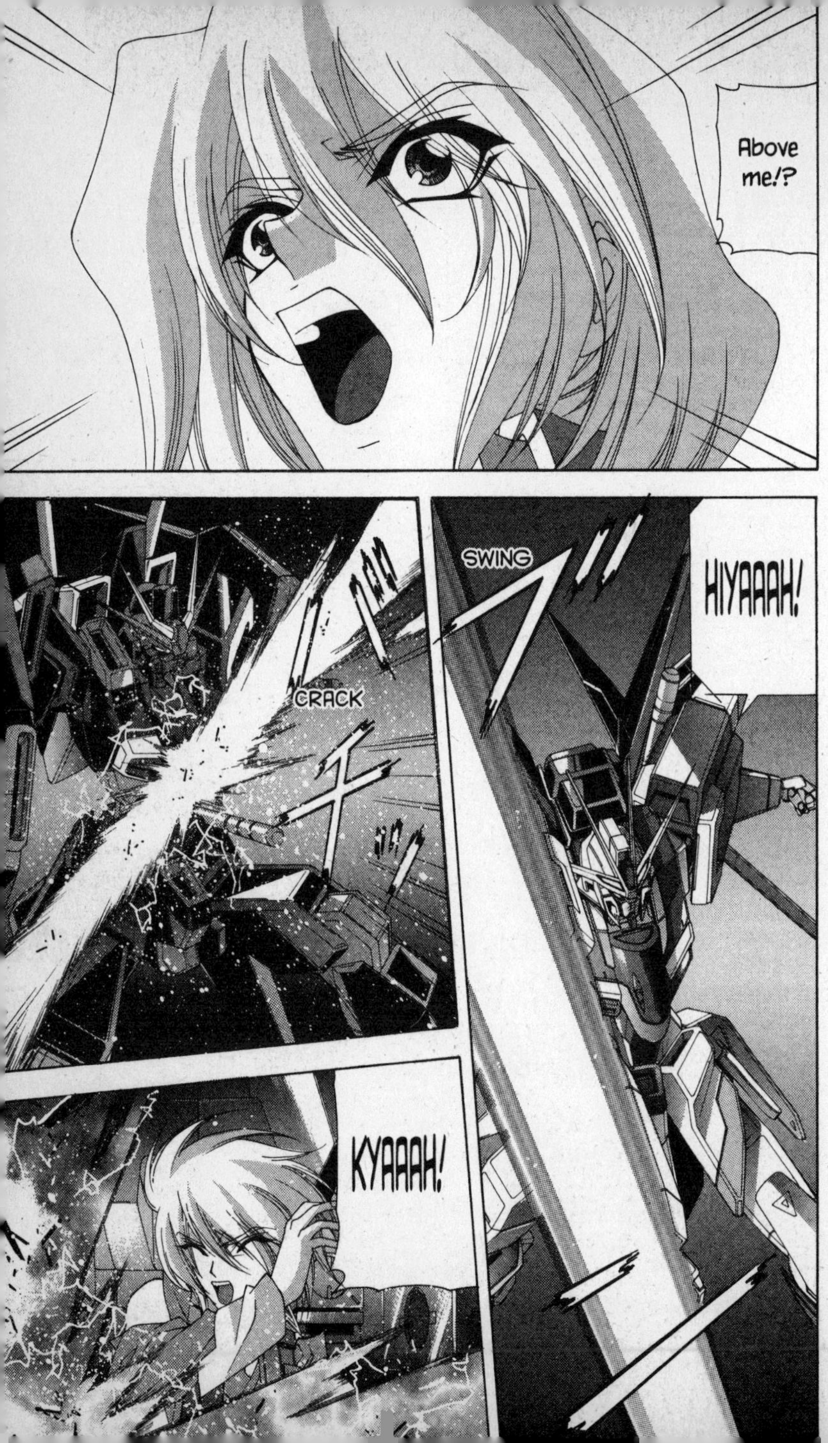
Above me!?
HIYAAAH!
SWING
CRACK
KYAAAH!

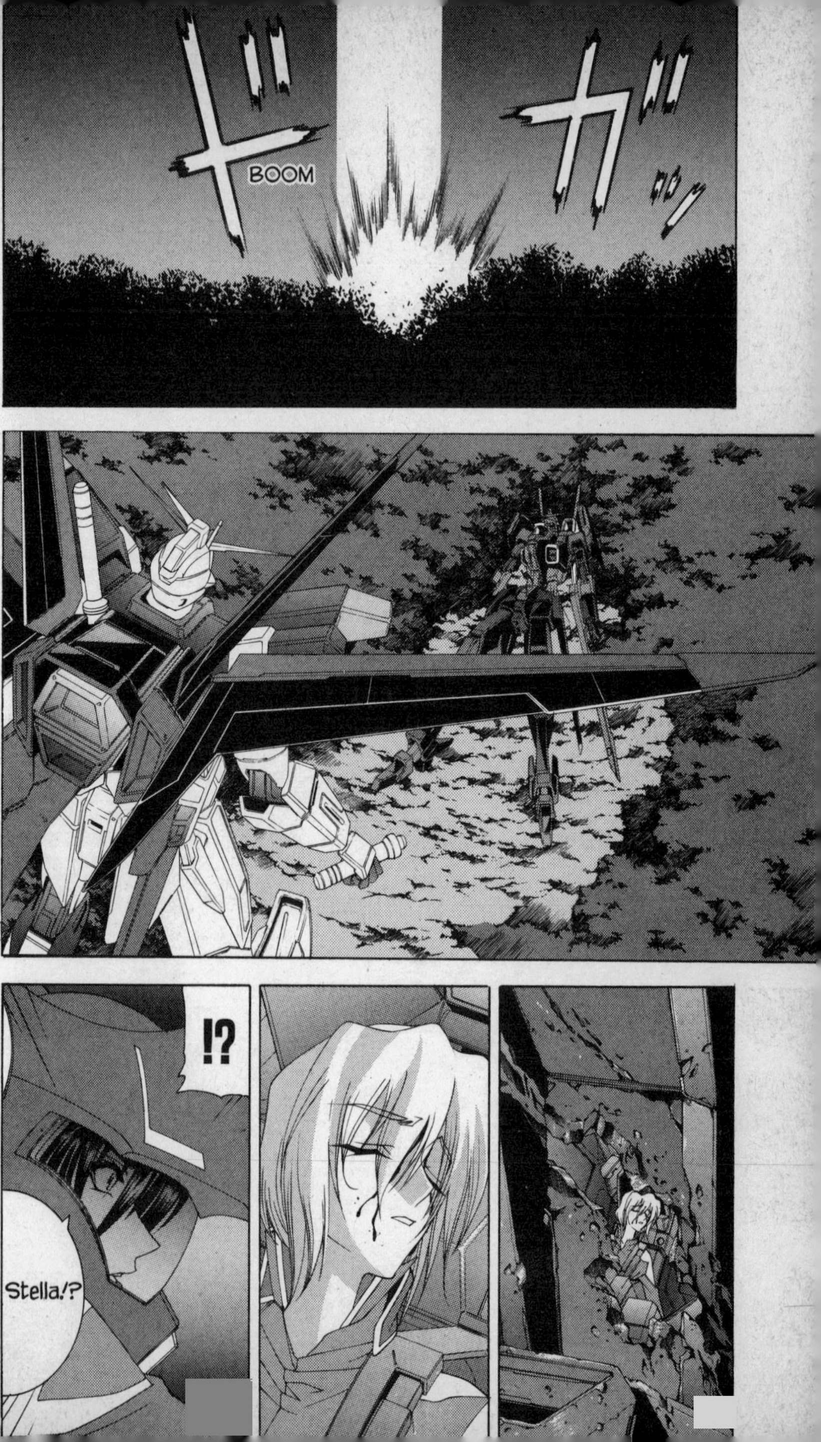
BOOM
!?
Stella!?

They are in stable condition.

How are Rey and the unidentified pilot doing?

After a few more tests, they'll be sure.

The medical officer believes that Rey suffered from a stress-induced breakdown.

I can't do that, ma'am.

If you aren't comfortable, stay on the ship.

I don't believe you should physically lead the investigation.

I think this is a bad idea.

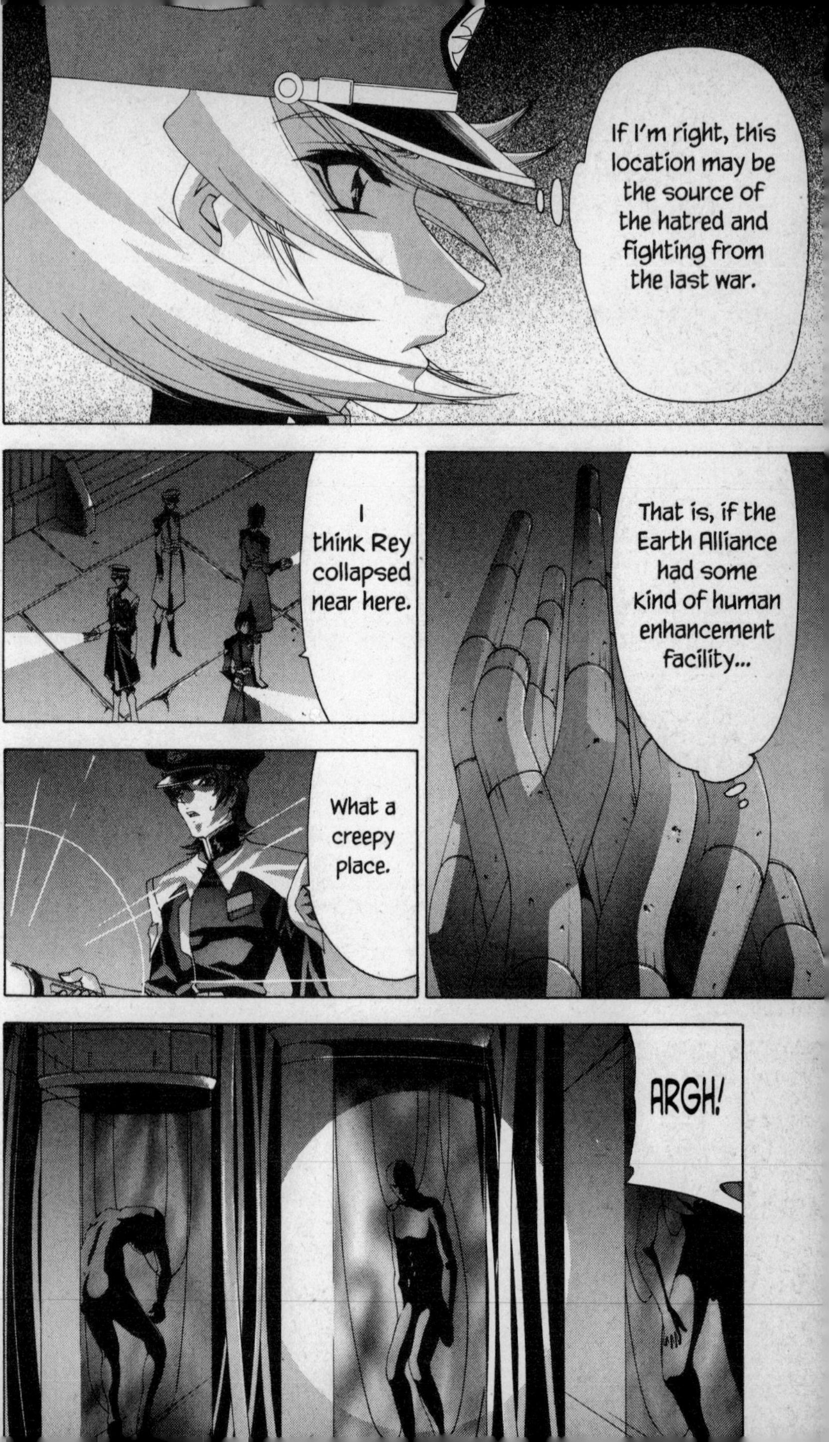
If I'm right, this location may be the source of the hatred and fighting from the last war.
That is, if the Earth Alliance had some kind of human enhancement facility...
I think Rey collapsed near here.
What a creepy place.
ARGH!

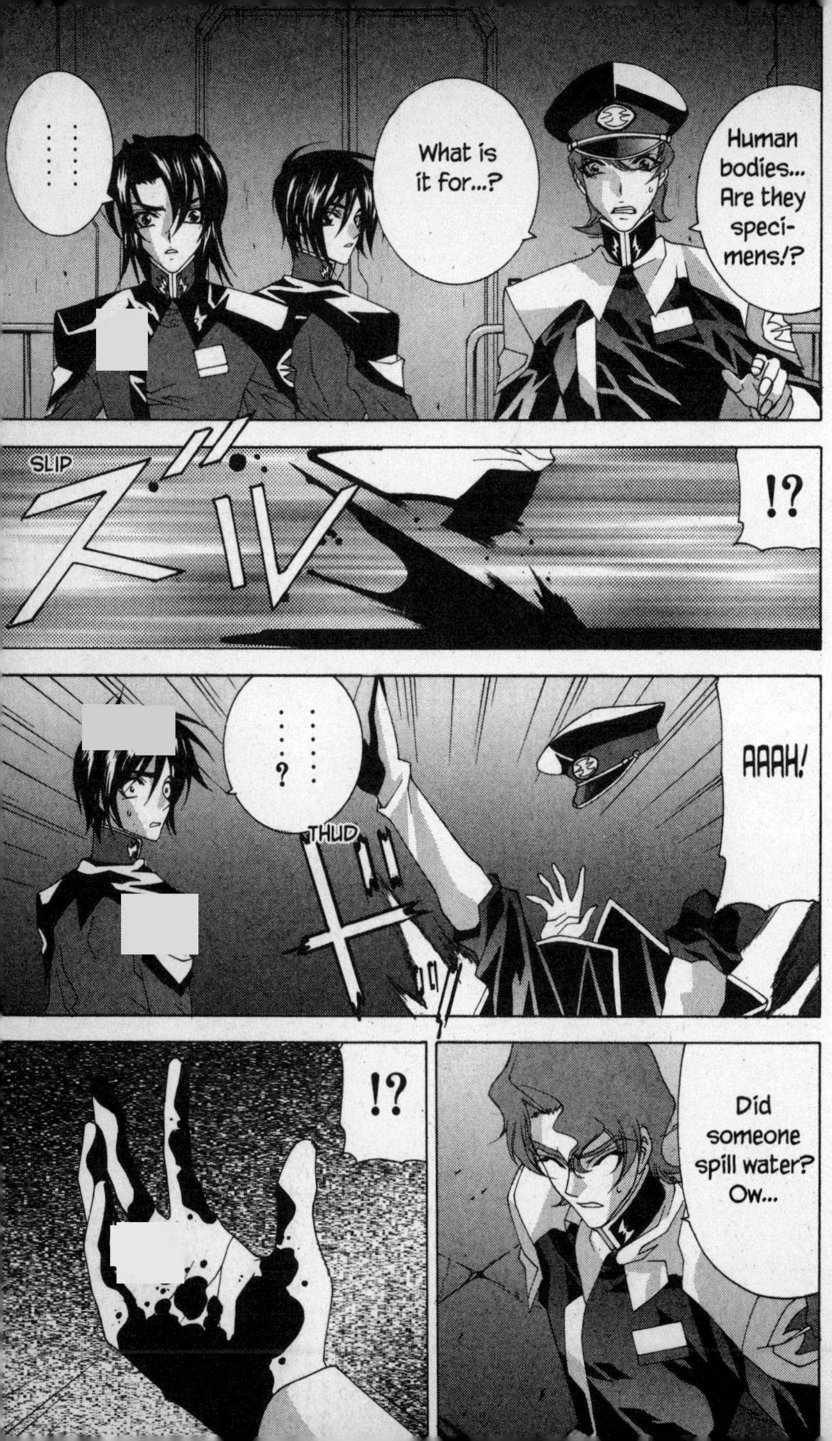
Human bodies... Are they speci-mens!?
What is it for...?
......
!?
SLIP
AAAH!
......?
THUD
Did someone spill water? Ow...
!?

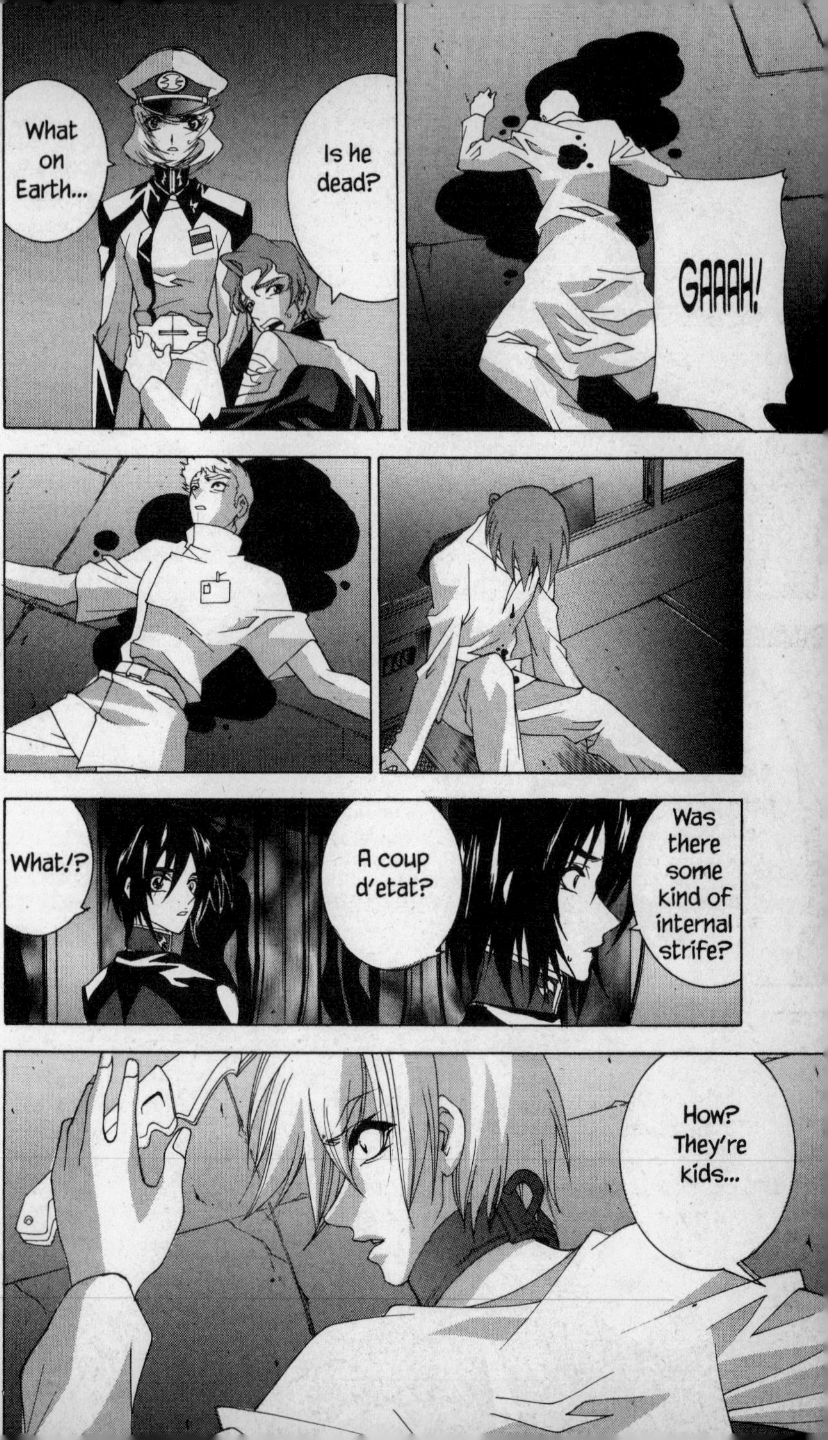
GAAAH!
Is he dead?
What on Earth...
Was there some kind of internal strife?
A coup d'etat?
What!?
How? They're kids...

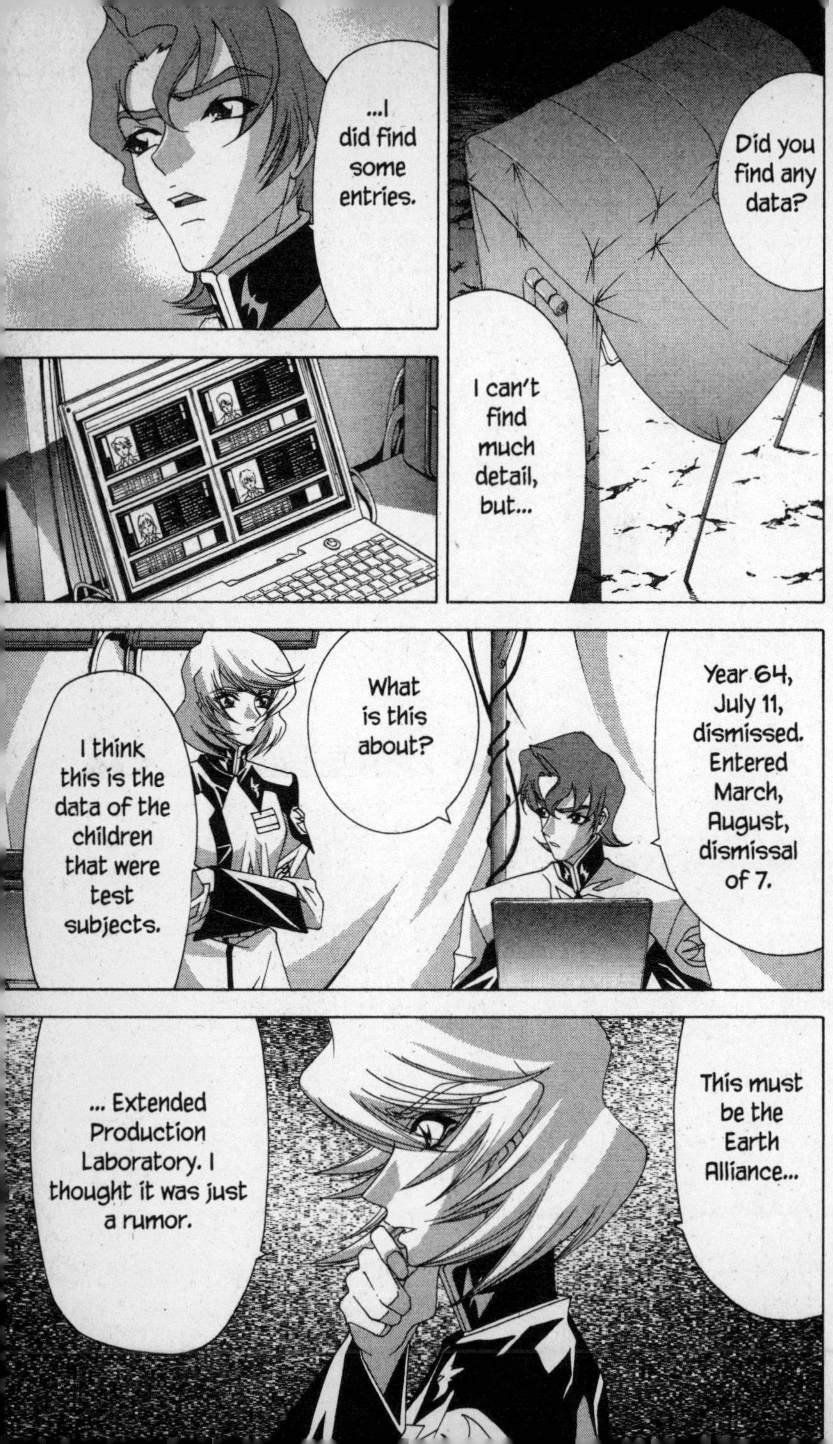
Did you find any data?
...I did find some entries.
I can't find much detail, but...
Year 64, July 11, dismissed. Entered March, August, dismissal of 7.
What is this about?
I think this is the data of the children that were test subjects.
This must be the Earth Alliance...
... Extended Production Laboratory. I thought it was just a rumor.

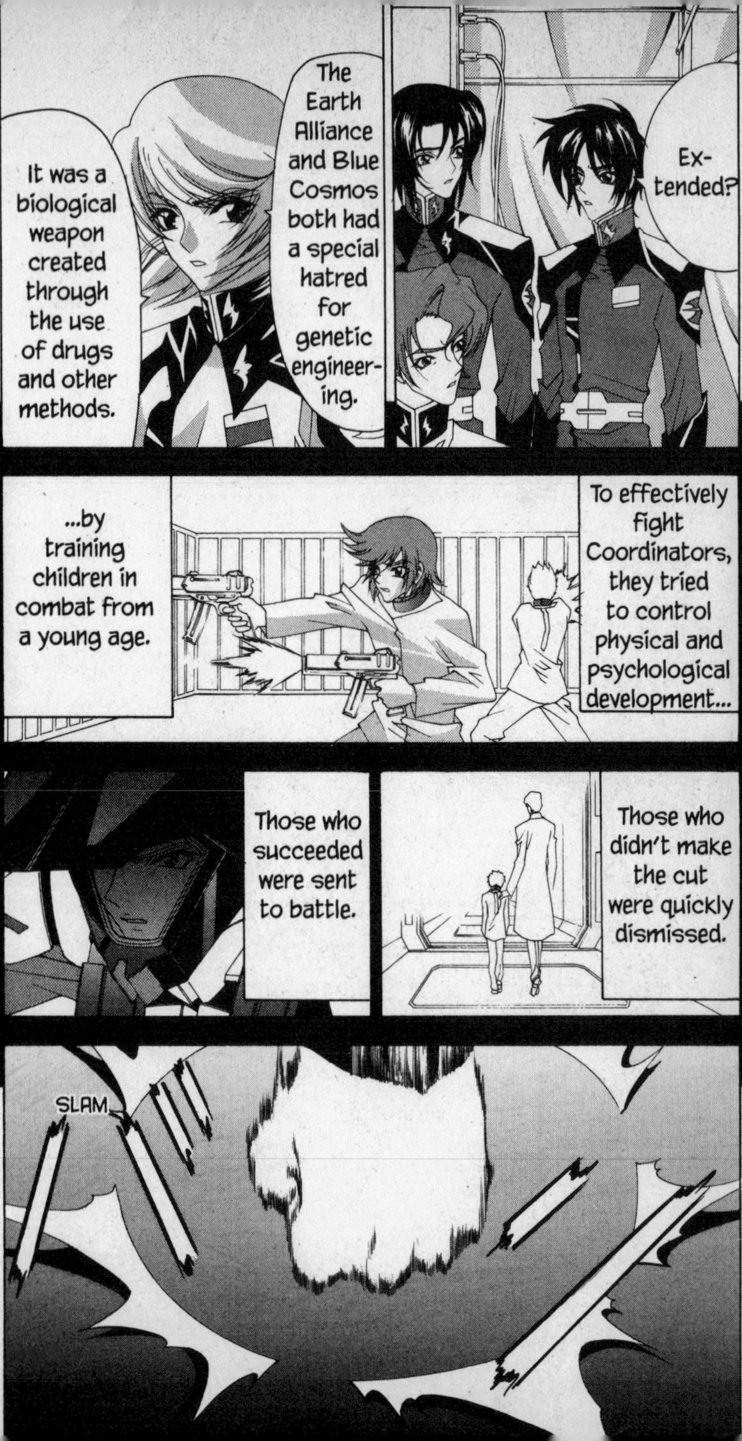
Ex-tended?
The Earth Alliance and Blue Cosmos both had a special hatred for genetic engineer-ing.
It was a biological weapon created through the use of drugs and other methods.
To effectively fight Coordinators, they tried to control physical and psychological development...
...by training children in combat from a young age.
Those who didn't make the cut were quickly dismissed.
Those who succeeded were sent to battle.
SLAM

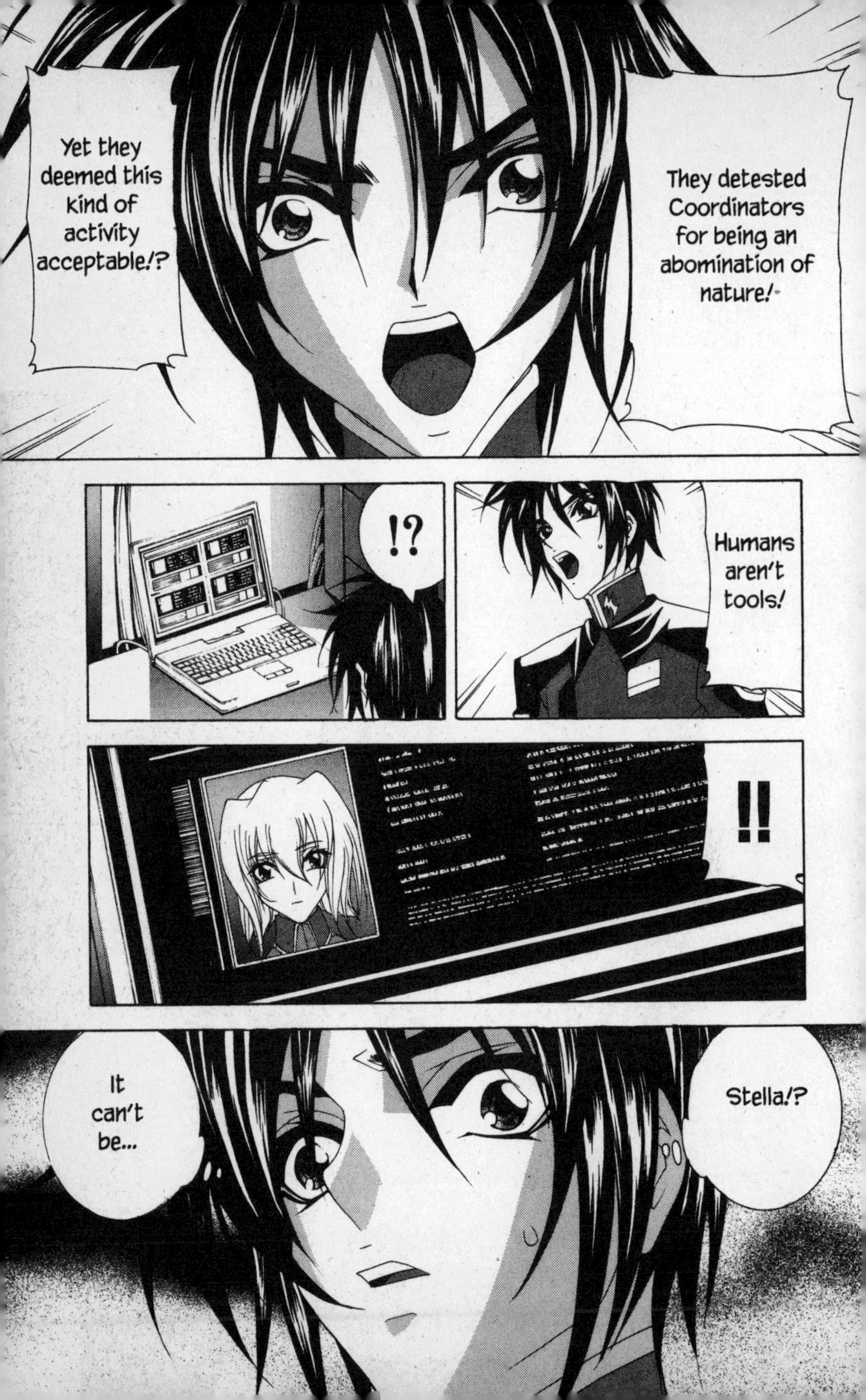
They detested Coordinators for being an abomination of nature!
Yet they deemed this kind of activity acceptable!?
Humans aren't tools!
!?
!!
Stella!?
It can't be...

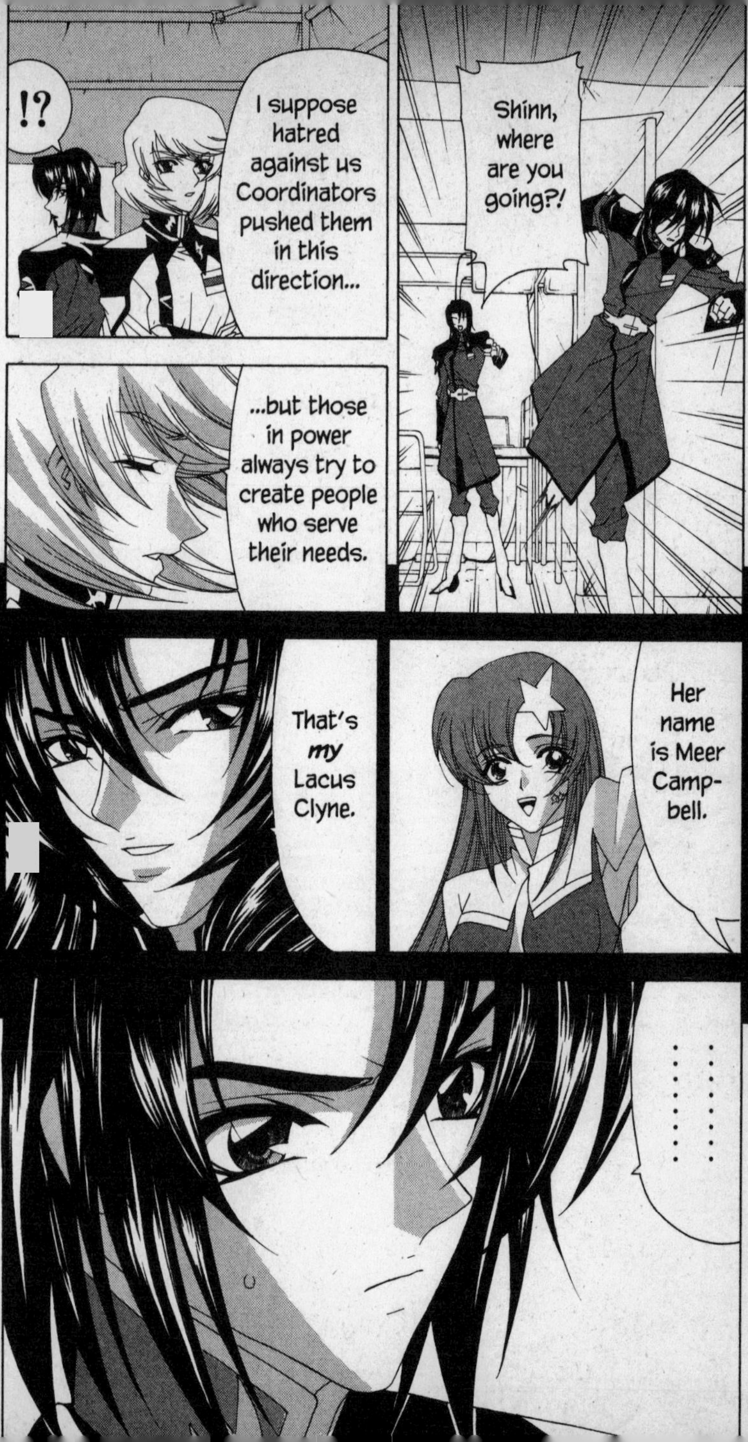
!?
I suppose hatred against us Coordinators pushed them in this direction...
...but those in power always try to create people who serve their needs.
Shinn, where are you going?!
That's *my* Lacus Clyne.
Her name is Meer Campbell.
......
......

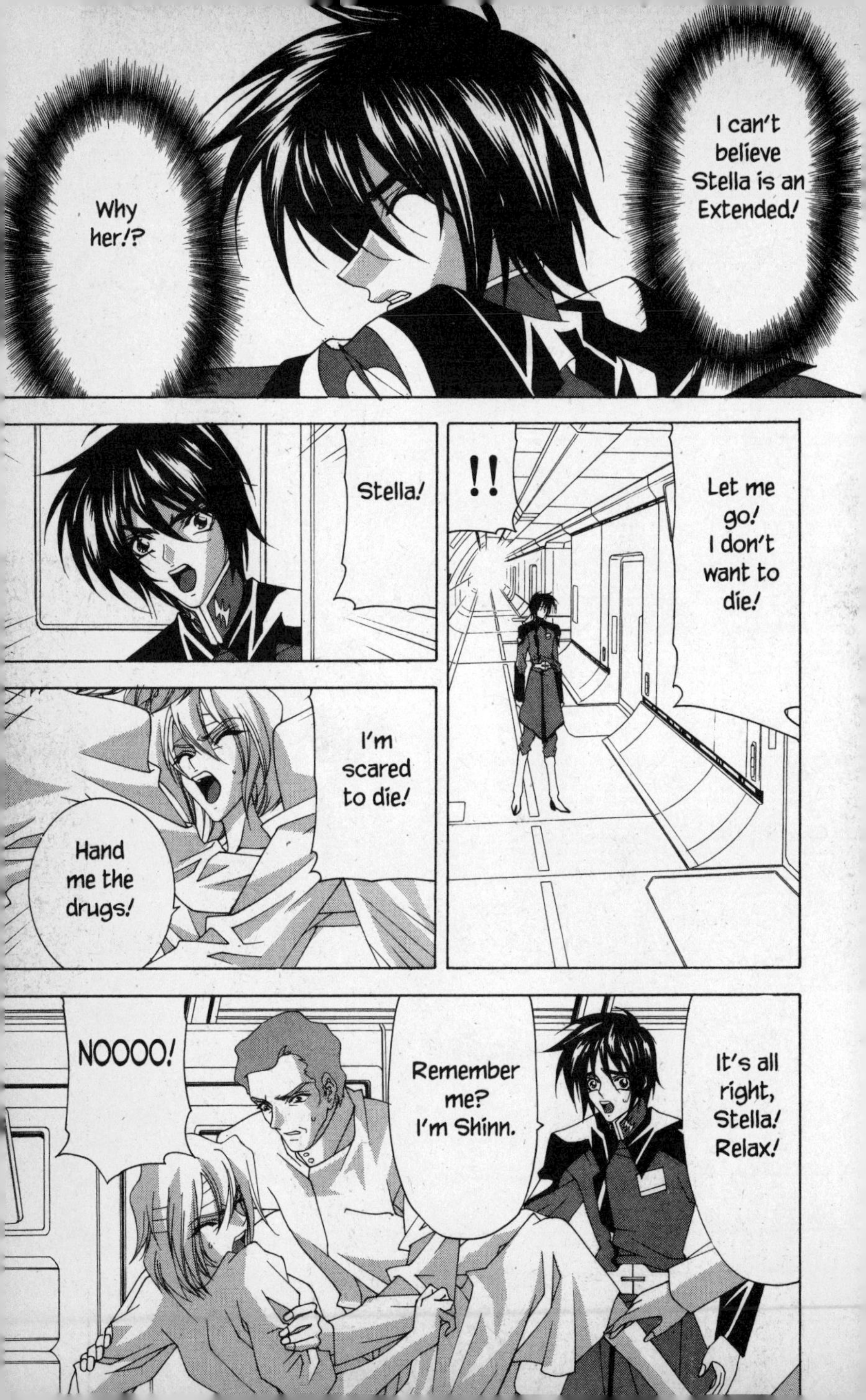

I can't believe Stella is an Extended!
Why her!?
Let me go! I don't want to die!
!!
Stella!
I'm scared to die!
Hand me the drugs!
It's all right, Stella! Relax!
Remember me? I'm Shinn.
NOOOO!

Wait...

Help me, Neo!

I don't know who you are!

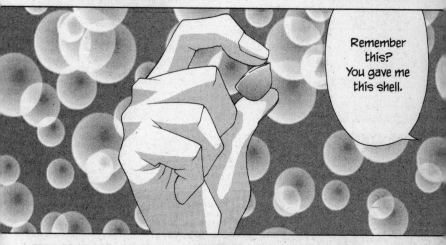

Remember this? You gave me this shell.

I don't remember you!

Let me go!

What!?

I don't remember.

∙ ∙ ∙ ∙ ∙

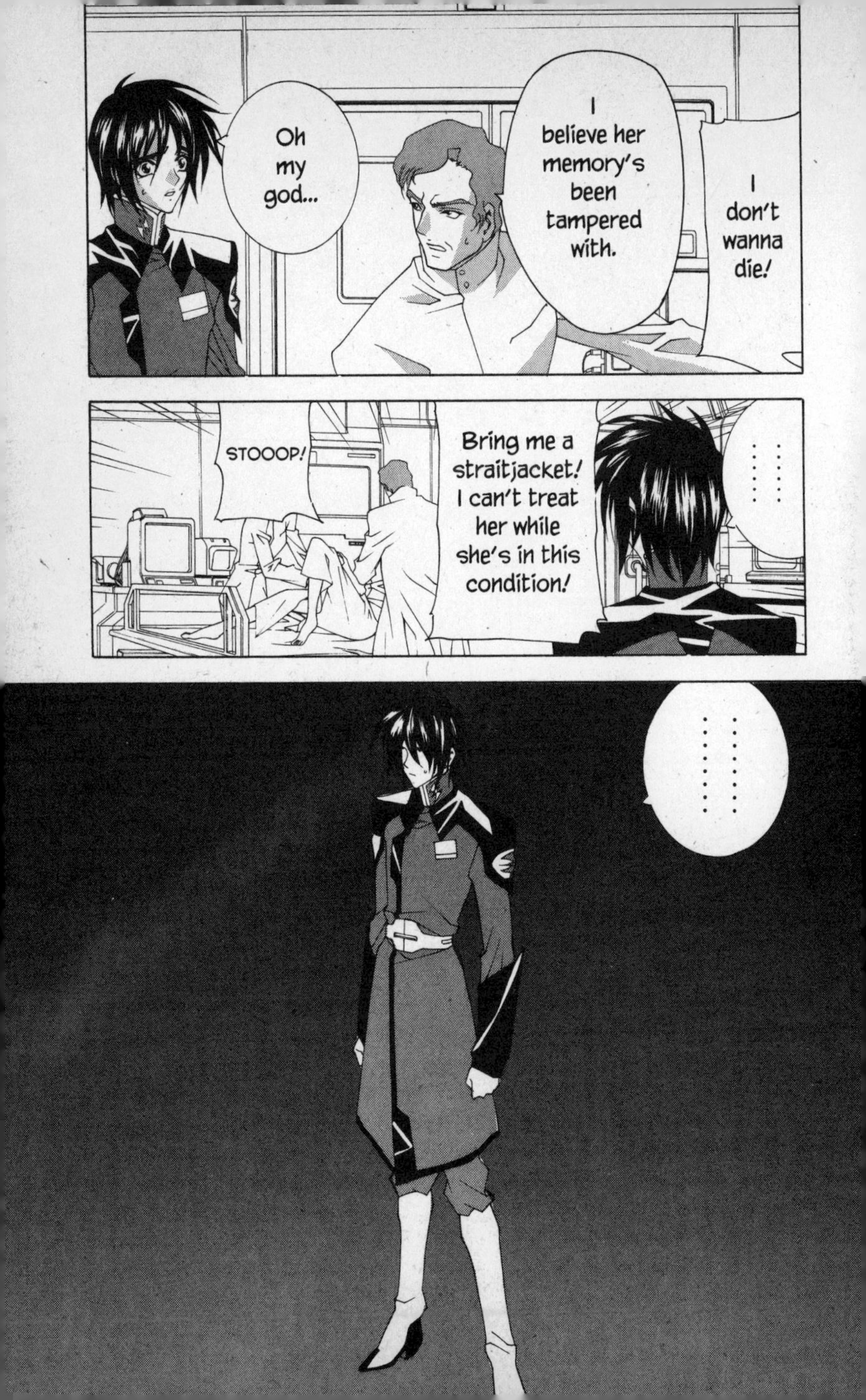
I don't wanna die!
I believe her memory's been tampered with.
Oh my god...
......
Bring me a straitjacket! I can't treat her while she's in this condition!
STOOOP!
......

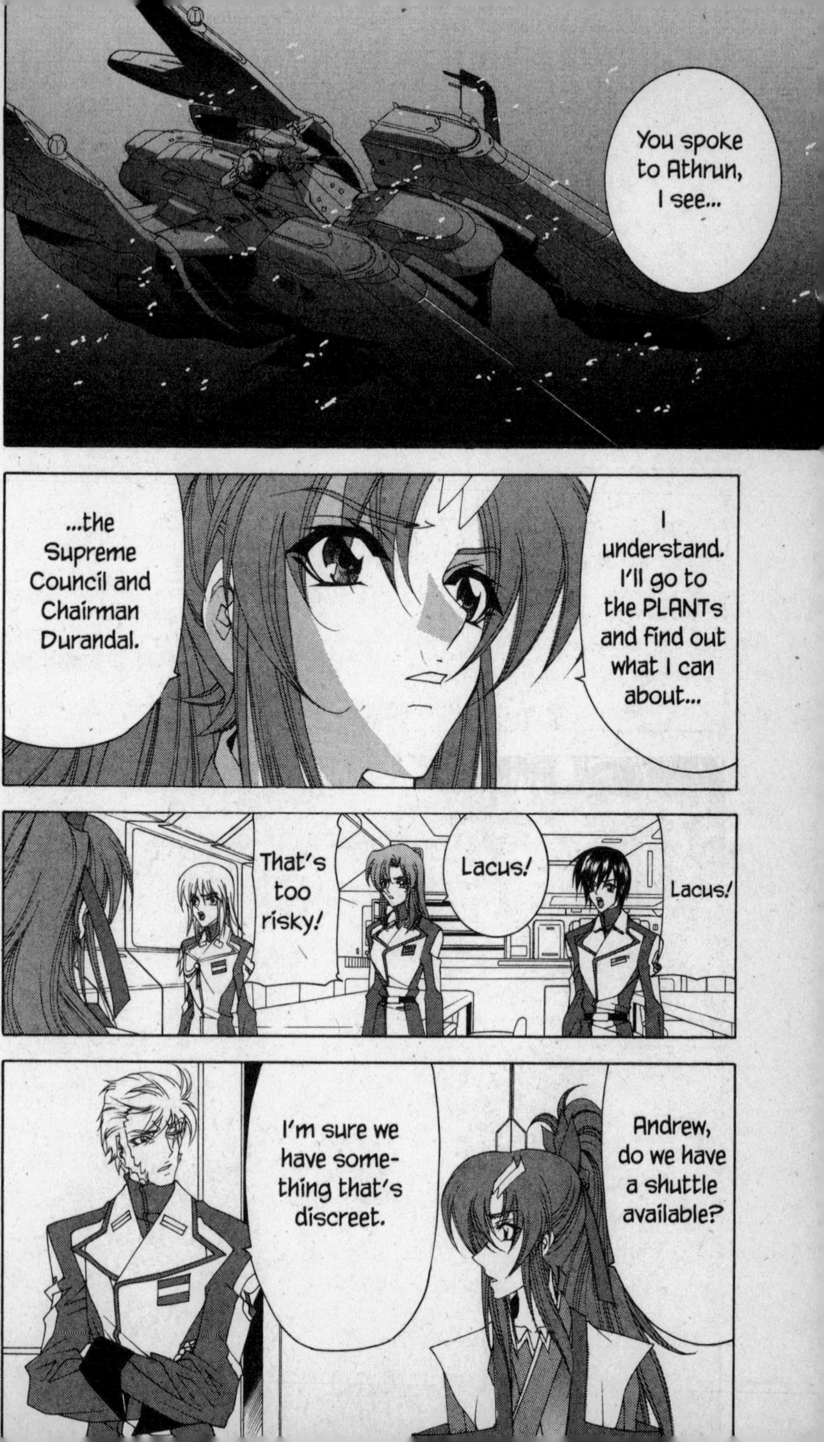
You spoke to Athrun, I see...
I understand. I'll go to the PLANTs and find out what I can about...
...the Supreme Council and Chairman Durandal.
Lacus!
Lacus!
That's too risky!
Andrew, do we have a shuttle available?
I'm sure we have some-thing that's discreet.

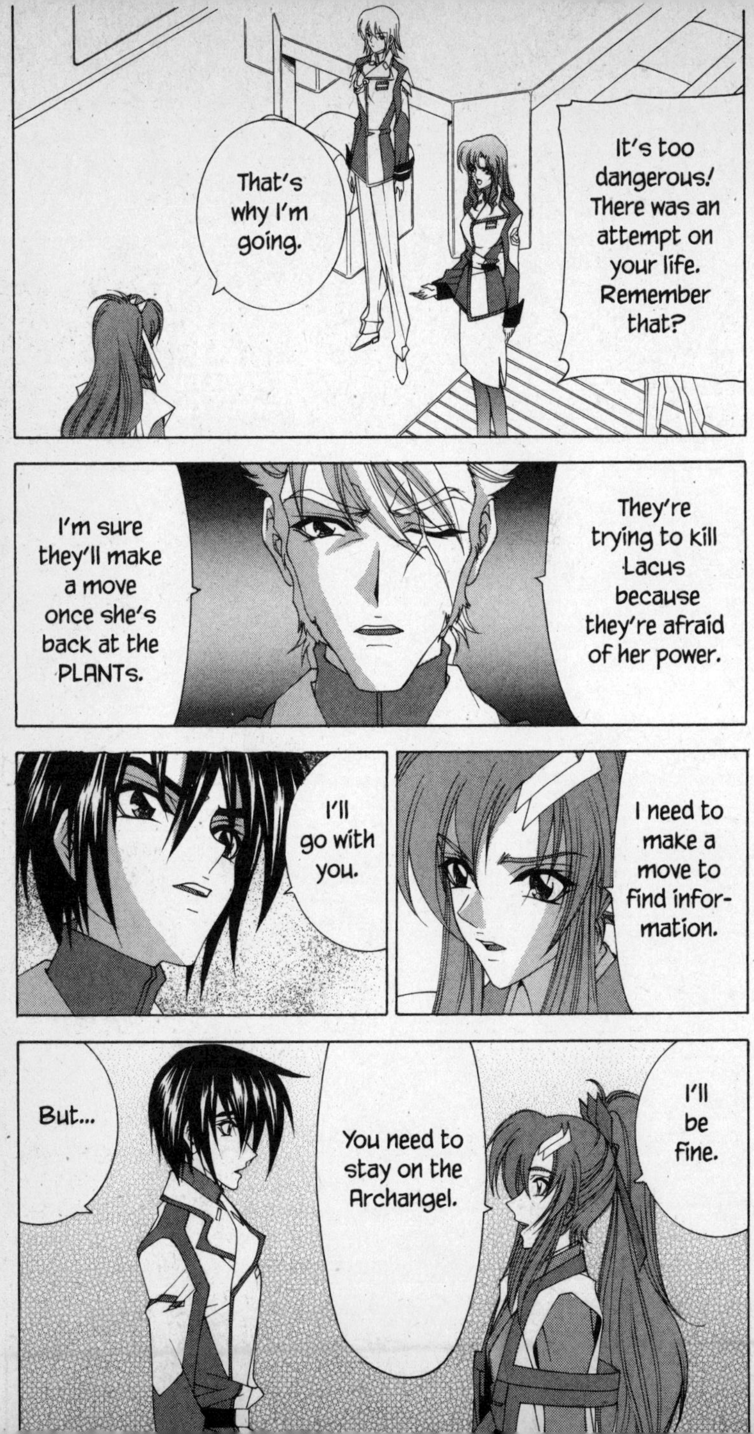
It's too dangerous! There was an attempt on your life. Remember that?
That's why I'm going.
They're trying to kill Lacus because they're afraid of her power.
I'm sure they'll make a move once she's back at the PLANTs.
I need to make a move to find information.
I'll go with you.
I'll be fine.
You need to stay on the Archangel.
But...

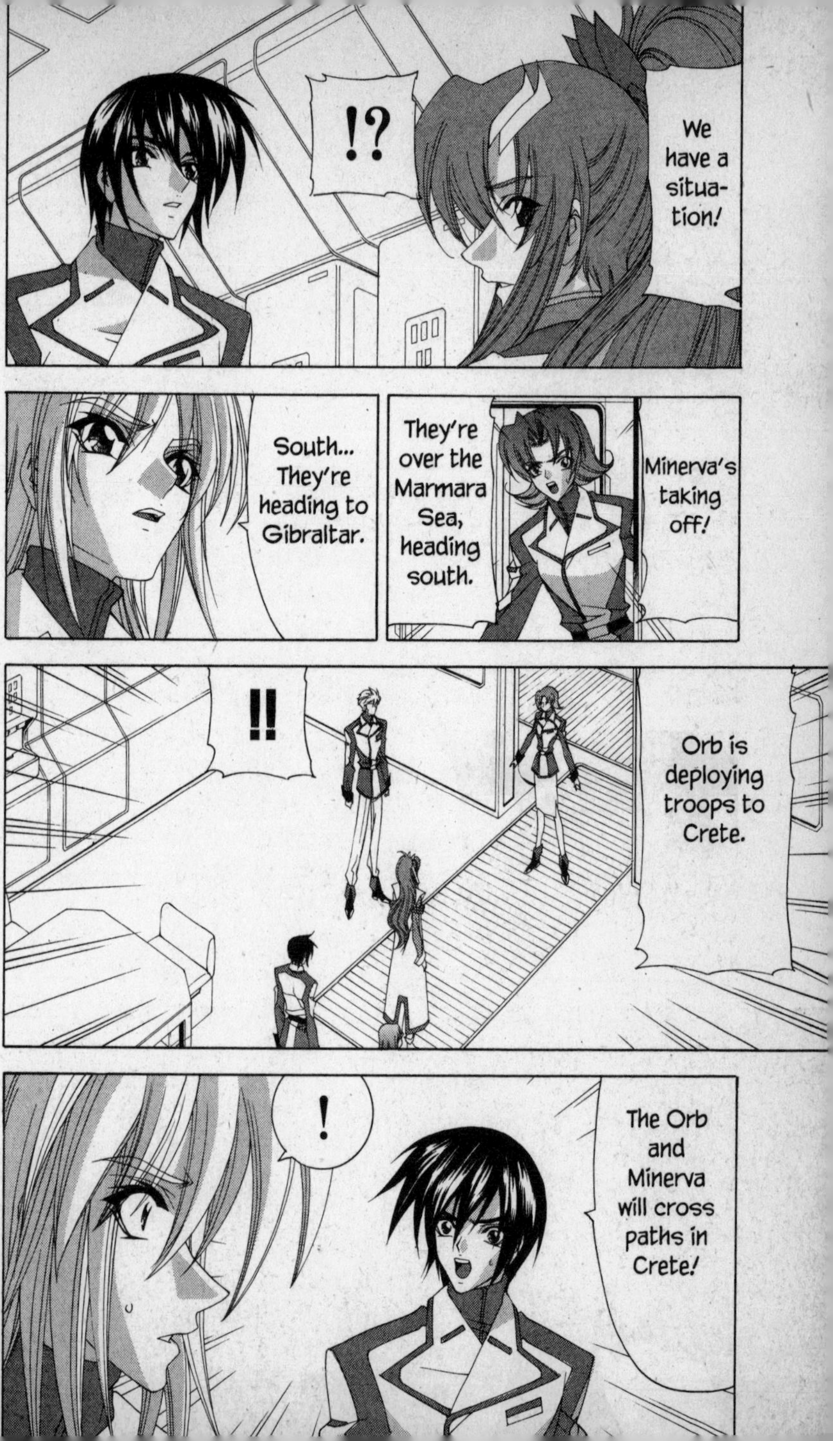
We have a situation!
!?
Minerva's taking off!
They're over the Marmara Sea, heading south.
South... They're heading to Gibraltar.
Orb is deploying troops to Crete.
!!
The Orb and Minerva will cross paths in Crete!
!

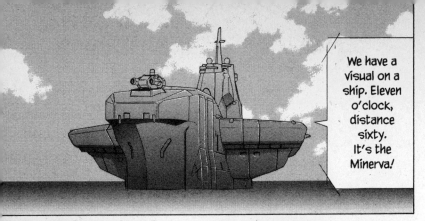

We have a visual on a ship. Eleven o'clock, distance sixty. It's the Minerva!

You erased Stella from Sting and Auel's memory, right?

Yes, according to the technicians.

Launch the Mobile Suit Troops.

Yes, sir!

!

DASH DASH DASH
カカカッ

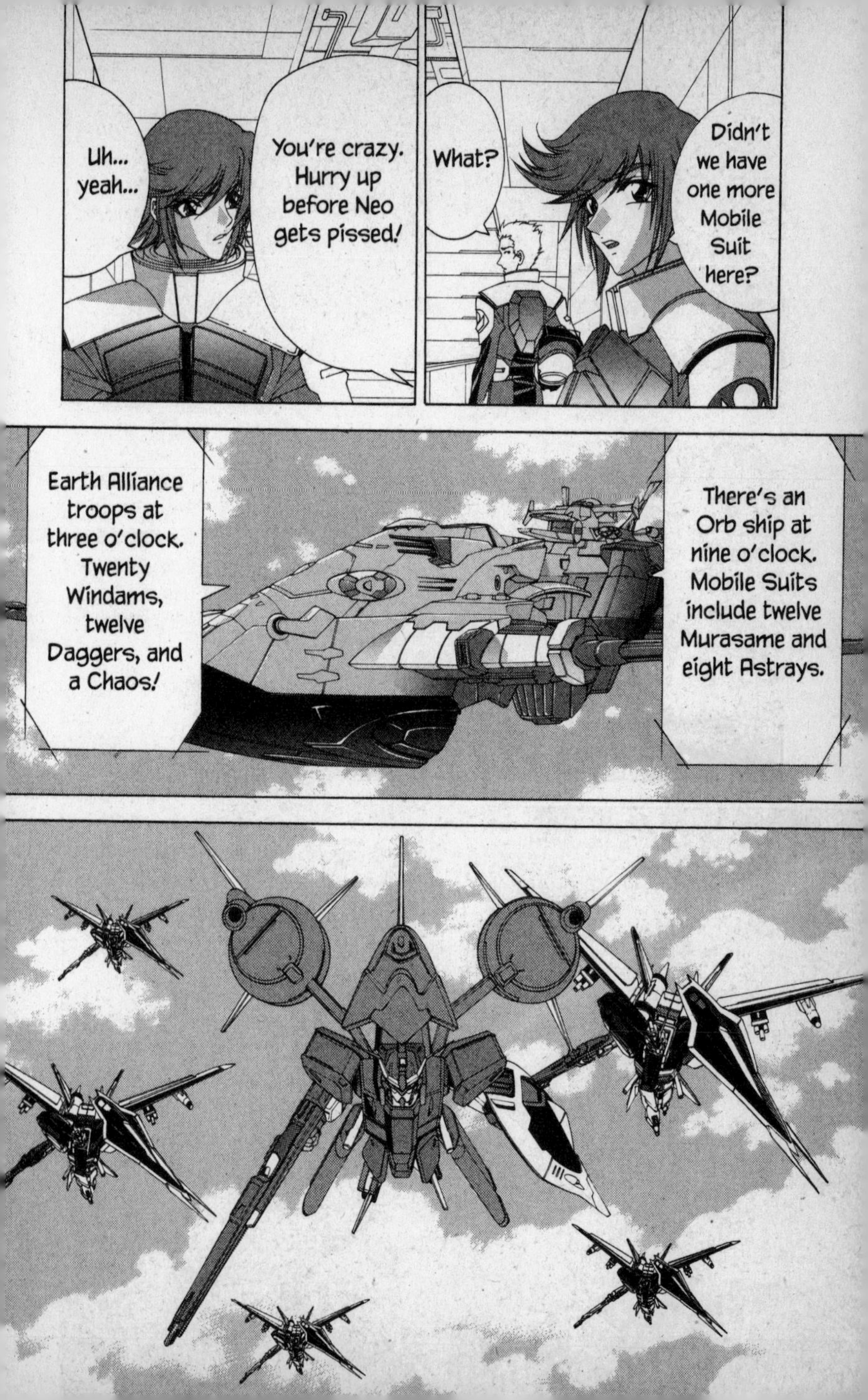
Didn't we have one more Mobile Suit here?
What?
You're crazy. Hurry up before Neo gets pissed!
Uh... yeah...
There's an Orb ship at nine o'clock. Mobile Suits include twelve Murasame and eight Astrays.
Earth Alliance troops at three o'clock. Twenty Windams, twelve Daggers, and a Chaos!

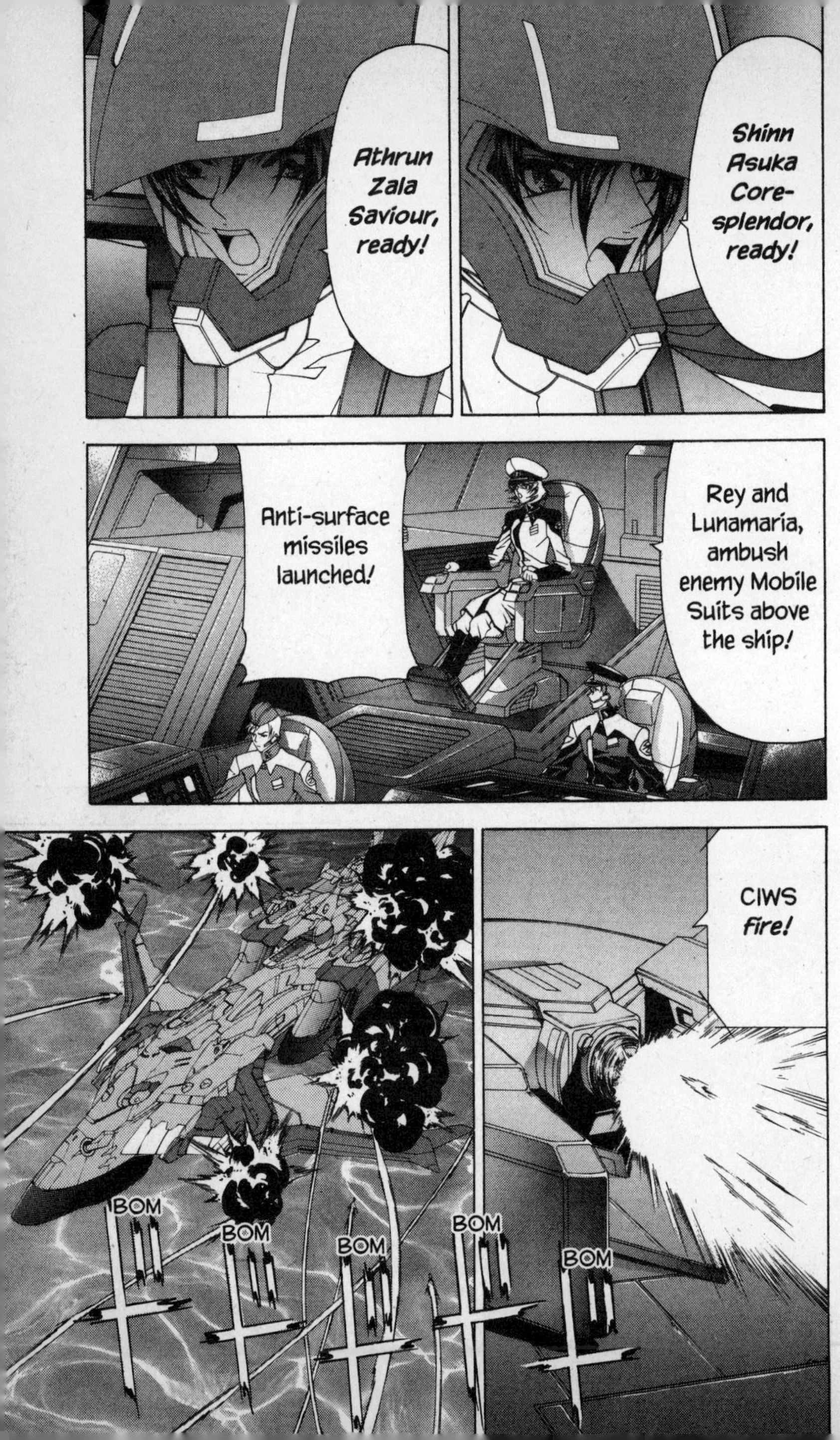
Shinn Asuka Core-splendor, ready!
Athrun Zala Saviour, ready!
Rey and Lunamaria, ambush enemy Mobile Suits above the ship!
Anti-surface missiles launched!
CIWS fire!
BOM
BOM
BOM
BOM
BOM

You bastards messed with Stella...

SHATTER

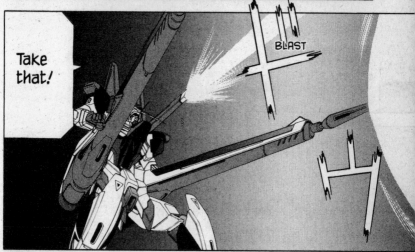

Take that!

BLAST

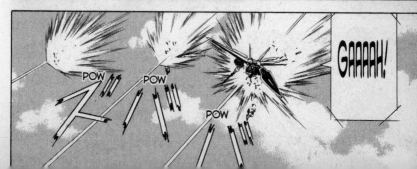

POW

POW

POW

GAAAAH!

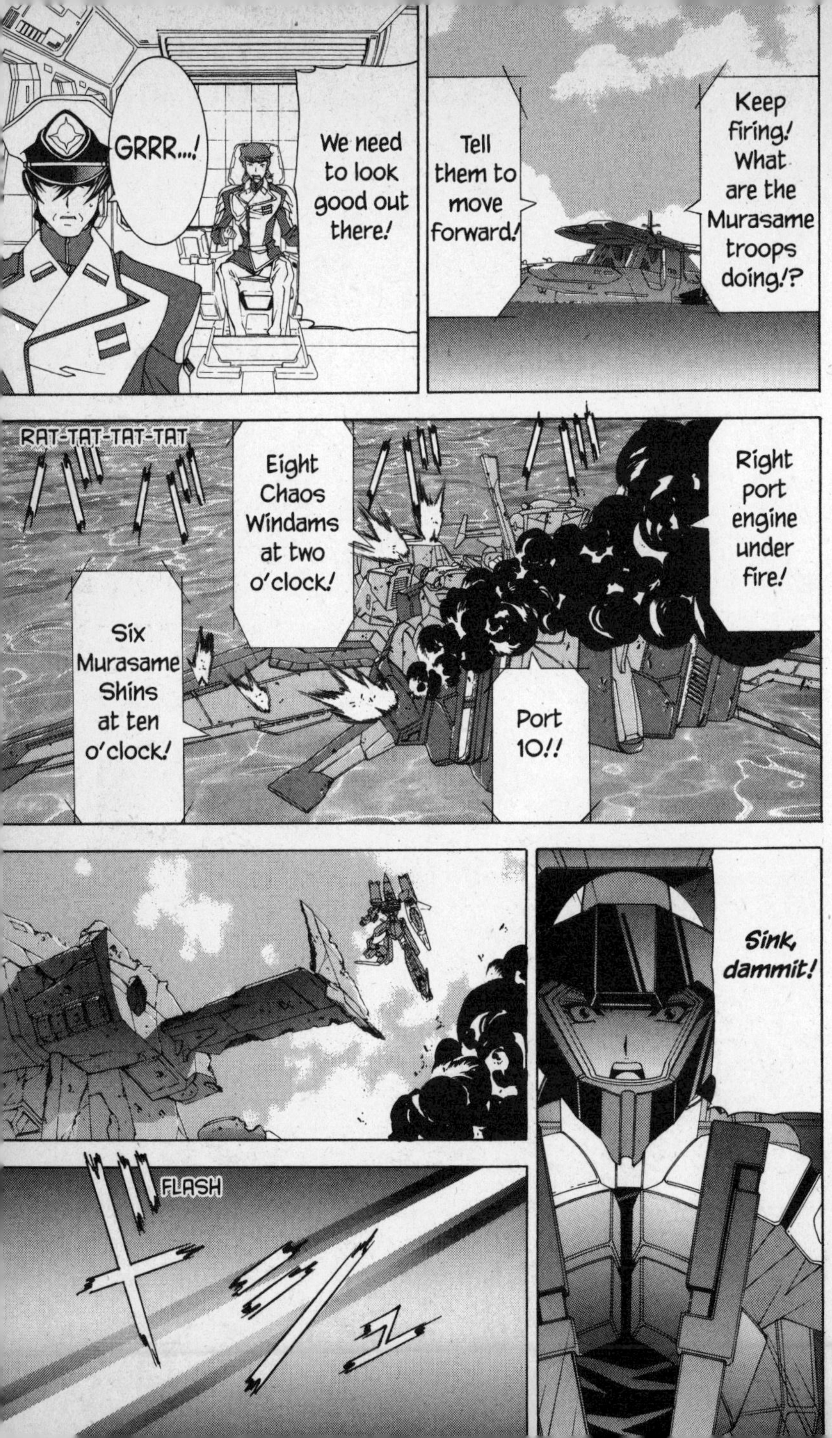
Keep firing! What are the Murasame troops doing!?
Tell them to move forward!
We need to look good out there!
GRRR...!
Right port engine under fire!
Eight Chaos Windams at two o'clock!
RAT-TAT-TAT-TAT
Port 10!!
Six Murasame Shins at ten o'clock!
Sink, dammit!
FLASH

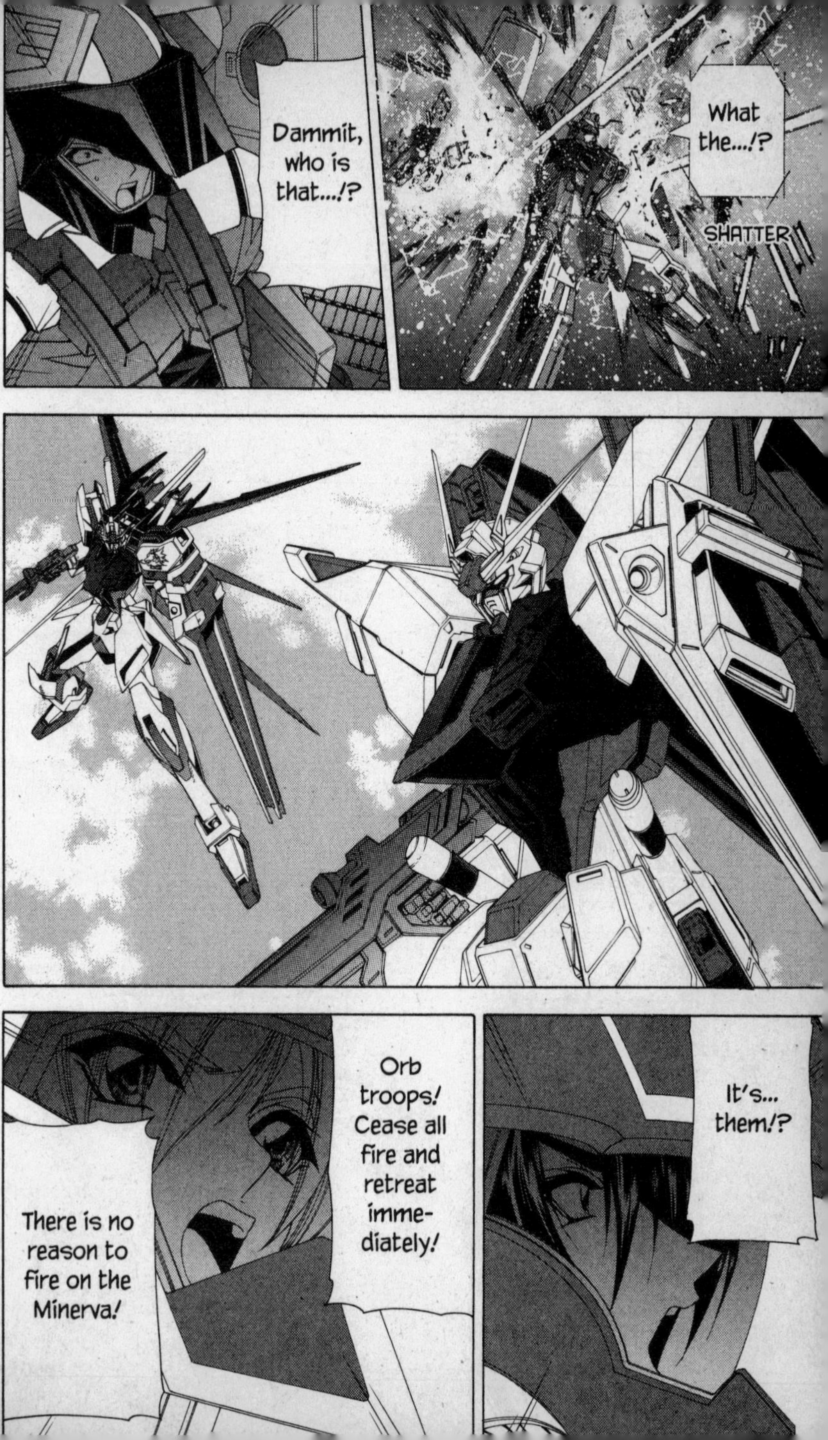
What the...!?
SHATTER
Dammit, who is that...!?
It's... them!?
Orb troops! Cease all fire and retreat imme-diately!
There is no reason to fire on the Minerva!

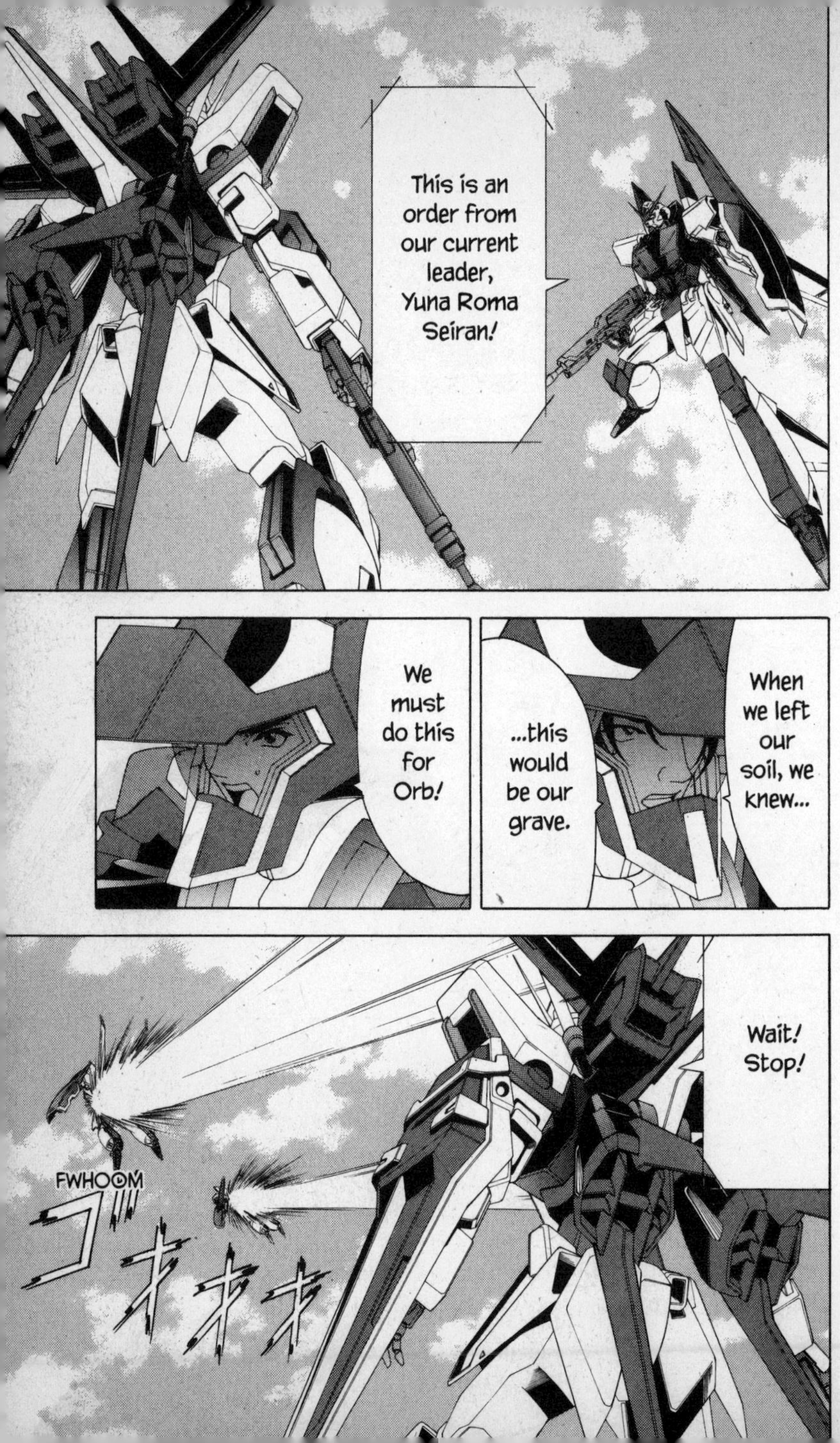
This is an order from our current leader, Yuna Roma Seiran!
When we left our soil, we knew...
...this would be our grave.
We must do this for Orb!
Wait! Stop!
FWHOOM
ゴオオオ

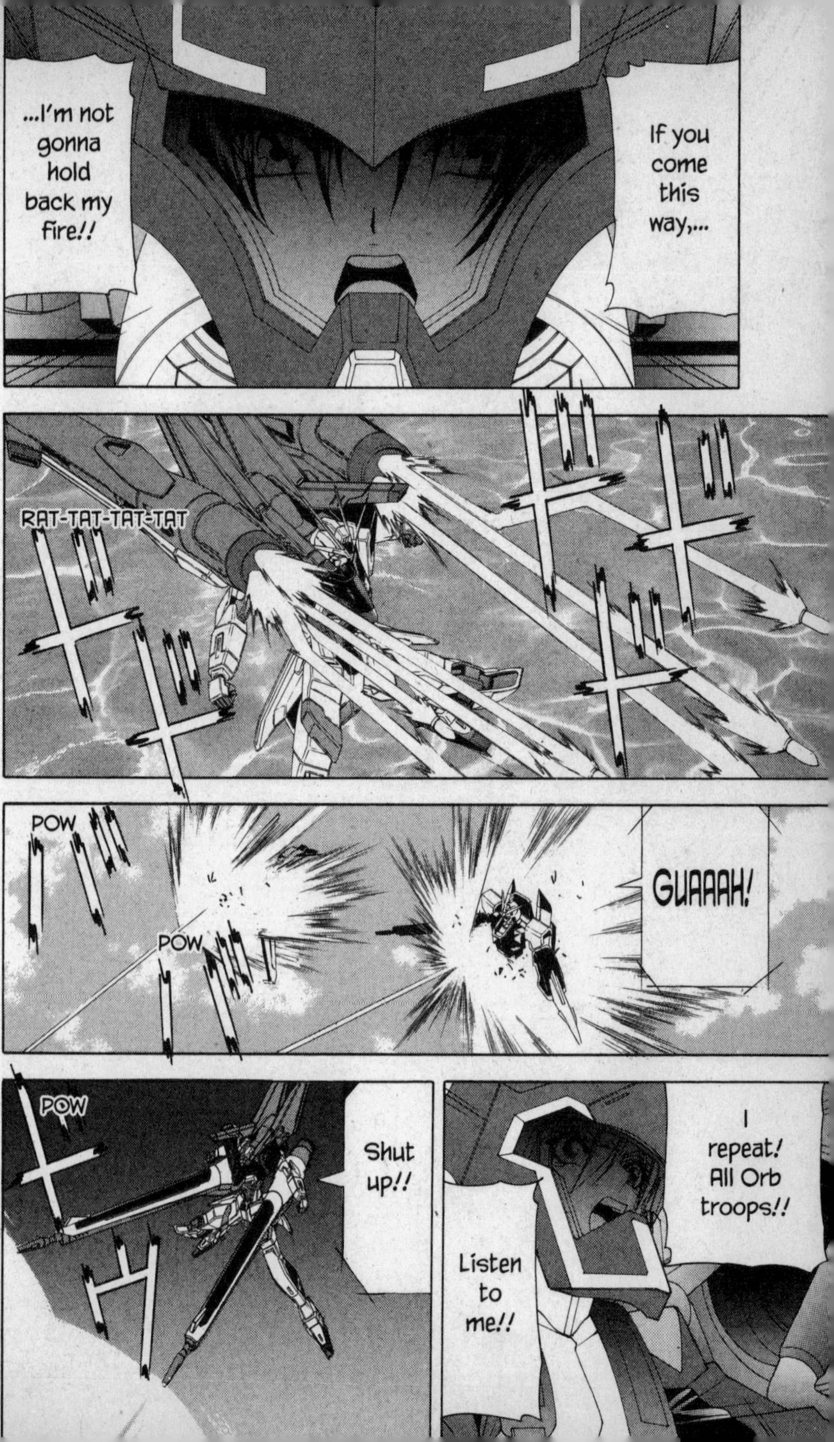
If you come this way,...
...I'm not gonna hold back my fire!!
RAT-TAT-TAT-TAT
GUAAAH!
POW
POW
I repeat! All Orb troops!!
Listen to me!!
Shut up!!
POW

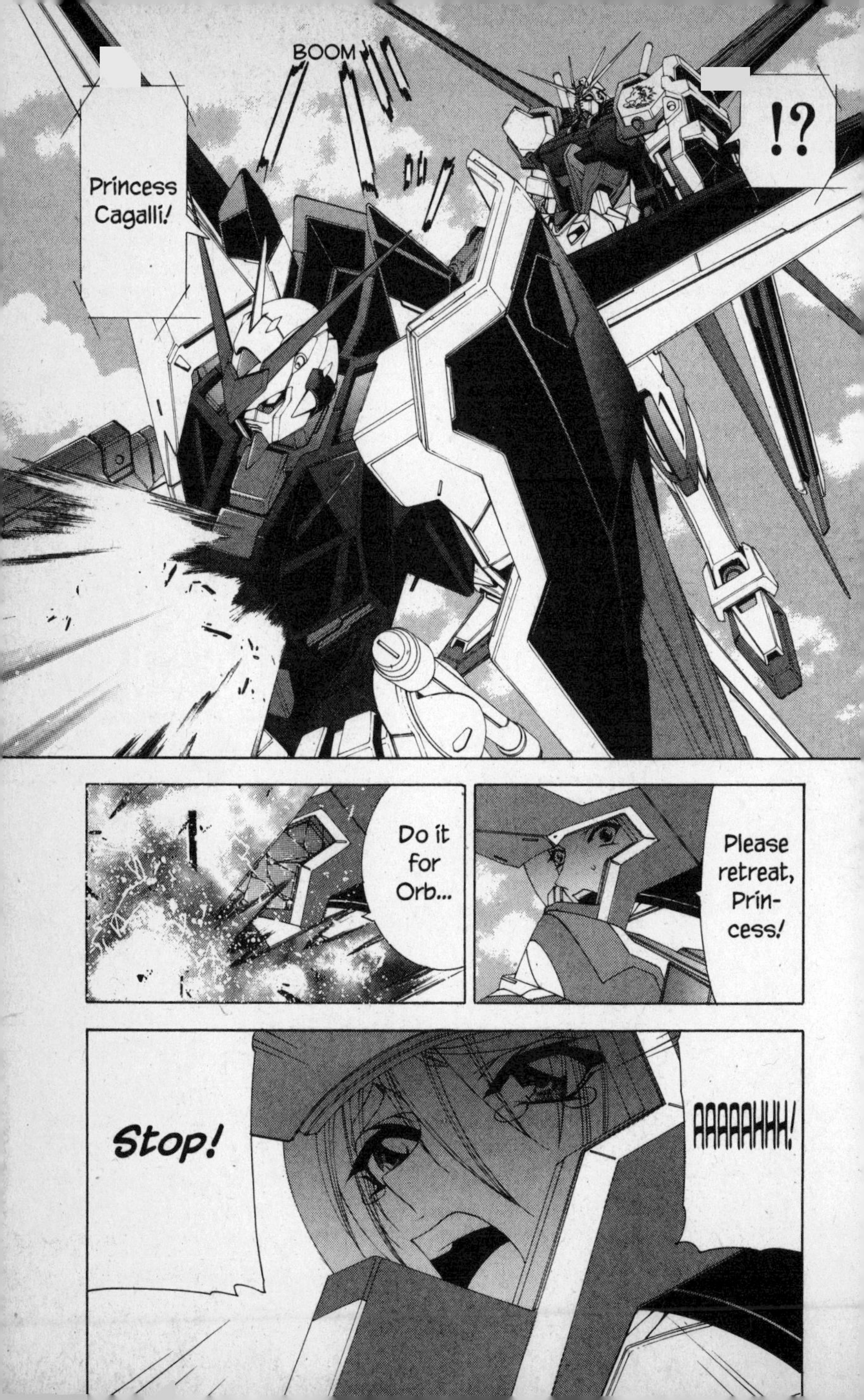
!?
BOOM
Princess Cagalli!
Please retreat, Prin-cess!
Do it for Orb...
AAAAAHHH!
Stop!

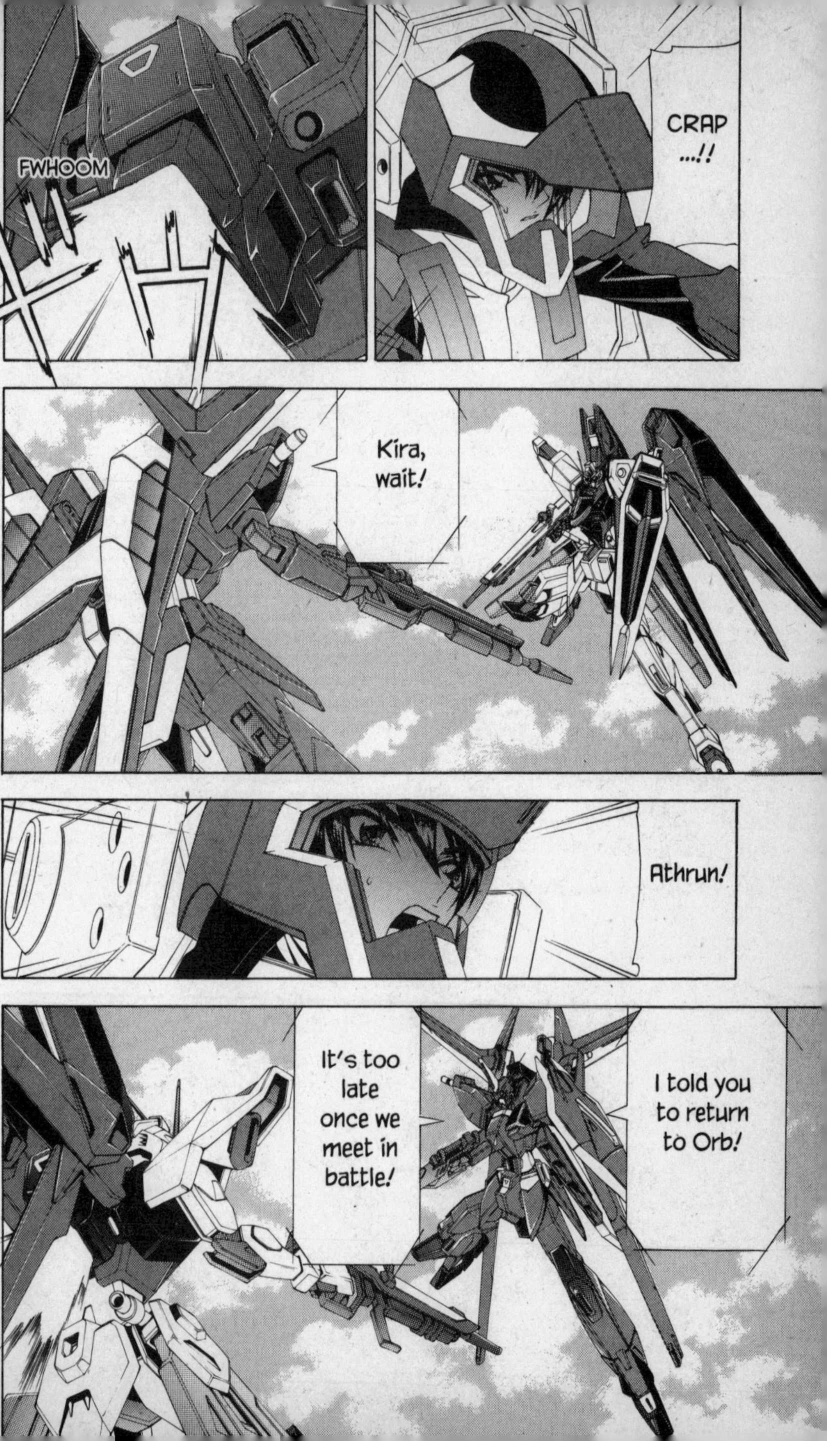
CRAP ...!!
FWHOOM
Kira, wait!
Athrun!
I told you to return to Orb!
It's too late once we meet in battle!

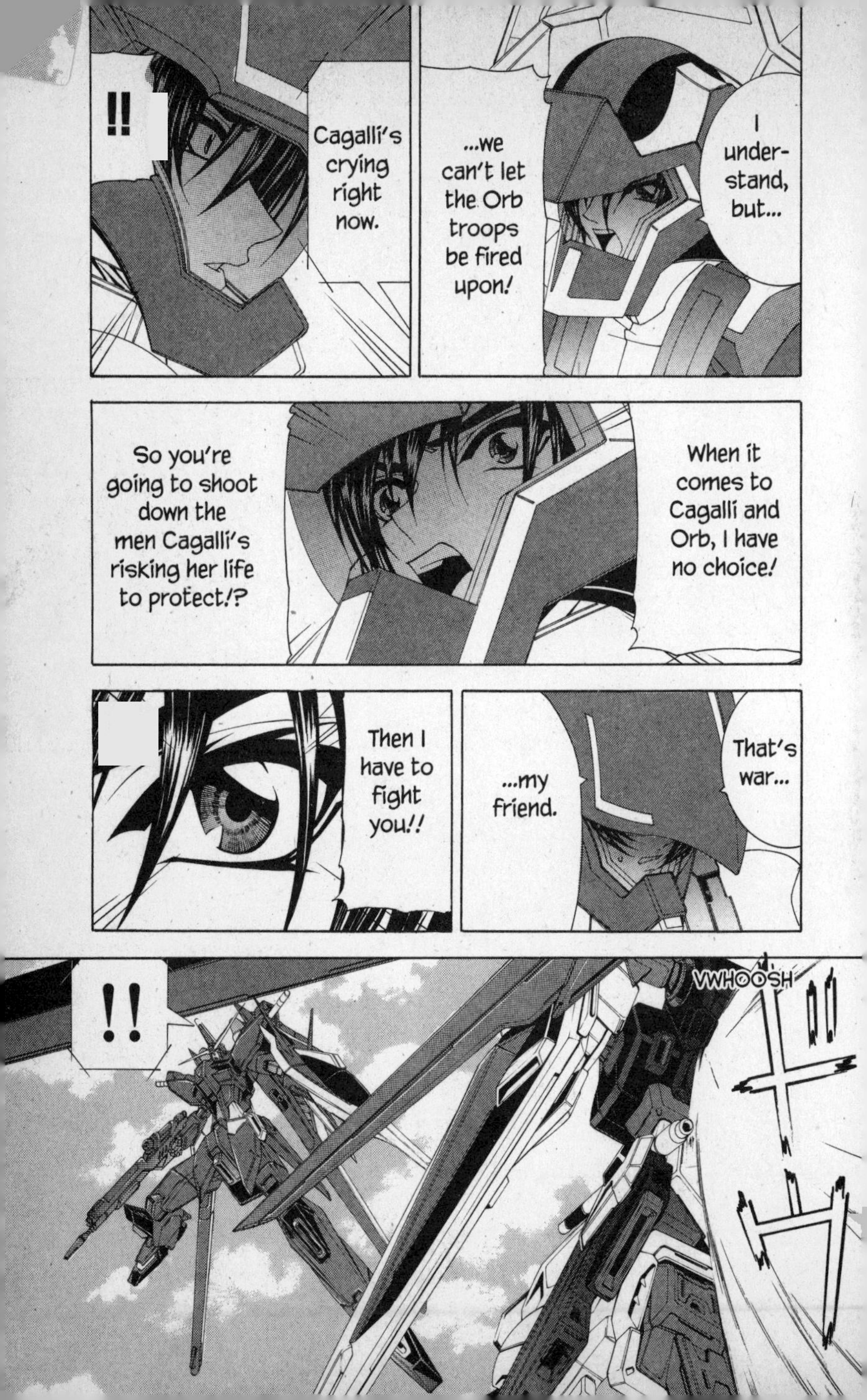
I under-stand, but...
...we can't let the Orb troops be fired upon!
!!
Cagalli's crying right now.
When it comes to Cagalli and Orb, I have no choice!
So you're going to shoot down the men Cagalli's risking her life to protect!?
That's war...
...my friend.
Then I have to fight you!!
VWHOOSH
!!

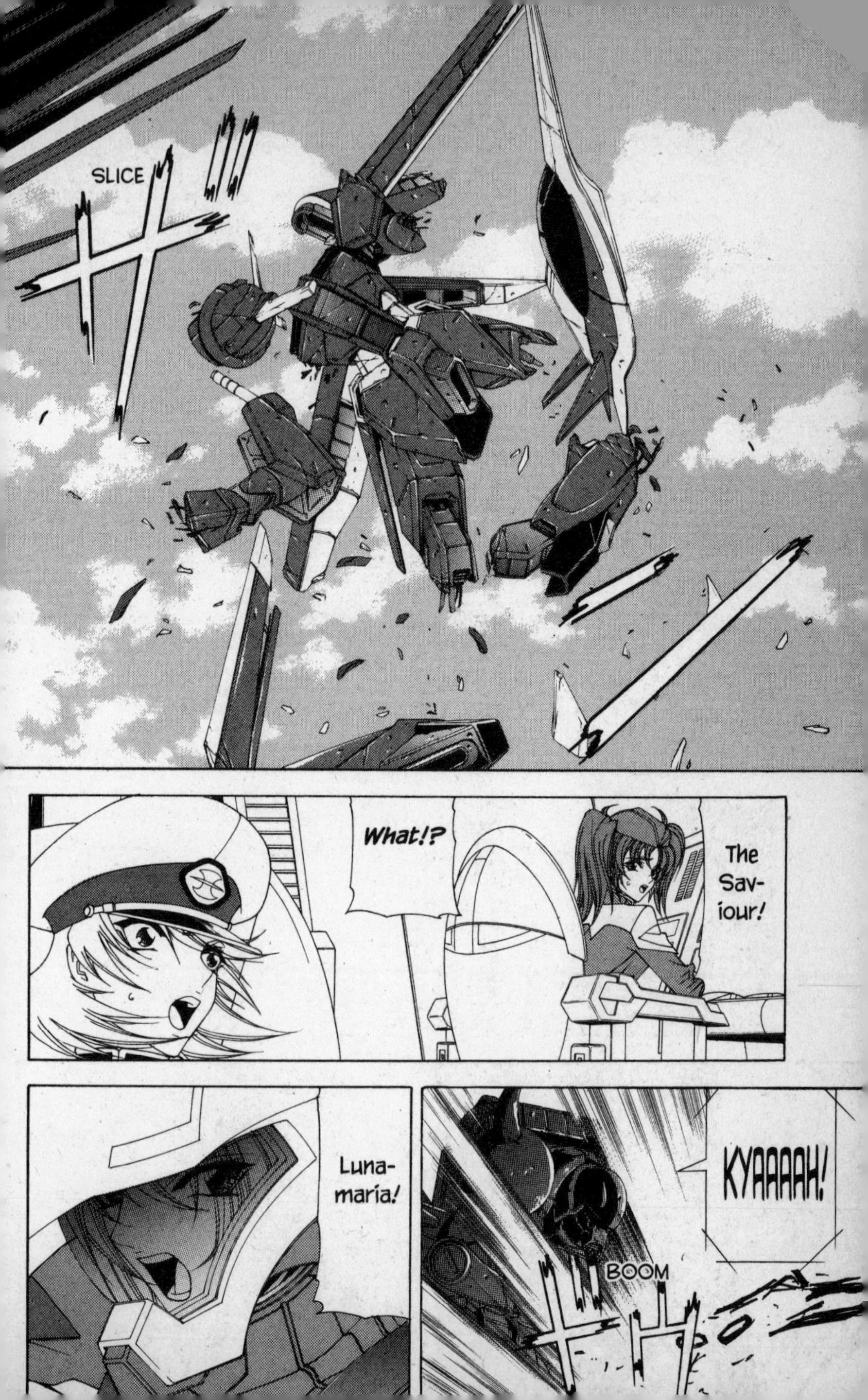
SLICE
The Sav-iour!
What!?
KYAAAAH!
BOOM
Luna-maria!

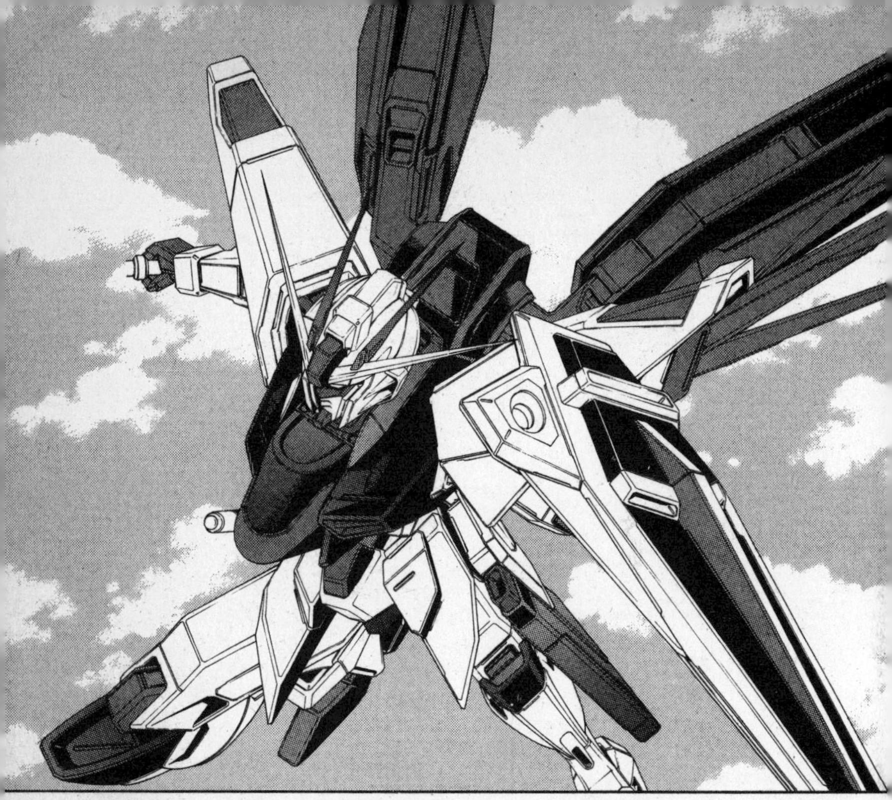

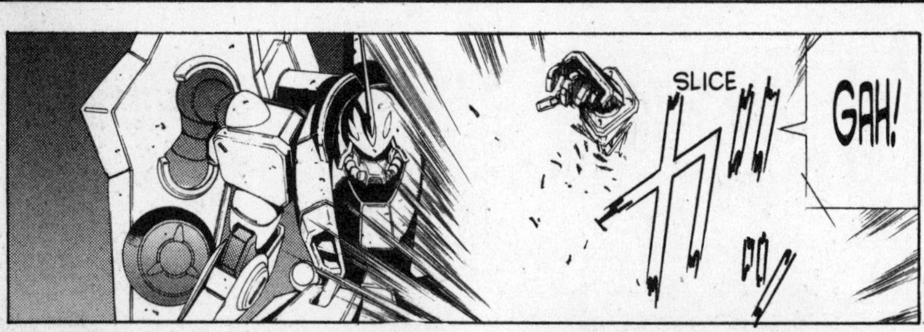
GAH!
SLICE

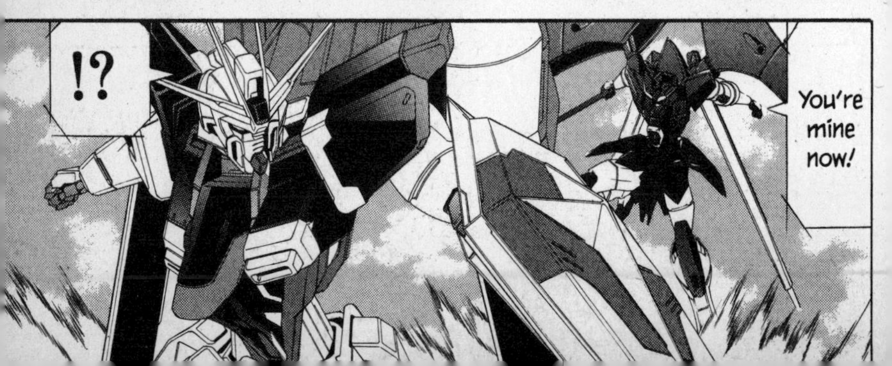
You're mine now!
!?

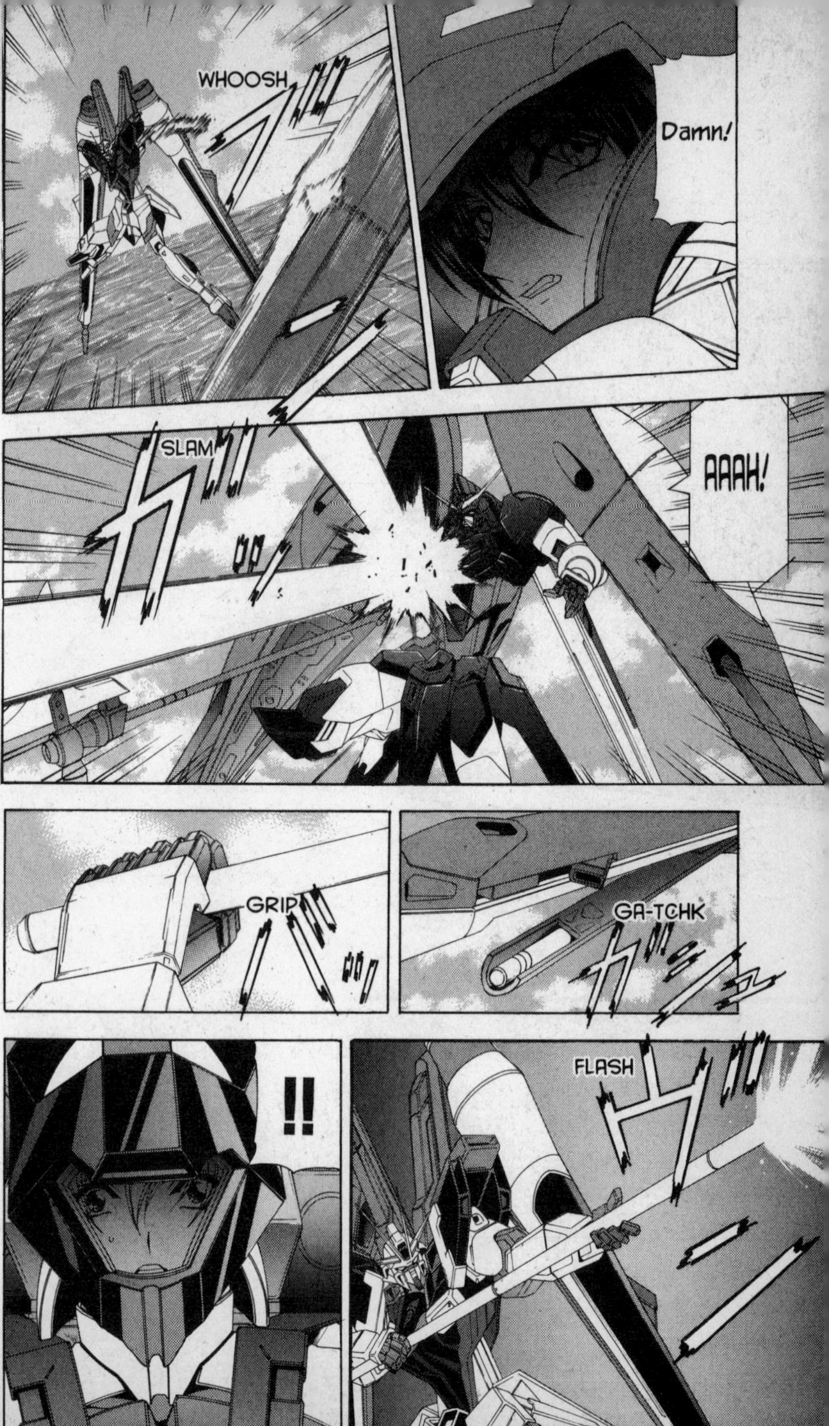
Damn!
WHOOSH
AAAH!
SLAM
GA-TCHK
GRIP
!!
FLASH

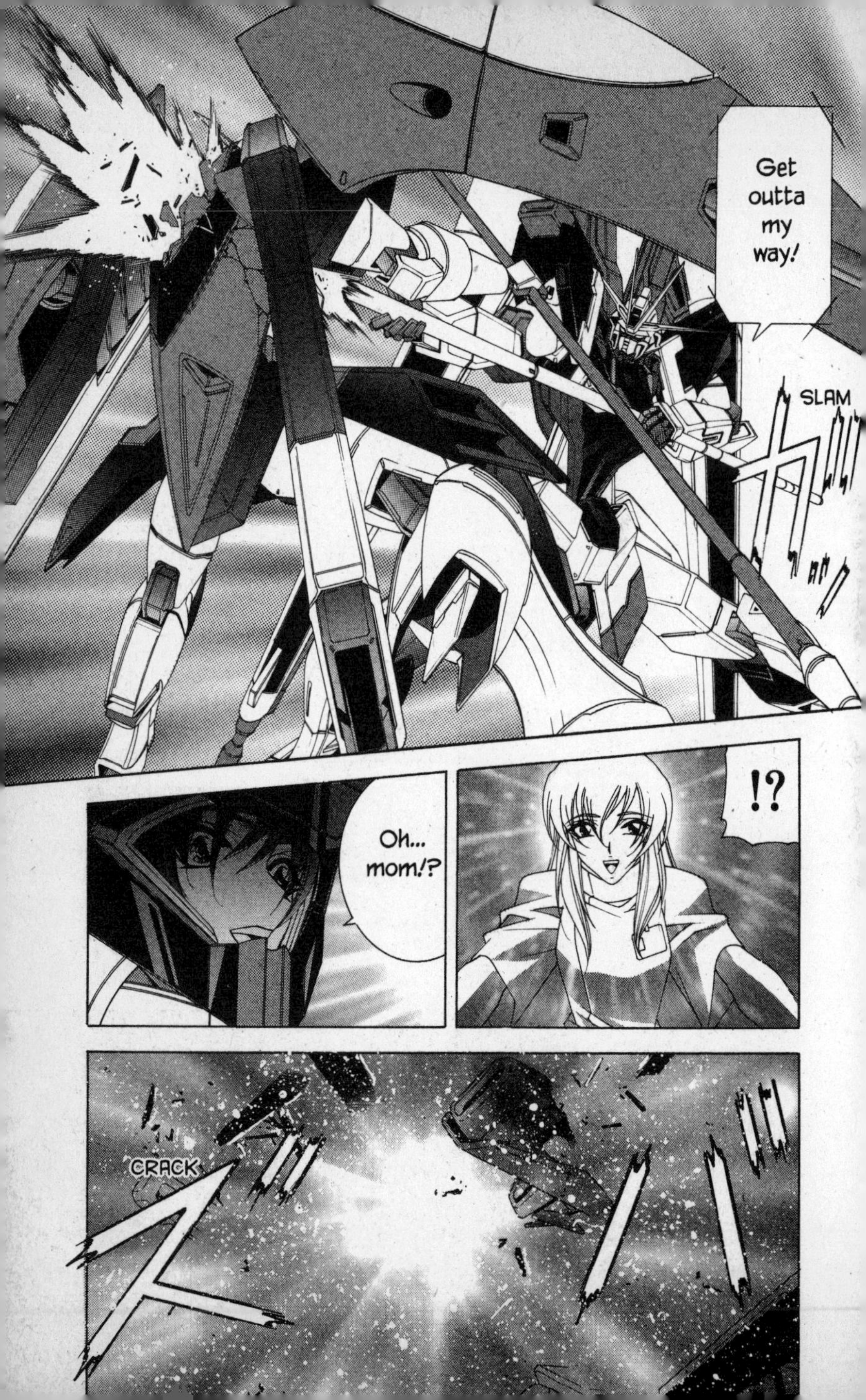
Get outta my way!
SLAM
!?
Oh... mom!?
CRACK

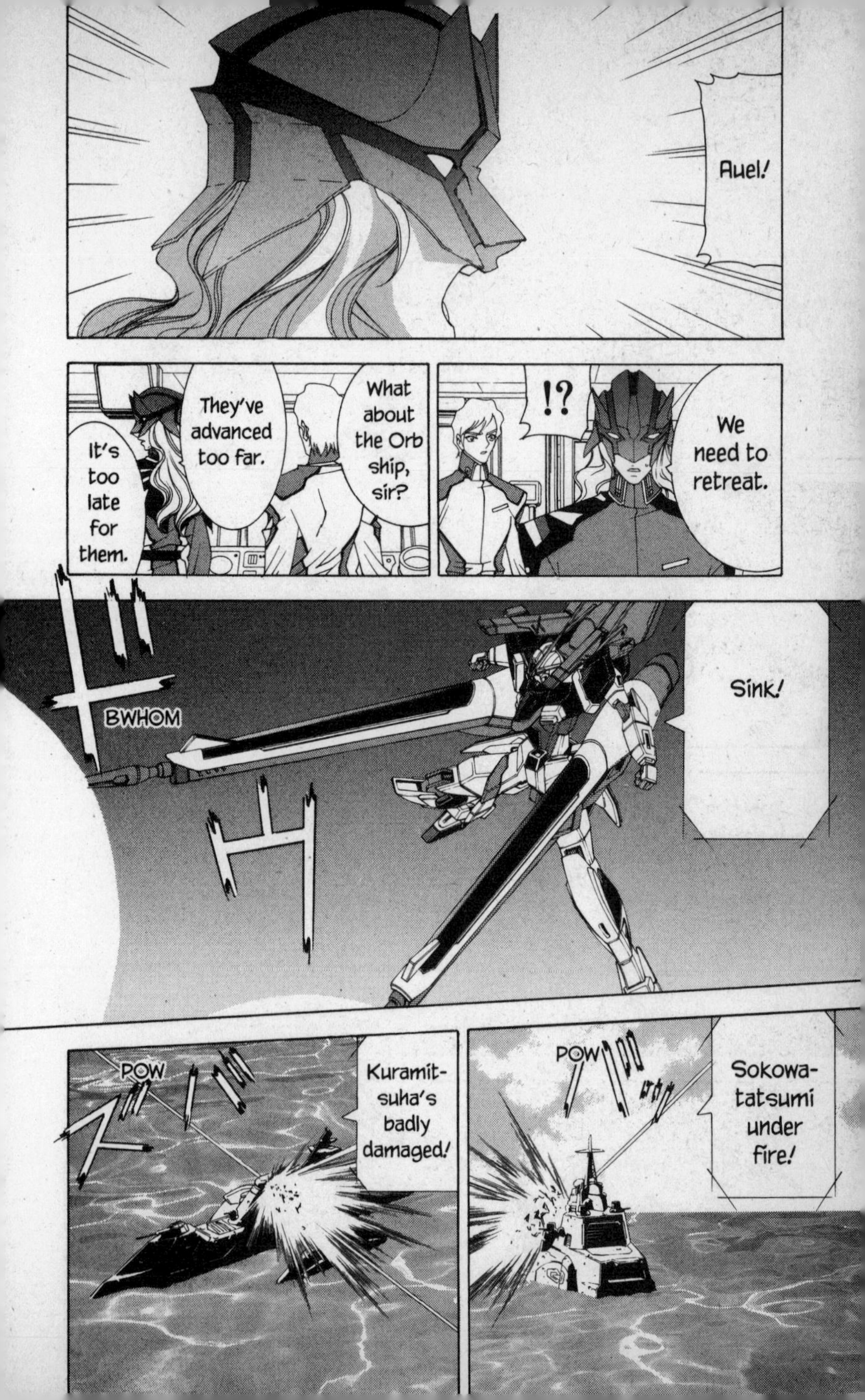
Auel!
We need to retreat.
!?
What about the Orb ship, sir?
They've advanced too far.
It's too late for them.
Sink!
BWHOM
POW
Sokowa-tatsumi under fire!
POW
Kuramit-suha's badly damaged!

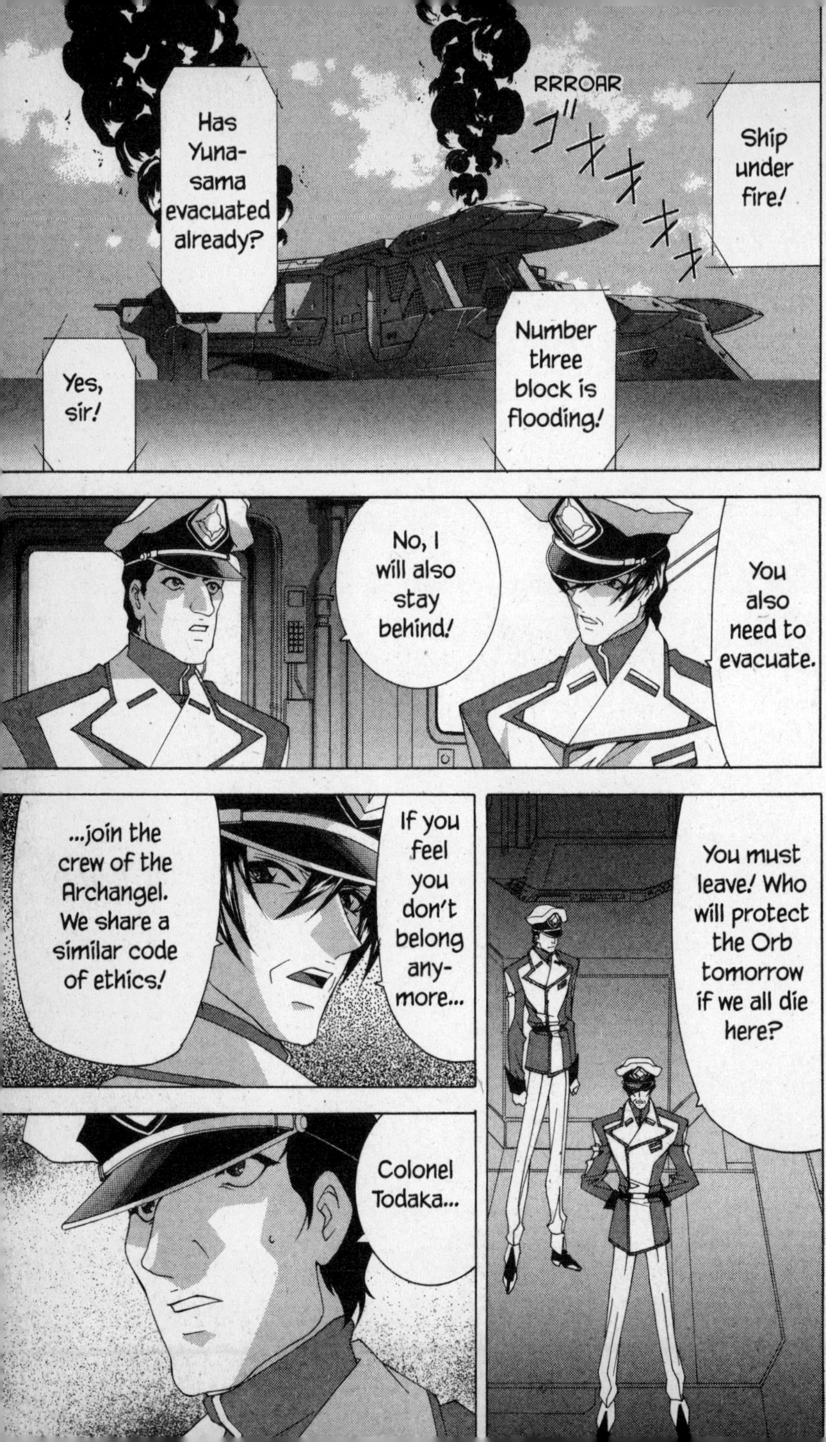
Ship under fire!
RRROAR
ゴオオオオ
Has Yuna-sama evacuated already?
Number three block is flooding!
Yes, sir!
You also need to evacuate.
No, I will also stay behind!
You must leave! Who will protect the Orb tomorrow if we all die here?
If you feel you don't belong anymore...
...join the crew of the Archangel. We share a similar code of ethics!
Colonel Todaka...

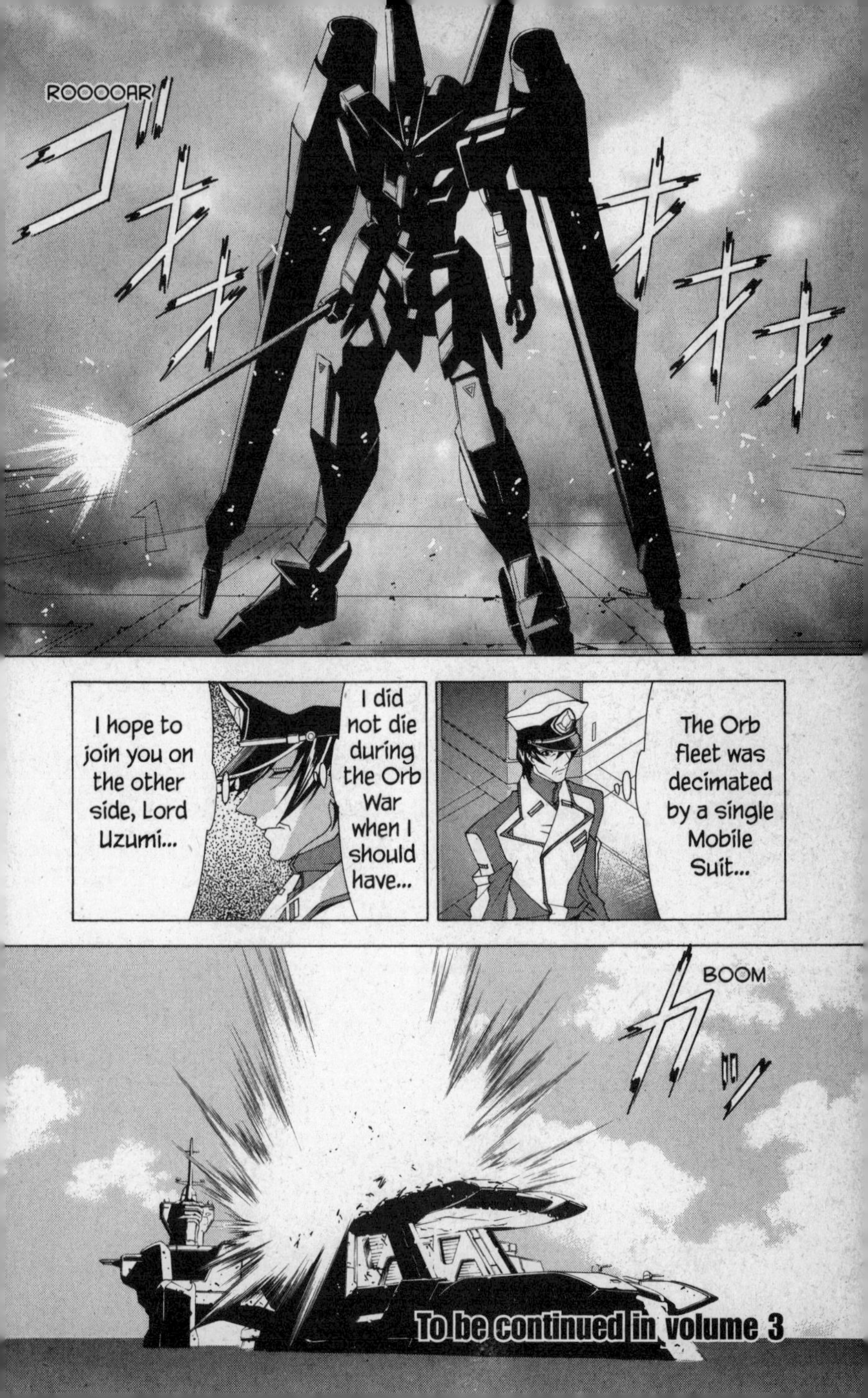
ROOOOAR
The Orb fleet was decimated by a single Mobile Suit...
I did not die during the Orb War when I should have...
I hope to join you on the other side, Lord Uzumi...
BOOM
To be continued in volume 3

Special Bonus

Bonus Pages
Mecha Parts Description

Special Edition
Gundam Seed Destiny
Series Preview Manga

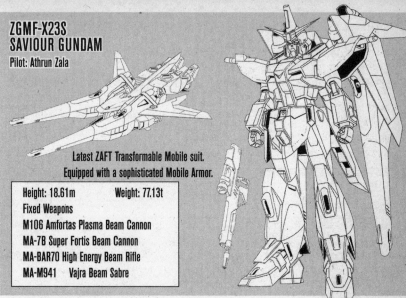

ZGMF-X23S
SAVIOUR GUNDAM
Pilot: Athrun Zala

Latest ZAFT Transformable Mobile suit.
Equipped with a sophisticated Mobile Armor.

Height: 18.61m	Weight: 77.13t

Fixed Weapons

M106 Amfortas Plasma Beam Cannon

MA-7B Super Fortis Beam Cannon

MA-BAR70 High Energy Beam Rifle

MA-M941   Vajra Beam Sabre

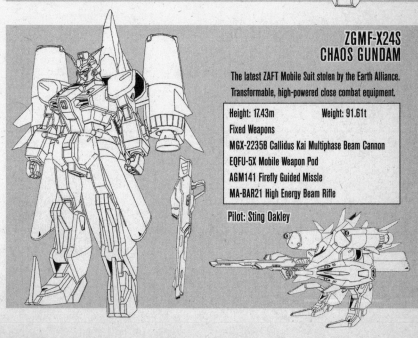

ZGMF-X24S
CHAOS GUNDAM

The latest ZAFT Mobile Suit stolen by the Earth Alliance.
Transformable, high-powered close combat equipment.

Height: 17.43m	Weight: 91.61t

Fixed Weapons

MGX-2235B Callidus Kai Multiphase Beam Cannon

EQFU-5X Mobile Weapon Pod

AGM141 Firefly Guided Missle

MA-BAR21 High Energy Beam Rifle

Pilot: Sting Oakley

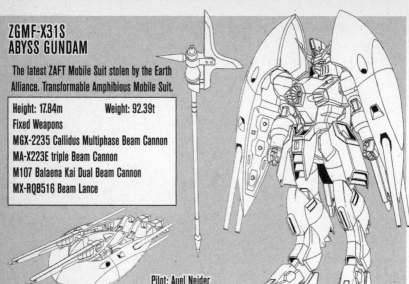

ZGMF-X31S
ABYSS GUNDAM

The latest ZAFT Mobile Suit stolen by the Earth Alliance. Transformable Amphibious Mobile Suit.

Height: 17.84m Weight: 92.39t
Fixed Weapons
MGX-2235 Callidus Multiphase Beam Cannon
MA-X223E triple Beam Cannon
M107 Balaena Kai Dual Beam Cannon
MX-RQB516 Beam Lance

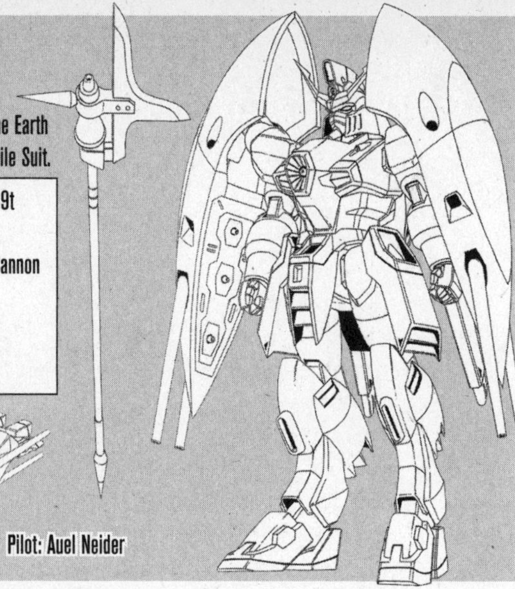

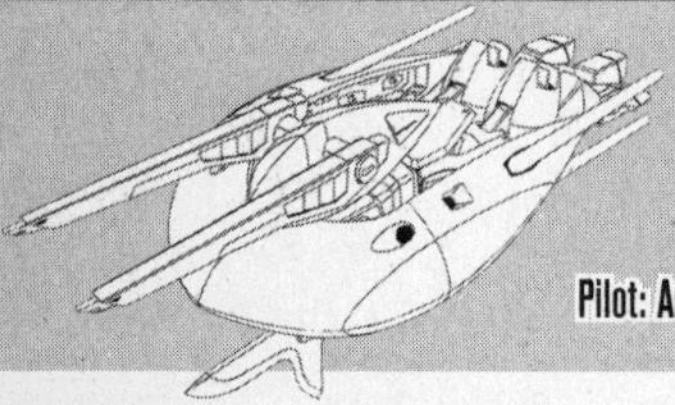

Pilot: Auel Neider

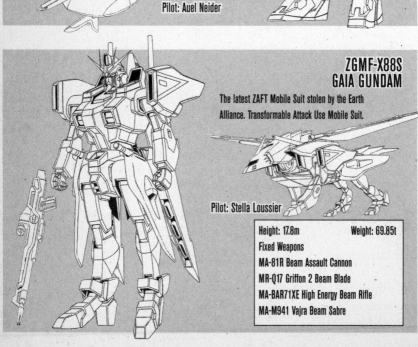

ZGMF-X88S
GAIA GUNDAM

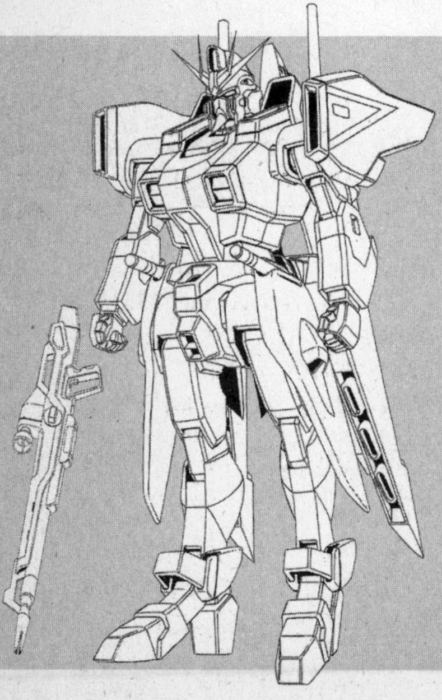

The latest ZAFT Mobile Suit stolen by the Earth Alliance. Transformable Attack Use Mobile Suit.

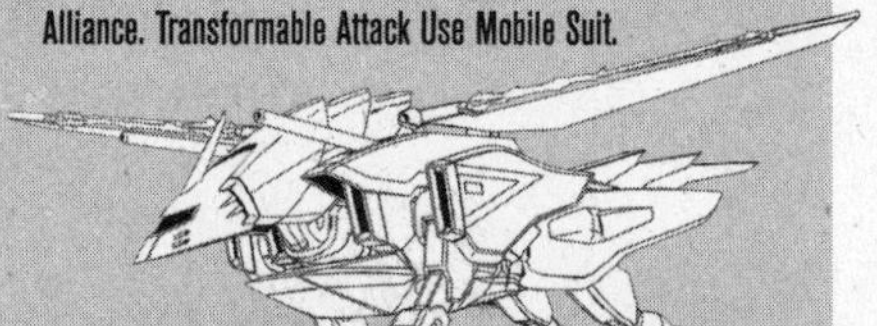

Pilot: Stella Loussier

Height: 17.8m Weight: 69.85t
Fixed Weapons
MA-81R Beam Assault Cannon
MR-Q17 Griffon 2 Beam Blade
MA-BAR71XE High Energy Beam Rifle
MA-M941 Vajra Beam Sabre

BONUS PAGE
MECHA PARTS DESCRIPTION

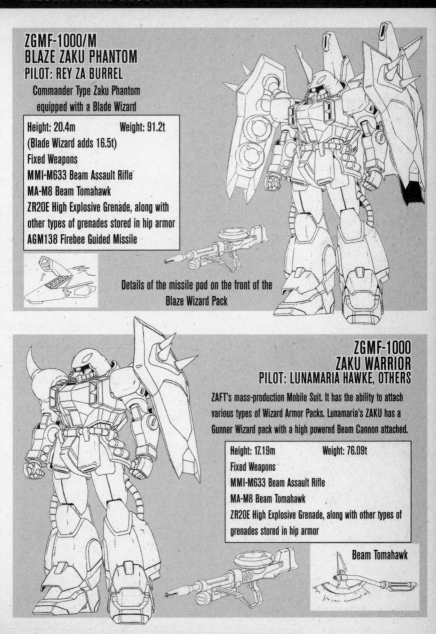

ZGMF-1000/M
BLAZE ZAKU PHANTOM
PILOT: REY ZA BURREL

Commander Type Zaku Phantom equipped with a Blade Wizard

Height: 20.4m Weight: 91.2t
(Blade Wizard adds 16.5t)
Fixed Weapons
MMI-M633 Beam Assault Rifle
MA-M8 Beam Tomahawk
ZR20E High Explosive Grenade, along with other types of grenades stored in hip armor
AGM138 Firebee Guided Missile

Details of the missile pod on the front of the Blaze Wizard Pack

ZGMF-1000
ZAKU WARRIOR
PILOT: LUNAMARIA HAWKE, OTHERS

ZAFT's mass-production Mobile Suit. It has the ability to attach various types of Wizard Armor Packs. Lunamaria's ZAKU has a Gunner Wizard pack with a high powered Beam Cannon attached.

Height: 17.19m Weight: 76.09t
Fixed Weapons
MMI-M633 Beam Assault Rifle
MA-M8 Beam Tomahawk
ZR20E High Explosive Grenade, along with other types of grenades stored in hip armor

Beam Tomahawk

ZGMF-X2000
GOUF IGNITED

ZAFT's latest Mobile Suit. The armor is
optimal for close combat situations.

Height: 19.2m	Weight: 72.13t

Fixed Weapons
M181SE Draupnir 4-barrel Gun
(Machine guns on both wrists)
MA-M757 Slayer whip
MM-558 Tempest Beam Sword

Beam Sword is extendable.
It is stored inside the
shield.

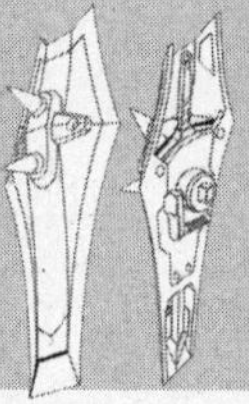

Pilot: Heine Westenfluss,
others

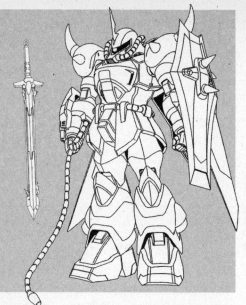

UMF-SS0-3
ASH
PILOT: ZAFT SPECIAL FORCES

ZAFT's Special
Forces Mobile
Suit used
for covert
operations.
Its special
feature is
the beam
claws.

Height: 20.7m	Weight: 50.59t

Fixed Weapons
MX-RQB505 Beam Claw
PJP3 Dual Photon Maser Cannon
MA-M1217R High Energy Beam Cannon
GMF22X prototype propeller and multipurpose Missile
Launcher

Mobile Armor for
aquatic activities

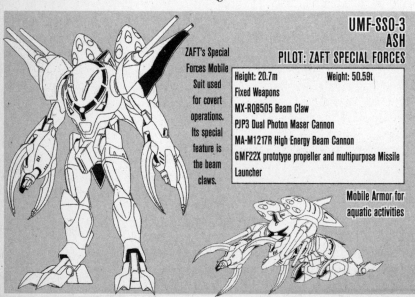

BONUS PAGE
MECHA PARTS DESCRIPTION

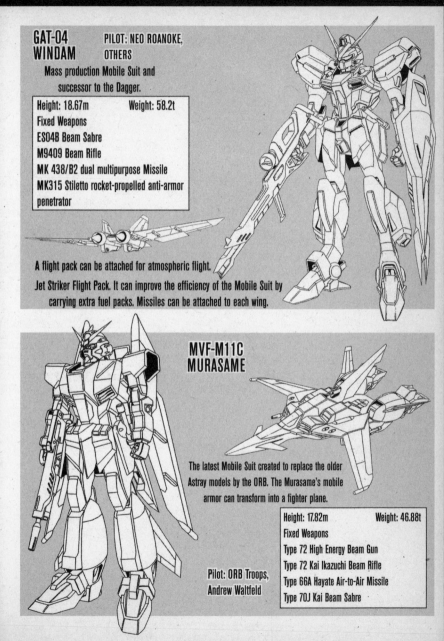

GAT-04 WINDAM

PILOT: NEO ROANOKE, OTHERS

Mass production Mobile Suit and successor to the Dagger.

Height: 18.67m
Weight: 58.2t
Fixed Weapons
ES04B Beam Sabre
M9409 Beam Rifle
MK 438/B2 dual multipurpose Missile
MK315 Stiletto rocket-propelled anti-armor penetrator

A flight pack can be attached for atmospheric flight.

Jet Striker Flight Pack. It can improve the efficiency of the Mobile Suit by carrying extra fuel packs. Missiles can be attached to each wing.

MVF-M11C MURASAME

The latest Mobile Suit created to replace the older Astray models by the ORB. The Murasame's mobile armor can transform into a fighter plane.

Height: 17.82m
Weight: 46.88t
Fixed Weapons
Type 72 High Energy Beam Gun
Type 72 Kai Ikazuchi Beam Rifle
Type 66A Hayate Air-to-Air Missile
Type 70J Kai Beam Sabre

Pilot: ORB Troops, Andrew Waltfeld

About the Creators

Yoshiyuki Tomino

Gundam was created by Yoshiyuki Tomino. Prior to Gundam, Tomino had worked on the original *Astro Boy* anime, as well as *Princess Knight* and *Brave Raideen*, among others. In 1979, he created and directed *Mobile Suit Gundam*, the very first in a long line of Gundam series. The show was not immediately popular and was forced to cut its number of episodes before going off the air, but as with the American show *Star Trek*, the fans still had something to say on this matter. By 1981, the demand for Gundam was so high that Tomino oversaw the re-release of the animation as three theatrical movies (a practice still common in Japan, and rarely, if ever, seen in the United States). It was now official: Gundam was a blockbuster.

Tomino would go on to direct many Gundam series, including *Gundam ZZ*, *Char's Counterattack*, *Gundam F91*, and *Victory Gundam*, all of which contributed to the rich history of the vast Gundam universe. In addition to Gundam, Tomino created *Xabungle*, *L. Gaim*, *Dunbine*, and *Garzey's Wing*. His most recent anime is *Brain Powered*, which was released by Geneon in the United States.

Masatsugu Iwase

Masatsugu Iwase writes and draws the manga adaptation of *Gundam SEED* and *Gundam SEED Destiny*. *Gundam SEED* was his first work published in the United States. This manga creator is better known in Japan, however, for his work on *Calm Breaker*, a hilarious parody of anime, manga, and Japanese pop culture.

Preview of *Gundam SEED Destiny* volume 3

We're pleased to present you with a preview from *Gundam Seed Destiny*, volume 3. This volume will be available in English on March 27, 2007, but for now you'll have to make do with Japanese!

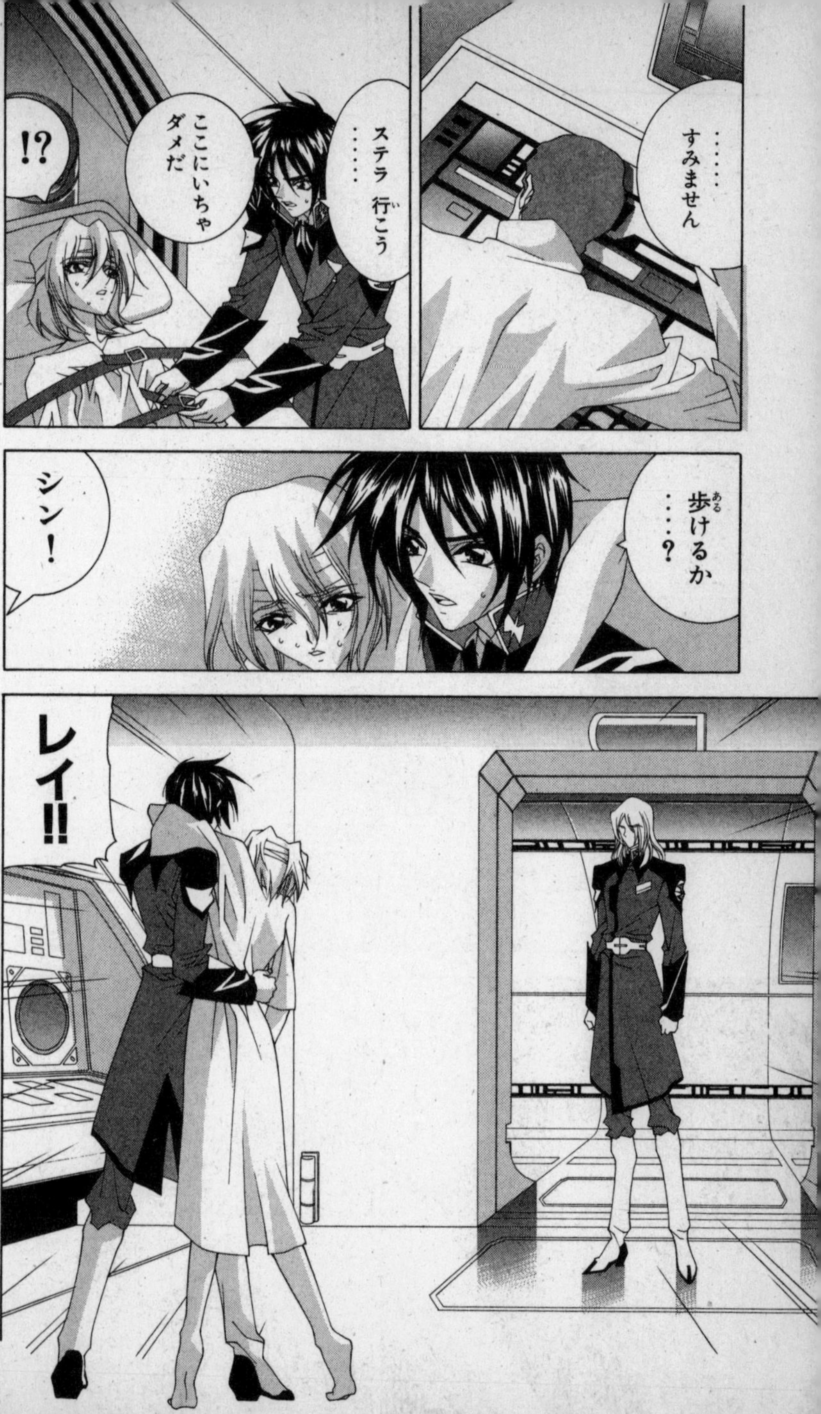
……すみません
ステラ 行こう……
ここにいちゃダメだ
!?
歩けるか・・・?
シン!
レイ!!

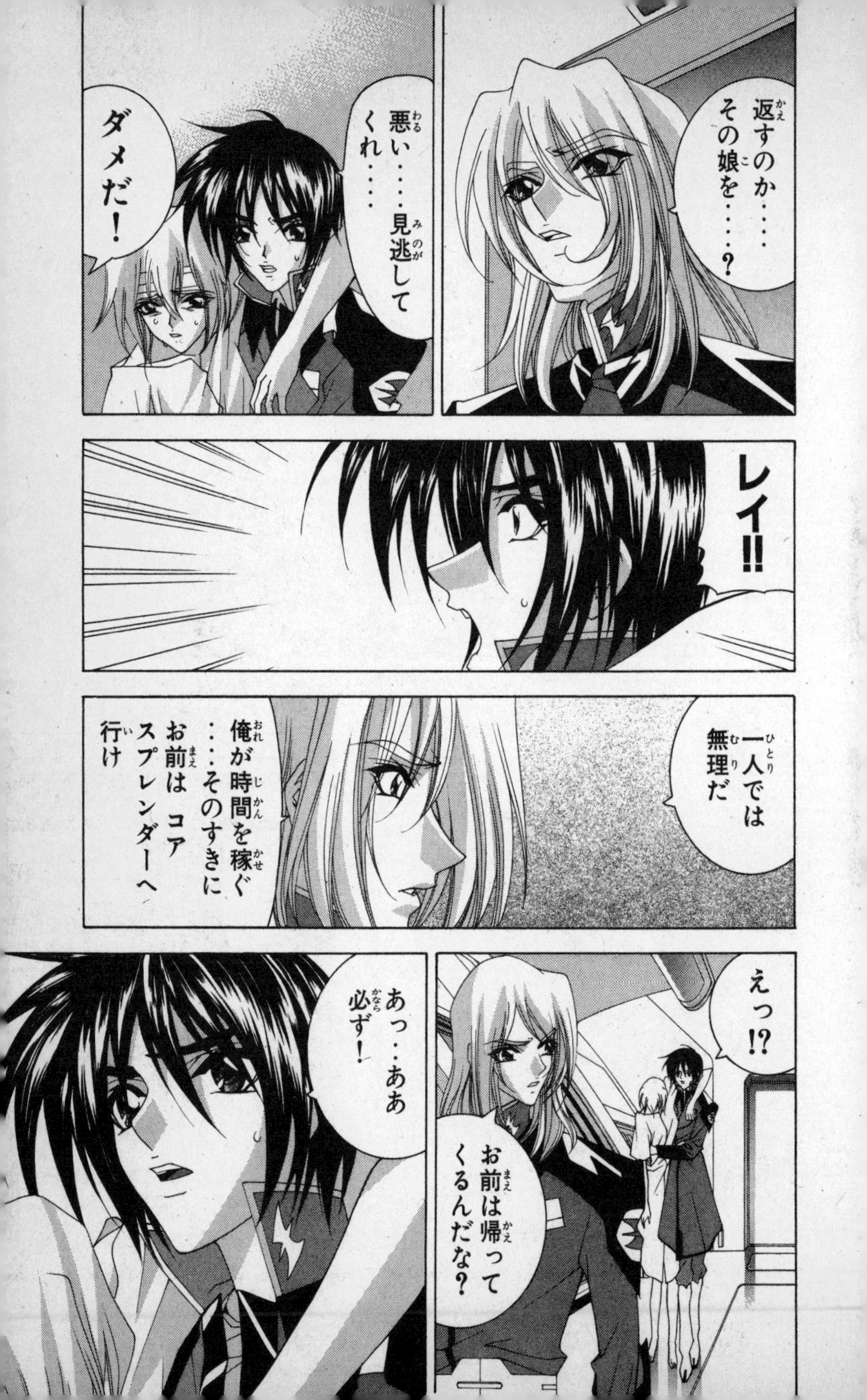
返すのか……その娘を……？
悪い……見逃してくれ……
ダメだ！
レイ!!
一人では無理だ
俺が時間を稼ぐ……そのすきにお前は コアスプレンダーへ行け
えっ!?
お前は帰ってくるんだな？
あっ…ああ 必ず！

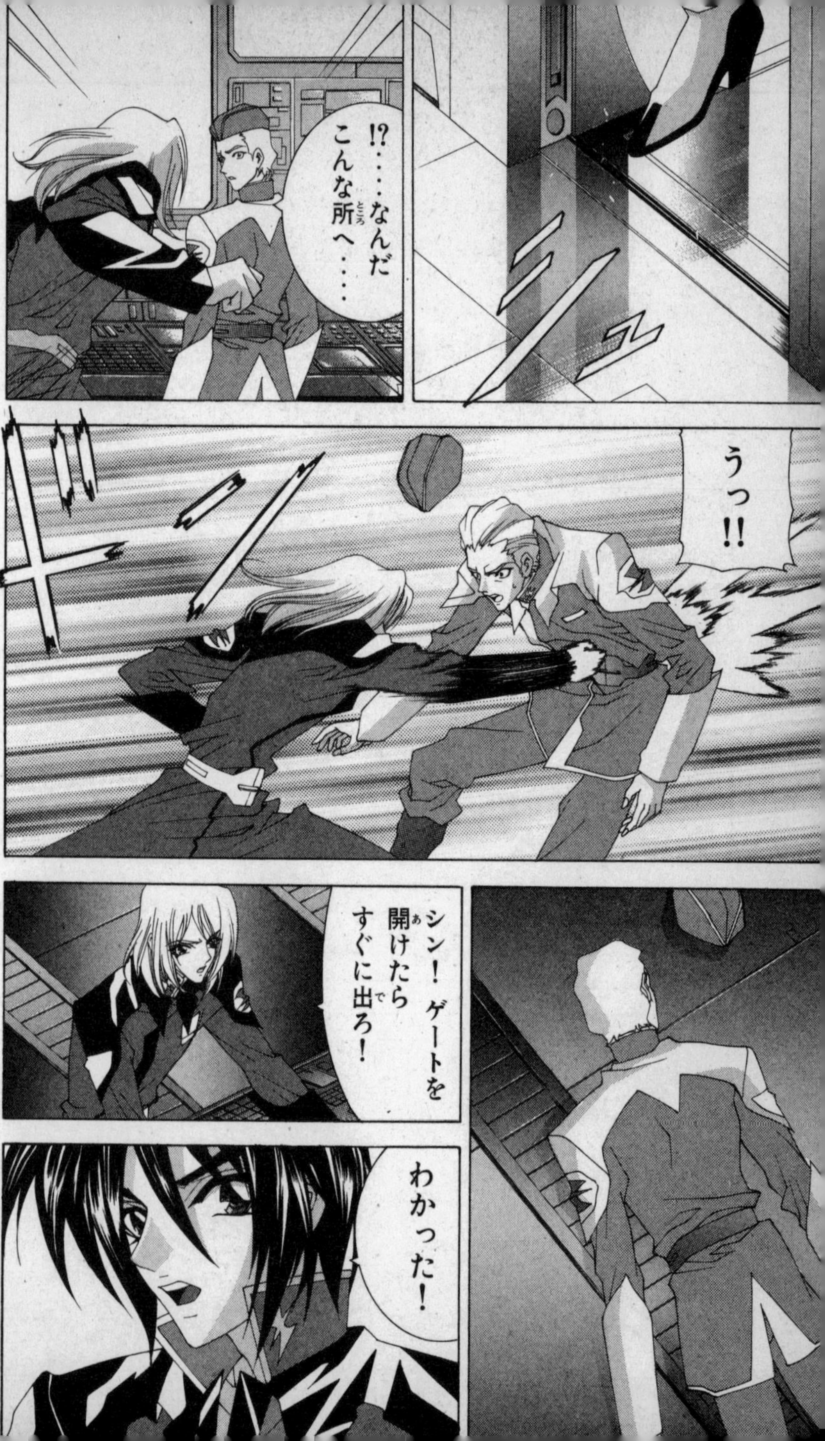
!?……なんだ
こんな所へ……
うっ!!
シン! ゲートを
開けたら
すぐに出ろ!
わかった!

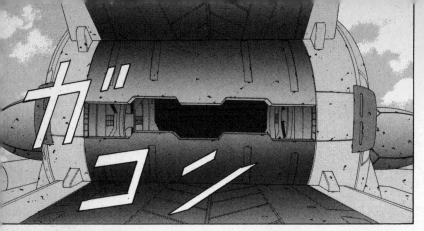

大変です！
シン・アスカが
エクステンデッドを
連れて、コア
スプレンダーで……

なんですって!?

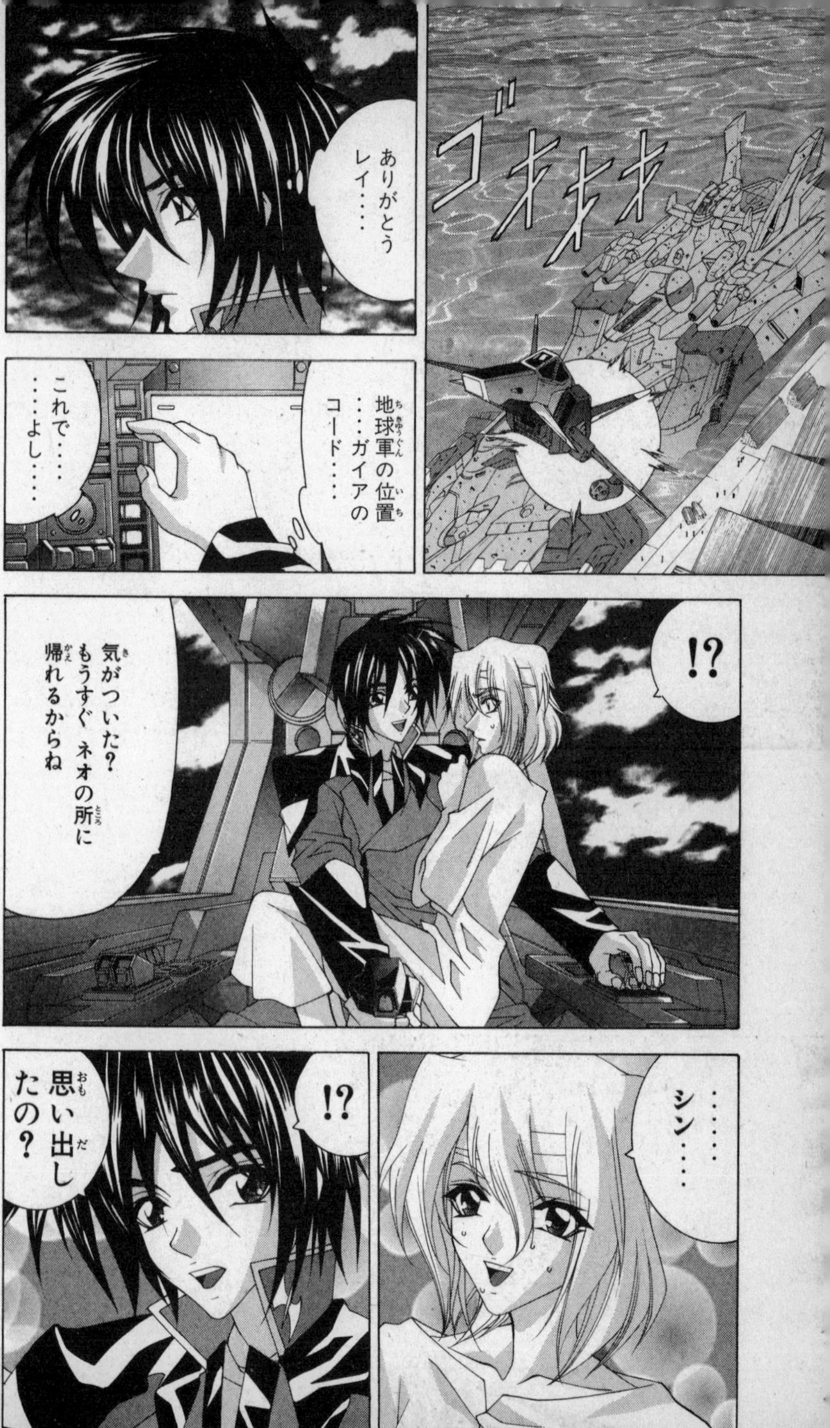
ゴォォォ
ありがとう レイ・・・・
地球軍の位置・・・ガイアのコード・・・・
これで・・・・・・・よし・・・・
!?
気がついた？ もうすぐ ネオの所に帰れるからね
・・・・・・シン・・・・
!?
思い出したの？

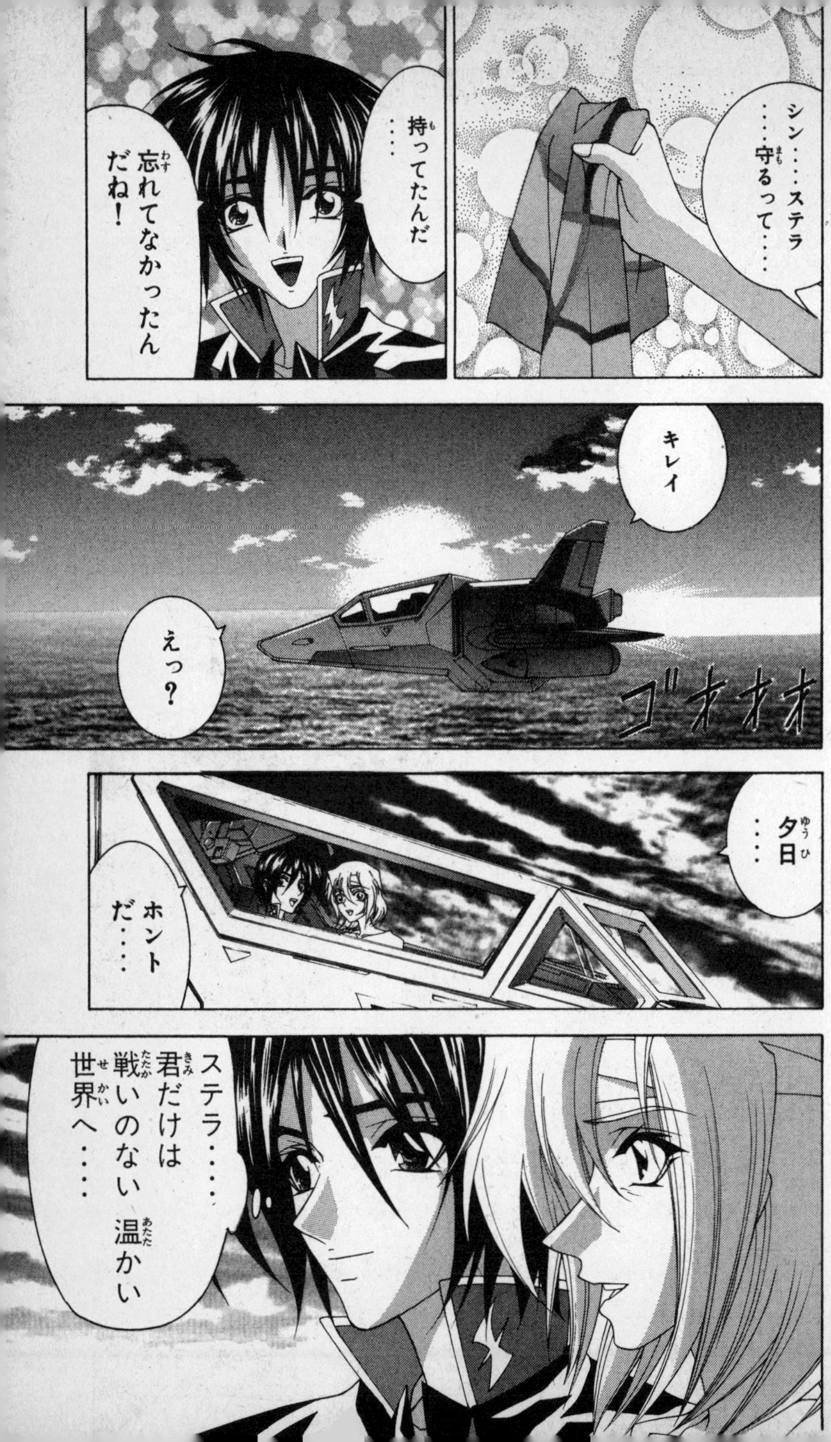
シン……ステラ……守るって……
持ってたんだ……
忘れてなかったんだね！
キレイ
えっ？
ゴオオオ
夕日……
ホントだ……
ステラ……君だけは戦いのない温かい世界へ……

School Rumble

BY JIN KOBAYASHI

SUBTLETY IS FOR WIMPS!

She . . . is a second-year high school student with a single all-consuming question: Will the boy she likes ever really notice her?

He . . . is the school's most notorious juvenile delinquent, and he's suddenly come to a shocking realization: He's got a huge crush, and now he must tell her how he feels.

Life-changing obsessions, colossal foul-ups, grand schemes, deep-seated anxieties, and raging hormones—School Rumble portrays high school as it really is: over-the-top comedy!

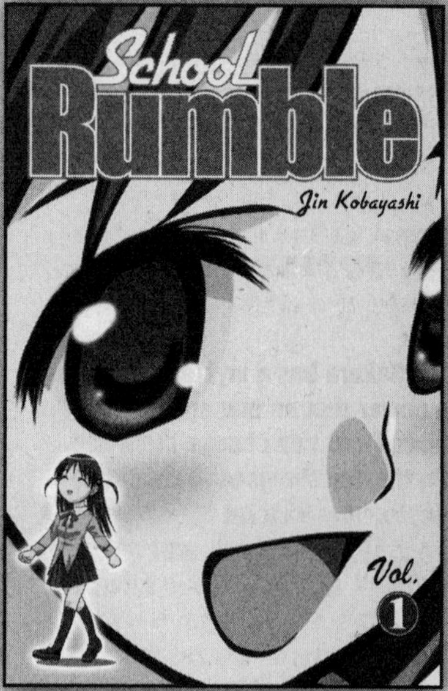
School Rumble
Jin Kobayashi
Vol. 1

Ages: 16 +

Special extras in each volume! Read them all!

DEL REY

VISIT WWW.DELREYMANGA.COM TO:
- Read sample pages
- View release date calendars for upcoming volumes
- Sign up for Del Rey's free manga e-newsletter
- Find out the latest about new Del Rey Manga series

RESERVoir CHRoNiCLE

TSUBASA

BY CLAMP

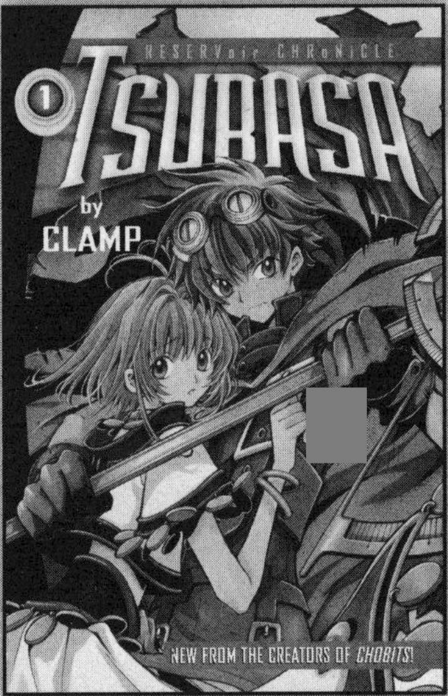

RESERVoir CHRoNiCLE
1
TSUBASA
by
CLAMP
NEW FROM THE CREATORS OF *CHOBITS*!

Ages: 13+

Sakura is the princess of Clow. Syaoran is her childhood friend, and leader of the archaeological dig that cost him his father. Fans of Cardcaptor Sakura will recognize the names and the faces, but these aren't the people you know. This is an alternate reality where everything is familiar and strange at the same time.

Sakura has a mysterious power, a power that no one understands, a power that can change the world. On the day she goes to the dig to declare her love for Syaoran, a mysterious symbol is uncovered that will have vast repercussions for Sakura and Syaoran. It marks the beginning of a quest that will take Syaoran and his friends through worlds that will be familiar to any CLAMP fan, as our heroes encounter places and characters from X, Chobits, Magic Knight Rayearth, xxxHOLiC, and many more! But all that matters to Syaoran is his goal: saving Sakura.

Special extras in each volume! Read them all!

DEL REY

VISIT WWW.DELREYMANGA.COM TO:
- View release date calendars for upcoming volumes
- Sign up for Del Rey's free manga e-newsletter
- Find out the latest about new Del Rey Manga series

GHOST HUNT

MANGA BY SHIHO INADA
STORY BY FUYUMI ONO

The decrepit building was condemned long ago, but every time the owners try to tear it down, "accidents" start to happen—people get hurt, sometimes even killed. Mai Taniyama and her classmates have heard the rumors that the creepy old high school is haunted. So, one rainy day they gather to tell ghost stories, hoping to attract one of the suspected spirits. No ghosts materialize, but they do meet Kazuya Shibuya, the handsome young owner of Shibuya Psychic Research, hired to investigate paranormal activity at the school. Also brought to the scene are an exorcist, a Buddhist monk, a woman who can speak with the dead, and an outspoken Shinto priestess. Surely one of them will have the talents to solve this mystery. . . .

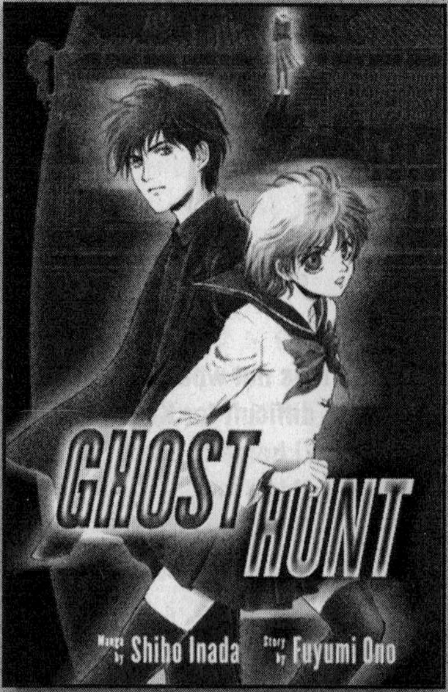
GHOST HUNT
Shiho Inada
Fuyumi Ono

Ages: 13 +

Special extras in each volume! Read them all!

DEL REY

VISIT WWW.DELREYMANGA.COM TO:
- Read sample pages
- View release date calendars for upcoming volumes
- Sign up for Del Rey's free manga e-newsletter
- Find out the latest about new Del Rey Manga series

BY AKIRA SEGAMI

MISSION IMPOSSIBLE

The young ninja Kagetora has been given a great honor—to serve a renowned family of skilled martial artists. But on arrival, he's handed a challenging assignment: teach the heir to the dynasty, the charming but clumsy Yuki, the deft moves of self-defense and combat.

Yuki's inability to master the martial arts is not what makes this job so difficult for Kagetora. No, it is Yuki herself. Someday she will lead her family dojo, and for a ninja like Kagetora to fall in love with his master is a betrayal of his duty, the ultimate dishonor, and strictly forbidden. Can Kagetora help Yuki overcome her ungainly nature . . . or will he be overcome by his growing feelings?

Ages: 13+

Special extras in each volume! Read them all!

VISIT WWW.DELREYMANGA.COM TO:
• Read sample pages
• View release date calendars for upcoming volumes
• Sign up for Del Rey's free manga e-newsletter
• Find out the latest about new Del Rey Manga series

KURO GANE

BY KEI TOUME

AN EERIE, HAUNTING SAMURAI ADVENTURE

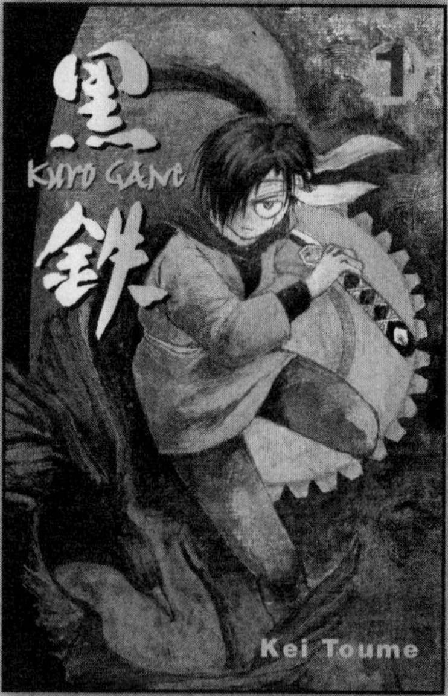
1
黒
KURO GANE
鉄
Kei Toume

Teen: Ages 13 +

Avenging his father's murder is a matter of honor for the young samurai Jintetsu. But it turns out that the killer is a corrupt government official—and now the powers that be are determined to hunt Jintetsu down. There's only one problem: Jintetsu is already dead.

Torn to pieces by a pack of dogs, Jintetsu's ravaged body has been found by Genkichi, outcast and master inventor. Genkichi gives the dead boy a new, indestructible steel body and a talking sword—just what he'll need to face down the gang that's terrorizing his hometown and the mobster who ordered his father's hit. But what about Otsuki, the beautiful girl he left behind? Steel armor is defense against any sword, but it can't save Jintetsu from the pain in his heart.

Special extras in each volume! Read them all!

DEL REY

VISIT WWW.DELREYMANGA.COM TO:
- Read sample pages
- View release date calendars for upcoming volumes
- Sign up for Del Rey's free manga e-newsletter
- Find out the latest about new Del Rey Manga series

Subscribe to

You are going the wrong way!

Manga is a completely different
type of reading experience.

To start at the beginning, go to the end!

That's right! Authentic manga is read the traditional Japanese
way—from right to left. Exactly the opposite of how American
books are read. It's easy to follow: Just go to the other end of
the book, and read each page—and each panel—from right side
to left side, starting at the top right. Now you're experiencing
manga as it was meant to be.

TOMARE! [STOP!]